Film Censorship in the Asia-Pacific Region

Film censorship has always been a controversial matter, particularly in jurisdictions with restrictive state-based censorship systems. This book reviews the film censorship systems in the Asia-Pacific region by comparing the systems used in Malaysia, Hong Kong and Australia. It identifies the key issues and concerns that arise from the design and implementation of the systems by examining the censorship laws, policies, guidelines and processes. The book evaluates film practitioners' and censors' opinions of, and experiences in, dealing with those issues and goes on to develop reform proposals for the Malaysian film censorship system.

Saw Tiong Guan currently teaches at the Faculty of Law, University of Malaya, Malaysia. He obtained his doctorate degree from the University of Melbourne and is an advocate and solicitor of the High Court of Malaya. He is also a film director and producer.

I0894962

Routledge Advances in Asia-Pacific Studies

Environment, Education and Society in the Asia-Pacific
Local traditions and global discourses
David Yencken, John Fien and Helen Sykes

Ageing in the Asia-Pacific Region
David R. Phillips

Caring for the Elderly in Japan and the US
Practices and policies
Susan Orpett Long

Human Rights and Gender Politics
Asia-Pacific perspectives
Edited by Anne Marie Hilsdon, Martha Macintyre, Vera Mackie and Maila Stivens

Human Rights in Japan, South Korea and Taiwan
Ian Neary

Cultural Politics and Asian Values
The tepid war
Michael D. Barr

Social Policy in East and Southeast Asia
Education, health, housing and income maintenance
M. Ramesh

Sino-Japanese Relations
Facing the past, looking to the future?
Caroline Rose

Directors of Urban Change in Asia
Edited by Peter J.M. Nas

Education Reform and Education Policy in East Asia
Ka Ho Mok

The Strong and the Weak in Japanese Literature
Discrimination, egalitarianism, nationalism
Fuminobu Murakami

Civilization, Nation and Modernity in East Asia
Chih-Yu Shih

Diminishing Conflicts in Asia and the Pacific
Robin Jeffrey, Edward Aspinall and Anthony Regan

Health Transitions and the Double Disease Burden in Asia and the Pacific
Histories of responses to non-communicable and communicable diseases
Edited by Milton J. Lewis and Kerrie L. MacPherson

Film Censorship in the Asia-Pacific Region
Malaysia, Hong Kong and Australia compared
Saw Tiong Guan

Film Censorship in the Asia-Pacific Region

Malaysia, Hong Kong and Australia compared

Saw Tiong Guan

Routledge
Taylor & Francis Group
LONDON AND NEW YORK

First published 2013
by Routledge
2 Park Square, Milton Park, Abingdon, Oxfordshire OX14 4RN

Simultaneously published in the USA and Canada
by Routledge
711 Third Avenue, New York, NY 10017

First issued in paperback 2015

Routledge is an imprint of the Taylor & Francis Group, an informa business

British Library Cataloguing in Publication Data
A catalogue record for this book is available from the British Library

Library of Congress Cataloging in Publication Data
Saw, Tiong Guan.
Film censorship in the Asia-Pacific Region : Malaysia, Hong Kong, and Australia compared / Saw Tiong Guan.
p. cm. -- (Routledge Advances in Asia-Pacific Studies ; 15)
Includes bibliographical references and index.
1. Motion pictures--Law and legislation--Pacific Area. 2. Motion pictures--Censorship--Pacific Area. I. Title.
KVC728.M67S29 2013
344.505′31--dc23
2012031252

ISBN 13: 978-1-138-95041-2 (pbk)
ISBN 13: 978-0-415-65689-4 (hbk)

Typeset in Times
by Saxon Graphics Ltd, Derby

For my mother,
who taught me how to write,
and
for Piyasak Vitayaburananont,
who keeps me writing.

Contents

Table of cases

Abrams v United States
250 US 616 (1919) (Supreme Court, United States of America)

Adultshop.com Ltd v Members of the Classification Review Board and anor.
[2008] 169 FCR 31 (Federal Court, Australia)

Alberts v California
354 US 476 (1957) (Supreme Court, United States of America)

Anisminic Ltd v Foreign Compensation Commission
[1969] 2 AC 147 (House of Lords, United Kingdom)

Associated Provincial Picture Houses Ltd v Wednesbury Corporation
[1948] 1 KB 223 (Court of Appeal, England and Wales)

Attorney-General v Guardian Newspapers Ltd (No 2)
[1990] 1 AC 109 (House of Lords, United Kingdom)

Australian Capital Television v Commonwealth
(1992) 177 CLR 106 (High Court, Australia)

Badan Peguam Malaysia v Kerajaan Malaysia
[2008] 2 MLJ 285 (Federal Court, Malaysia)

Brandenburg v Ohio
395 US 444 (1969) (Supreme Court, United States of America)

Burstyn Inc. v Wilson
343 US 495 (1952) (Supreme Court, United States of America)

Chaplinsky v New Hampshire
315 US 568 (1942) (Supreme Court, United States of America)

Che Omar Che Soh v Public Prosecutor
[1988] 2 MLJ 55 (Supreme Court, Malaysia)

Chief Constable of the North Wales Police v Evans
[1982] 1 WLR 1155 (House of Lords, United Kingdom)

Coleman v Power
[2004] 220 CLR 1 (High Court, Australia)

Council of Civil Service Unions v Minister for the Civil Service
[1985] AC 374 (House of Lords, United Kingdom)

Crowe v Graham
(1968) 121 CLR 375 (High Court, Australia)

Director of Public Prosecutions v Whyte
[1972] 3 All ER 12 (House of Lords, United Kingdom)

Dr Mohd Nasir bin Hashim v Menteri Dalam Negeri Malaysia
[2006] 6 MLJ 213 (Court of Appeal, Malaysia)

Family Voice Australia v Members of the Classification Review Board
[2011] FCA 1014 (Federal Court, Australia)

George John v Goh Eng Wah Bros Filem Sdn Bhd
[1988] 1 MLJ 319 (High Court, Malaysia)

Ginzburg v United States
383 US 463 (1966) (Supreme Court, United States of America)

Government of Malaysia v Jagdis Singh
[1987] 2 MLJ 185 (Supreme Court, Malaysia)

Haji Laugan Tarki bin Mohd Noor v Mahkamah Anak Negeri Penampang
[1988] 2 MLJ 85 (Supreme Court, Malaysia)

Harpers Trading (M) Sdn Bhd v National Union of Commercial Workers
[1991] 1 MLJ 417 (Supreme Court, Malaysia)

Hoh Kiang Ngan v Mahkamah Perusahaan Malaysia
[1995] 3 MLJ 378 (Federal Court, Malaysia)

Hong Leong Equipment Sdn Bhd v Liew Fook Chuan
[1996] 1 MLJ 481 (Court of Appeal, Malaysia)

Hotel Equatorial (M) Sdn Bhd v National Union of Hotel, Bar and Restaurant Workers
[1984] 1 MLJ 363 (Federal Court, Malaysia)

Huang v Secretary of State for the Home Department
[2007] 2 AC 167 (House of Lords, United Kingdom)

In re Amin [On appeal from Regina v Entry Clearance Officer, Bombay, Ex parte Amin]
[1983] 2 AC 818 (House of Lords, United Kingdom)

Jacobellis v Ohio
378 US 184 (1964) (Supreme Court, United States of America)

Katherine Lim KH Sr v Ketua Pengarah Perkhidmatan Perubatan Malaysia
[1997] 2 MLJ 538 (Court of Appeal, Malaysia)

Kerajaan Negeri Selangor v Sagong Tasi
[2005] 4 CLJ 169 (Court of Appeal, Malaysia)

Ketua Pengarah Kastam v Ho Kwan Seng
[1977] 2 MLJ 152 (Federal Court, Malaysia)

Knuller (Publishing, Printing and Promotions) Ltd v Director of Public Prosecutions
[1973] AC 435 (House of Lords, United Kingdom)

Kumpulan Perangsang Selangor Bhd v Zaid bin Hj Mohd Noh
[1997] 1 MLJ 789 (Supreme Court, Malaysia)

Lange v Australian Broadcasting Corporation
(1997) 189 CLR 520 (High Court, Australia)

Lee Kwan Woh v Public Prosecutor
[2009] 5 MLJ 301 (Federal Court, Malaysia)

Lim Cho Hock v Government of the State of Perak
[1980] 2 MLJ 148 (High Court, Malaysia)

Majlis Perbandaran Pulau Pinang v Syarikat Berkerjasama-sama Serbaguna Sungai Gelugor, Dalam Tanggungan
[1999] 3 MLJ 1 (Federal Court, Malaysia)

Miller v California
413 US 15 (1973) (Supreme Court, United States of America)

Minister of Finance, Government of Sabah v Petrojasa Sdn Bhd
[2008] 4 MLJ 641 (Federal Court, Malaysia)

Minister of Home Affairs v Persatuan Aliran Kesedaran Malaysia
[1990] 1 MLJ 351 (Supreme Court, Malaysia)

Minister of Labour, Malaysia v Chan Meng Yuen
[1992] 2 MLJ 337 (Supreme Court, Malaysia)

Mohamed bin Ismail v Tan Sri Othman Saat
[1982] 2 MLJ 133 (High Court, Malaysia)

Nationwide News Pty Ltd v Wills
(1992) 177 CLR 1 (High Court, Australia)

Om Kumar v Union of India
(2001) 2 SCC 386 (Supreme Court, India)

O'Reilly v Mackman
[1983] 2 AC 237 (House of Lords, United Kingdom)

Otto-Preminger Institute v Austria
(1994) 19 EHRR 34 (European Court of Human Rights)

Paris Adult Theatre v Slaton
413 US 49 (1973) (Supreme Court, United States of America)

Public Service Board of New South Wales v Osmond
(1986) 159 CLR 656 (High Court, Australia)

QSR Brands v Suruhanjaya Sekuriti
[2006] 3 MLJ 164 (Court of Appeal, Malaysia)

R v Barnsley Metropolitan Borough Council, Ex parte Hook
[1976] 3 All ER 452 (Court of Appeal, England and Wales)

R v Butler
[1992] 89 DLR (4th) 449 (Supreme Court, Canada)

R v Calder & Boyars Ltd
[1969] 1 QB 151 (Court of Appeal, England and Wales)

R v Hicklin
(1868) LR 3 QB 360 (Court of Appeal, England and Wales)

R v Hull University Visitor, Ex parte Page
[1993] AC 682 (House of Lords, United Kingdom)

R v Northumberland Compensation Appeal Tribunal, Ex parte Shaw
[1952] 1 All ER 122 (Court of Appeal, England and Wales)

R v Panel on Take-Over and Mergers, Ex parte Datafin Plc
[1987] QB 815 (Court of Appeal, England and Wales)

R v Secretary of State for the Environment, Ex parte Nottinghamshire County Council
[1986] AC 240 (House of Lords, United Kingdom)

R v Secretary of State for the Home Department, Ex parte Brind
[1991] 1 AC 696 (House of Lords, United Kingdom)

R v Secretary of State for Trade and Industry, Ex parte Lonrho Plc
[1989] 1 WLR 525 (Court of Appeal, England and Wales)

R v Stanley
[1965] 2 QB 327 (Court of Criminal Appeal, England)

Rama Chandran R v The Industrial Court of Malaysia
[1997] 1 MLJ 145 (Federal Court, Malaysia)

Robin Tan Pang Heng v Ketua Pengarah Kesatuan Sekerja Malaysia
[2002] 1 MLJ 466 (High Court, Malaysia)

Rohana bte Ariffin v Universiti Sains Malaysia
[1989] 1 MLJ 487 (High Court, Malaysia)

Roth v United States
354 US 476 (1957) (Supreme Court, United States of America)

Schenk v United States
249 US 47 (1919) (Supreme Court, United States of America)

Sivarasa Rasiah v Badan Peguam Malaysia & Anor
[2010] 2 MLJ 333 (Federal Court, Malaysia)

South East Asia Fire Bricks Sdn Bhd v Non-Metallic Mineral Products Mfg Employees Union
[1980] 2 MLJ 165 (Privy Council appeal from Malaysia)

Syarikat Kenderaan Melayu Kelantan Bhd v Transport Workers' Union
[1995] 2 MLJ 336 (Court of Appeal, Malaysia)

Tan Tek Seng v Suruhanjaya Perkhidmatan Pendidikan
[1996] 1 MLJ 261 (Court of Appeal, Malaysia)

United Engineers (M) Bhd v Lim Kit Siang
[1988] 2 MLJ 12 (Supreme Court, Malaysia)

Village Roadshow Corporation Ltd v Sheehan
(1987) 17 FCR 324 (Federal Court, Australia)

Whitney v California
274 US 357 (1927) (Supreme Court, United States of America)

Wingrove v United Kingdom
(1997) 24 EHRR 1 (European Court of Human Rights)

Table of statutes and rules

Malaysia

Cinematograph Films Ordinance 1952
Communications and Multimedia Act 1998
Courts of Judicature Act 1964
Federal Constitution
Film (Censorship) Act 1952
Film Censorship Act 2002
Internal Security Act 1960
Industrial Relations Act 1967
Malaysian Communications and Multimedia Commission Act 1998
National Film Development Corporation of Malaysia Act 1981
National Film Development Corporation (Compulsory Screening Scheme) Regulations 2005
National Language Act 1963
Printing Presses and Publications Act 1984
Rules of the Court of Appeal 1994
Rules of the Federal Court 1995
Rules of the High Court 1980
Sedition Act 1948
Specific Relief Act 1950

Hong Kong Special Administrative Region

Basic Law of the Hong Kong Special Administrative Region
Broadcasting Ordinance
Control of Obscene and Indecent Articles Ordinance
Film Censorship Ordinance
Film Censorship (Amendment) Ordinance 1994
Film Censorship Regulations 1953
Places of Public Entertainment Ordinance

Australia

Administrative Appeals Tribunal Act 1975
Administrative Decisions (Judicial Review) Act 1977
Australian Constitution
Broadcasting Services Act 1992
Censorship Act 1996 (Western Australia)
Classification (Publications, Films and Computer Games) Act 1995
  Classification of Publications, Films and Computer Games Act 1995 (Northern Territory)
  Classification (Publications, Films and Computer Games) (Enactment) Act 1995 (Australian Capital Territory)
  Classification (Publications, Films and Computer Games) (Enforcement) Act 1995 (Victoria)
  Classification (Publications, Films and Computer Games) Enforcement Act 1995 (New South Wales)
  Classification (Publications, Films and Computer Games) Enforcement Act 1995 (South Australia)
  Classification (Publications, Films and Computer Games) Enforcement Act 1995 (Tasmania)
Classification (Publications, Films and Computer Games) Regulations 2005
Customs Act 1901
Customs (Cinematograph Films) Regulations
Film and Video Tape Classification Act 1984 (New South Wales)
Income Tax Act 1936
Screen Australia Act 2008

England

Human Rights Act 1998
Obscene Publications Act 1857
Obscene Publications Act 1959
Video Recordings Act 1984

India

Constitution of India

United States of America

First Amendment to the United States Constitution

International and regional covenants

European Convention on Human Rights and Fundamental Freedoms
International Covenant on Civil and Political Rights

Films

The Adventures of Barry McKenzie (Bruce Beresford, 1972)
Amok (Adman Salleh, 1995)
Anakku Sazali (*My Son Sazali*, Phani Majumdar, 1956)
Apa Khabar Orang Kampung (*Village People Radio Show*, Amir Muhammad, 2007)
At the End of Daybreak (Ho Yuhang, 2009)
Bad Boy Bubby (Rolf de Heer, 1993)
Baise Moi (*Rape Me*, Virginie Despentes, 2000)
Beijing Rocks (Mabel Cheung, 2001)
Big Bullet (Benny Chan, 1996)
The Bird House (Khoo Eng Yow, 2006)
The Boat People (Ann Hui, 1982)
Brokeback Mountain (Ang Lee, 2005)
Bruce Almighty (Tom Shadyac, 2003)
Cageman (Jacob Cheung, 1992)
Caligula (Tinto Brass, 1979)
Crocodile Dundee (Peter Faiman, 1986)
Daredevil (Mark Steven Johnson, 2003)
Days of Being Wild (Wong Kar Wai, 1990)
The Devil's Playground (Fred Schepisi, 1976)
Double Tap (Lo Chi Leung, 2000)
Election (Johnnie To, 2005)
Embun (Erma Fatima, 2002)
The Eye (Danny Pang and Oxide Pang, 2002)
Fantasia / Fantasi (Aziz M. Osman, 1992)
Full Metal Jacket (Stanley Kubrick, 1987)
Gerak Khas: The Movie (Yusof Haslam, 2001)
Gone in Sixty Seconds (Dominic Sena, 2000)
Hang Jebat (Hussain Haniff, 1961)
Hantu Bonceng (Ahmad Idham, 2011)
Happy Bigamist (Anthony Chan, 1987)
Happy Together (Wong Kar Wai, 1997)
Histeria (*Hysteria*, James Lee, 2009)

The Home Song Stories (Tony Ayres, 2007)
The Human Centipede II (Tom Six, 2011)
I Don't Want to Sleep Alone (Tsai Ming-liang, 2006)
In the Mood for Love (Wong Kar Wai, 2000)
Infernal Affairs (Andrew Lau and Alan Mak, 2002)
Irreversible (Gaspar Noe, 2002)
Istana Berdarah (*Palace of Blood*, Hussain Haniff, 1964)
Jedda (Charles Chauvel, 1955)
Jogho (*Champion*, U-Wei Haji Saari, 1997)
Kaki Bakar (*The Arsonist*, U-Wei Haji Saari, 1995)
Kami (Effendee Mazlan, 2008)
The Killer (John Woo, 1989)
Laila Majnum (B. S. Rajhans, 1933)
Lantana (Ray Lawrence, 2001)
Lan Yu (Stanley Kwan, 2001)
Lelaki Komunis Terakhir (*The Last Communist*, Amir Muhammad, 2006)
Les Amants (*The Lovers*, Louis Malle, 1958)
Love Conquers All (Tan Chui Mui, 2006)
Lolita (Adrian Lyne, 1997)
Lust, Caution (Ang Lee, 2007)
Made in Hong Kong (Fruit Chan, 1997)
Malaysian Gods (Amir Muhammad, 2008)
Matinya Seorang Patriot (*Death of a Patriot*, Rahim Razali, 1984)
Mekanik (*Mechanic*, Othman Hafsham, 1983)
Mission: Impossible II (John Woo, 2000)
Muallaf (*The Convert*, Yasmin Ahmad, 2008)
Mukhsin (Yasmin Ahmad, 2007)
Naked Killers (Wong Jing, 1992)
New Police Story (Benny Chan, 2004)
Ocean's Eleven (Steven Soderbergh, 2001)
Paloh (Adman Salleh, 2003)
Penarik Becha (*The Rickshaw Man*, P Ramlee, 1955)
Perempuan, Isteri & ... (*Woman, Wife & Whore*, U-Wei Haji Saari, 1993)
The Piano (Jane Campion, 1993)
The Piano Teacher (Michael Haneke, 2001)
Picnic at Hanging Rock (Peter Weir, 1975)
Pontianak Harum Sundal Malam (*Pontianak: A Scent of Tuberose*, Shuhaimi Baba, 2004)
Puteri Gunung Ledang (*Princess of Mount Ledang*, Saw Teong Hin, 2004)
Rabbit Proof Fence (Phillip Noyce, 2002)
Rain Dogs (Ho Yuhang, 2006)
Remp-it (Ahmad Idham, 2006)
Ringgit Kasyorga (*Dollar to Heaven*, Shuhaimi Baba, 1995)
Rogue (Li Beihai, 1925)
Romance (Catherine Breillat, 1999)

Rouge (Stanley Kwan, 1987)
Salo o le 120 giornate di Sodoma (*Salo, the 120 Days of Sodom*, Pier Paolo Pasolini, 1975)
Saving Private Ryan (Steven Spielberg, 1999)
Schindler's List (Steven Spielberg, 1993)
Senario (*Scenario*, Aziz M. Osman, 1999)
Sepet (*Chinese Eye*, Yasmin Ahmad, 2004)
Serbian Film (Srdjan Spasojevic, 2010)
Sex and Zen (Michael Mak, 1991)
Shine (Scott Hicks, 1996)
Shortbus (John Cameron Mitchell, 2006)
The Soong Sisters (Mabel Cheung, 1997)
Stealing a Roast Duck (Liang Shaobo, 1909)
Stone Bros (Richard J. Frankland, 2009)
Stork (Tim Burstall, 1971)
The Story of the Kelly Gang (Charles Tait, 1906)
The Story of Woo Viet (Ann Hui, 1981)
Strictly Ballroom (Baz Luhrmann, 1992)
Summer Snow (Ann Hui, 1995)
Susuk (Amir Muhammad, 2008)
The Sword (Patrick Tam, 1980)
Ten Canoes (Rolf de Heer, 2006)
Time and Tide (Tsui Hark, 2000)
Vive L'Amour (Tsai Ming-liang, 1994)
Walkabout (Nicholas Roeg, 1971)
The Wayward Cloud (Tsai Ming-liang, 2005)
What time is it there? (Tsai Ming-liang, 2001)
XX Ray (Aziz M. Osman, 1992)
XX Ray 2 (Aziz M. Osman, 1995)
Zoolander (Ben Stiller, 2001)
Zu: Warriors from the Magic Mountain (Tsui Hark, 1983)
1957: Hati Malaya (*1957: Heart of Malaya*, Shuhaimi Baba, 2007)
9 Songs (Michael Winterbottom, 2004)

Tables

Preface

Film censorship has always been a controversial matter, particularly in jurisdictions with restrictive state-based censorship systems. *Film Censorship in the Asia-Pacific Region* reviews the film censorship system in Malaysia by comparing it with the Hong Kong and Australian systems. It identifies key issues that arise from the systems by examining the laws, guidelines and administrative processes; evaluating film practitioners' and censors' opinions of, and experiences in, dealing with those issues in practice; and, finally, develops reform proposals for the Malaysian film censorship system. The rationale for comparing Malaysia with Hong Kong and Australia is threefold: there are broad similarities in the censorship schemes in these three jurisdictions; they share a common legal heritage; and yet the film industries differ markedly in their artistic and commercial achievements.

From both doctrinal and empirical research, it is suggested that the Malaysian film censorship system adversely affects that country's film industry and its film practitioners. Hence, reforms to the system are warranted. The book therefore investigates what changes to the Malaysian film censorship system appear likely to promote the artistic vibrancy and commercial viability of the country's film industry and makes systematic reform proposals.

In addition to proposing reforms to the film censorship system, the book also explores the availability and suitability of judicial review as a legal avenue for film practitioners to redress grievances occasioned by state censorship of film. The remedies available to film practitioners by way of judicial review application are examined, and the question of whether such application is the best option for film practitioners to tackle censorship problems is weighed against countervailing factors.

This book attempts to serve three functions. First, it offers original materials to enrich media law and film and media studies literature by analysing film censorship from a legal perspective, as well as considering film practitioners' and censors' opinions and experiences when dealing with censorship. Second, the book explains the need for, and the potential of, judicial review in film censorship matters. Third, the book develops law reform proposals and makes recommendations for changes to the Malaysian film censorship system in light of detailed analysis of the systems in Hong Kong and Australia. The suggested reform proposals may also be applicable to other jurisdictions facing similar censorship issues and weaknesses in their existing systems. The book consists of seven chapters. Chapter 1 deals with introductory matters and literature about freedom of expression, obscenity and censorship. Chapter 2 provides an overview of the Malaysian, Hong Kong and Australian film industries in their socio-legal contexts. Chapter 3 discusses the film censorship systems in the three jurisdictions under study by examining the relevant censorship laws, guidelines and processes. Chapter 4 identifies the key issues that arise in the systems and evaluates their likely effects on the film industries and practitioners. Chapter 5 focuses on the film practitioners' opinions of the key issues identified in Chapter 4. Chapter 6 examines the potential and viability of judicial review of film censorship decisions and, finally, Chapter 7 draws together the analysis and proposes reforms to the film censorship system.

Film Censorship in the Asia-Pacific Region emerges out of a doctoral thesis I completed in 2011 under the supervision of Professor Andrew Kenyon and Dr Amanda Whiting of the Melbourne Law School. Many people have assisted in the research that led to this book and I would like to thank, in particular, my supervisors and the interviewees who have generously shared their time, knowledge and experience with me. I thank my loving and supportive parents, Saw Chin Ting and Ti Lian Yuan; and my family, especially my sister Jo Anne who helped me in various ways while I worked on both this manuscript and my new film. Finally, I thank my close friends Wong Yew Leong, Yau Lap Ho, Azmi Sharom, Lim Wee Koon and Darren Parker, for whose ongoing support I am grateful.

Saw Tiong Guan
Kuala Lumpur
July 2012

1 Introduction

Setting the scene

This book sets out to review the film censorship system in Malaysia; identify the key issues and concerns that arise from the design and implementation of the system and analyse their effects on the film industry; evaluate film practitioners' opinions of, and experiences in, dealing with those censorship issues; and, finally, propose a film censorship system which appears capable of promoting the artistic vibrancy and commercial viability of the Malaysian film industry.

In the attempt to achieve these objectives, reference is made to the experiences of two other jurisdictions: Hong Kong and Australia. Three reasons account for this. First, while their film censorship systems have differences, the overall approach to film censorship in each of these three jurisdictions shares broad similarities. For example, they are 'state-based' as opposed to 'industry-based' systems, where the censorship of films is overseen by entities established under legislation and with direct connections to government ministries or departments. In contrast, the United States and United Kingdom have not been chosen as the comparative jurisdictions. The former's film censorship system is 'industry-based', where film ratings are handled by the Motion Picture Association of America. This is a body formerly known as the Motion Picture Producers and Distributors Association of America, set up in 1922 by the major film studios to resist the government's involvement by creating an arrangement of industry-based self-censorship known as the Production Code or the Hays Code.[1] The ratings currently applicable in the United States are G (General Audiences); PG (Parental Guidance Suggested); PG-13 (Parents Strongly Cautioned); R (Restricted); and NC-17 (No One 17 and Under Admitted). Films rated NC-17 are restricted to adults while films rated R may be viewed by persons at least 17 years of age or children accompanied by a parent or adult guardian. The United Kingdom has an independent non-governmental body, the British Board of Film Classification, formerly known as the British Board of Film Censors (BBFC), established in 1912 by the film industry as an independent entity with the aim of achieving uniformity in film classification, which operates outside the purview and control of both the British government and film industry.[2] Films may be classified U, PG, 12/12A, 15, 18 and 18R and the BBFC's classification decisions may be overridden by local council authorities. Films classified U, PG and 12 are unrestricted. However, audiences under 12 years of age must be accompanied by an adult in order to watch a 12A film. No one under the age of 15 may watch or purchase a film classified 15 and no one under the age of 18 may watch or purchase a film classified 18. Second, Malaysia, Hong Kong and Australia share the common law tradition, each with an entrenched judicial review process which appears to be the primary legal means by which film practitioners could have recourse to formal remedies to redress grievances caused by censorship of their films. Third, the film industries in Hong Kong and Australia are more vibrant and successful both in artistic and commercial terms than the one in Malaysia. Hong Kong and Australia have seen the production of critically acclaimed films recognized and celebrated internationally since the 1970s and revenues generated at their box offices have been enviable. Therefore, their experiences could provide illuminating comparisons and suggest recommendations for reform. While censorship is only one element underlying the film industry, the research suggests that the existing Hong Kong and Australian censorship systems – which are both transparent and more responsive to film practitioners' needs and the conditions of the industries and the societies – contributed to the vibrancy and achievements of their film industries.

At the outset, it is useful to explain a number of key terms in this book. The term 'film industry' is used to encompass the activities of film production, distribution and exhibition; 'film practitioners' is used to denote film directors, producers, distributors and exhibitors; while 'film' is confined to feature film, documentary and animation produced for commercial public release. This book focuses on censorship of films produced for exhibition in cinemas as well as distribution by way of sales and rental in Digital Versatile Disc (DVD) and Video Compact Disc (VCD) formats. It does not include censorship of films for the purposes of broadcasting on television, which is regulated under different laws.[3] The book places primary emphasis on the effects of film censorship and it is important to concede that a host of other factors, including genre, production budget, marketing strategy and popularity of the cast involved in a project, the size of domestic market and the standard of living of the society, and piracy are also likely to play significant roles in determining the viability of a country's film industry, particularly in its commercial sense. It is also noteworthy that there is no correlation between the artistic accomplishment of a film and its commercial realization in the market. In other words, a highly artistic film does not necessarily translate into box office success. The phrase 'artistic vibrancy and commercial viability of the film industry' is used to express two distinct realities that appear to be affected by censorship. In regard to the former, censorship can obstruct creative and experimental production, while in regard to the latter, censorship can make films less appealing to audiences and therefore reduce box office revenues.

Why do issues relating to a film censorship system matter to a country, film industry and society? Three Malaysian film practitioners' experiences emphasize the significance of this book.

Amir Muhammad, an independent filmmaker, had two of his recent films – *Lelaki Komunis Terakhir* (*The Last Communist*, 2006) and *Apa Khabar Orang*

Kampung (*Village People Radio Show*, 2007) – arbitrarily banned by the authorities while his latest film *Malaysian Gods* (2008) had its public exhibition in the country prohibited. The filmmaker thus lost an outlet to present his films to audiences and was deprived of the opportunity to recoup the production costs. Society was barred from seeing three thought-provoking films while within the film industry another 'deterrence' was firmly put in place to discourage other filmmakers being more critical and experimental with their creative works.

Aziz M. Osman's *Fantasia* (1992) was banned by the censors upon its completion. The film was only approved for public exhibition four years later, after its title had been changed and extensive alterations had been made to its content. The film was finally released as *Fantasi*, with its plot, message and theme markedly different from the originally intended version, and the production company suffered substantial financial losses. Tragically, the producer did not live to see his film released.

Tsai Ming-liang, a Malaysian-born internationally acclaimed *auteur,* chose to make films in Taiwan and France instead of his home country because of censorship concerns.[4] This has resulted in prestigious award-winning films such as *Vive L'Amour* (1994) and *The Wayward Cloud* (2005)[5] being considered as Taiwanese films in which Taiwanese, rather than Malaysians, can take pride and they are not considered part of Malaysian cinematic culture and heritage in international competition.

This book suggests possible reform to the Malaysian film censorship system by way of amendments to the Film Censorship Act 2002, revision to the censorship guidelines and changes to the censorship process. It also provides film practitioners with an understanding of the potential of judicial review in obtaining remedies against censorship authorities. Additionally, the book provides film regulators with information about the effects of censorship on film practitioners so that in carrying out their duties they will be better positioned to act in a more sensible and responsible manner. While the focus of the analysis remains Malaysian, some possible reforms to the Hong Kong and Australian systems are also outlined.

Structure of the book

This book is structured in three parts. The first part deals with introductory matters, literature about free speech, obscenity and censorship and the Malaysian, Hong Kong and Australian film industries. The second part focuses on the film censorship systems, which are principally made up of censorship laws, guidelines and administrative processes, in the three jurisdictions under study. This part identifies and compares the key issues that arise from the censorship systems and then discusses film practitioners' opinions of, and experiences in dealing with, those issues. From the analysis of the systems on paper and investigation of practice through fieldwork, the third part then considers two alternatives to tackle the adverse effects that the censorship system has on the film industry. These alternatives are applications for judicial review of censorship decisions and reforms to the existing film censorship system.

A total of seven chapters make up the three parts outlined above. Chapters 1 and 2 form the first part. After the introductory chapter, Chapter 2 serves as an introduction to the Malaysian, Hong Kong and Australian film industries in their socio-legal context. Its purpose is to provide readers with an overview of the three jurisdictions and their film industries to better understand the context in which the censorship systems operate. Chapter 2 discusses a brief history of, and the contemporary socio-legal settings in, Malaysia, Hong Kong and Australia. The chapter then looks at the background and development of each of the three film industries and explains the initiatives undertaken by their respective governments. Industry statistics, which include the number of films produced annually, the gross box office revenues, the number of cinema screens and details of cinema admissions are also presented where available.

The second part of the book comprises Chapters 3 to 5. Chapter 3 discusses the film censorship systems in Malaysia, Hong Kong and Australia by outlining the relevant legislation and guidelines. The chapter also elaborates the censorship mechanisms and processes. The comparative analysis of the film censorship laws and guidelines in each of the jurisdictions shows that they display marked differences and Chapter 4 highlights these differences and evaluates their likely effects. These key differences and issues are in regard to:

1 the suitability, competence and independence of film censors in carrying out their duties;
2 the exemption of films from censorship;
3 matters to be taken into account by censors in the course of making censorship decisions;
4 defects in film censorship guidelines;
5 the power of censors to require alteration to be made before a film is approved for exhibition and distribution, and the opportunity to discuss with censors the classification category of a film;
6 the provision of reasons for censorship decisions;
7 the parties to, and procedures of, an appeal against censorship decisions;
8 the availability of judicial review to aggrieved film practitioners.

These issues are intrinsically intertwined and inform the larger question: what are the adverse effects of the film censorship system on the film industry? Together Chapters 3 and 4 provide the basis for further investigation and evaluation of how the systems operate and affect the industries. It is recognized that before any conclusions can be drawn, it is pertinent to explore how these key issues are viewed and responded to by the parties who are most affected by them – the film practitioners and censors.

Chapter 5 thus continues by discussing the results of fieldwork, conducted to obtain film practitioners' opinions of the key issues identified in Chapter 4. Interviews were conducted with 36 film practitioners from Malaysia, Hong Kong and Australia and a representative from each of the censorship authorities. A number of factors account for the choice of conducting in-depth semi-structured interviews for this book. First, interviews with film practitioners (and regulators) appeared very likely to provide the sort of information crucial for the writing of this book. The interviews aimed to capture a range of opinions and experiences in order to deepen and contextualize the analysis carried out through doctrinal research in other chapters. As such, the sample size of 12 film practitioner interviewees in each jurisdiction was chosen to adequately assess a cross section of the film industry and to sufficiently represent the likely range of views of film practitioners from across the industry and from independent to mainstream practitioners. Second, interviews provided the most appropriate and viable empirical method and appeared to be the only primary source of information because Malaysian and Hong Kong film censorship reports are not publicly available, rendering impossible another plausible method of using documentary evidence. Other common research methods such as using multiple choice quantitative surveys or observing censorship processes in the three jurisdictions were not adopted as they were ill-suited to the complexities of censorship or inaccessible to observers. Third, interviews have a number of advantages that best suit the investigation being made. They provide a means of understanding the views and experiences of the interviewees in a way that could not be comprehensively understood through the use of other methods. They enable film practitioners to express their perspectives and recount their experiences in handling censorship concerns and problems. The process also allows for general comments and observations to be made by the interviewees. In addition, interviews enable the opinions and experiences of those subject to the censorship system to be drawn out and utilized in proposing reforms. The inclusion of interviews as part of the research ensures that the proposals for reform made are grounded in both artistic and commercial realities based on the interviewees' responses.

The third part of the book comprises two chapters – Chapters 6 and 7. This part considers two alternatives to deal with the adverse impact of the Malaysian film censorship system on the film industry. Chapter 6 focuses on judicial review of film censorship decisions as a possible legal means for aggrieved film practitioners to seek redress against the censorship authorities. The chapter explores the availability of judicial review to film practitioners by examining the effect of ouster clauses, the *locus standi* requirement and the rule of exhaustion of alternative remedies. The grounds of challenge, the remedies (both common law and statutory) that a successful applicant-film practitioner may obtain and whether judicial review is the best option for an aggrieved film practitioner are also discussed in this chapter. Finally, Chapter 7 draws together the analysis and proposes changes to the Malaysian film censorship system that appear likely to promote the artistic vibrancy and commercial viability of the country's film industry. The proposals for reform are developed from Malaysian film practitioners' input, the Hong Kong and Australian experiences as well as the author's own analysis. The chapter concludes by highlighting concerns that arise in relation to the Hong Kong and Australian film censorship systems, such as issues regarding film advertising, film censorship panel arrangements, appeal against classification decisions and reclassification of films.

Before beginning the analysis noted above, this chapter outlines aspects of the legal literature about freedom of expression to set out a key part of the wider framework pertaining to film censorship in the three jurisdictions. By the end of the book, it will be clear that a well-organized, transparent and responsive censorship system can operate without creating some of the difficulties or 'vices' emphasized in the free speech literature, such as the vagueness of the tests and standards to be applied in censoring materials.

Legal literature about freedom of expression, obscenity and censorship

It is possible to identify four common themes or topics that recur in legal writing about freedom of expression, obscenity and censorship.[6] They are the rationales for a free speech principle; the legitimacy of the state's role in regulating speech or expression; criticisms about definitions of key censorship terms and applicable tests; and the issue of what a censorship system needs for it to be reconcilable with the free speech principle.

Free speech is generally understood as speech that is not subjected to state regulation or suppression and the dichotomy between citizen and state is the focus of many free speech debates.[7] Historically, the free speech principle – a principle under which speech is entitled to special protection – began with, and developed through, the struggles for a free press.[8] Three rationales justifying the principle are commonly found in legal literature across jurisdictions.[9] They are the importance of free speech to the discovery of truth (free speech and truth), free speech as a necessity for an effective democracy (free speech and democracy), and free speech as an aspect of autonomy or self-determination and personal fulfilment (free speech and autonomy). These rationales are the subject of lengthy debates and criticisms. They are not settled,[10] but are nevertheless important as they form the philosophical foundations that determine the scope of the free speech principle and what it protects.[11]

Generally, the importance of free speech to the discovery of truth rationale has its roots in John Milton's *Aeropagitica: A Speech for the Liberty of Unlicensed Printing* which was subsequently taken up by John Stuart Mill and later by the US Supreme Court judges.[12] It is argued that truth can only be discovered where there is unrestricted discussion and competition between differing views in the open 'marketplace of ideas'. If the free circulation of ideas and exchange of information are restricted or suppressed, truth may be lost and displaced by falsehood.[13] Free speech is thought to support processes of deliberation that will lead to the discovery of truth, where true opinion will be identified and false ideas exposed through criticism,[14] for the betterment of the society. The second rationale argues that free speech is essential for a democracy to function effectively. It is argued that citizens have the right to receive information and views to be able to make informed decisions and to participate meaningfully in a democracy.[15] It follows that this rationale covers factual speech relating to politics and government. 'Non-political' speech such as literary or artistic expressions is not easily covered with this rationale. The truth and democracy rationales both see speech as a means to an end while the third rationale – free speech and autonomy – sees speech as having an inherent value[16] and being an integral aspect of every individual's right to self-determination and fulfilment.[17] It is asserted under this rationale that the ability to express one's ideas and views is an intrinsic part of being human. It enhances humanity and maintains human dignity and thus restriction or suppression of expression will inhibit autonomy and fulfilment.[18] This rationale covers a wide spectrum of expression and is at its strongest in protecting 'aesthetic and self-expressive speech'[19] making it a relevant rationale for this book.

The legitimacy of the state's role in regulating expression (by way of restriction or suppression) is also considered in much free speech and censorship literature. The discussion often notes provisions of international and regional instruments providing for freedom of expression such as Article 19 of the International Covenant on Civil and Political Rights (ICCPR) and Article 10 of the European Convention on Human Rights and Fundamental Freedoms (ECHR).[20] The right to freedom of expression as provided by these provisions is subject to qualifications or restrictions. For example, Article 19(2) of the ICCPR provides that 'everyone shall have the right to freedom of expression' and that right includes the 'freedom to seek, receive and impart information and ideas of all kinds' either orally, in writing or in print, in the form of art, or through any other media. However, clause (3) qualifies the right by subjecting it to restrictions 'provided by law' that are necessary 'for respect of the rights or reputations of others and for the protection of national security or of public order (*ordre public*) or of public health or morals'.[21] It is clear from these provisions that there is recognition at an international level that freedom of expression or free speech is not absolute. The exercise of the right to free speech is subject to laws promulgated by legislatures, where those laws comply with the limited allowable restrictions on speech provided for under these international provisions. As Barendt had observed, 'most proponents of strong free speech guarantees concede that its exercise may be restricted in some circumstances, for example, when it is likely to lead to imminent violence'.[22]

Besides international instruments, constitutional protection of freedom of expression is also discussed in the literature, depending on the jurisdiction and context of the analysis. The closest to an absolute constitutional protection of free speech is found in the First Amendment to the United States Constitution which provides that 'Congress shall make no law … abridging the freedom of speech or of the press …'[23] This provision is unqualified on its face and a literal interpretation would mean that no legal limitation can be placed on free speech. However, the US Supreme Court has on numerous occasions interpreted the First Amendment as subject to exceptions.[24] For example, the Court has ruled that 'hard-core pornography' is not 'speech' and therefore, not protected by the First Amendment.[25] Issues such as whether pornography (or sexually explicit materials) constitutes 'speech', the scope of protection under the First Amendment,[26] arguments for and against proscription of pornography, and whether pornography should be restricted or suppressed[27] are often the focus of censorship debates in America. This gives the US literature some relevance for this book, even given the atypical US approach to free speech.

The Malaysian Federal Constitution and the Hong Kong Special Administrative Region Basic Law each has a provision guaranteeing the right to freedom of expression. However, not surprisingly, there are also provisions within these documents that qualify the right. The Australian Constitution, which in any event does not contain a bill of rights, does not expressly guarantee the right to freedom of expression. However, the Australian High Court has, in a number of cases, held that there exists an implied freedom of political communication as an incident of the system of representative government established by the Constitution.[28] The constitutional protections of free speech in these three jurisdictions are further discussed in Chapter 2.

The third recurring theme in freedom of expression, obscenity and censorship literature concerns criticisms about the vagueness of definitions of key censorship terms as well as the weaknesses of the obscenity tests. This theme is often discussed within the context of the history of obscenity laws[29] which developed in England in the eighteenth century in a piecemeal fashion where the common law and statute each played an important role.[30]

The absence of precise definitions of 'obscenity',[31] 'pornography', and 'indecency' is discussed in most of the literature, with examples including work by Barendt, Robertson and Nicol, Schauer, Butler and Rodrick, Strossen and White.[32] It has been observed that 'both "obscenity" and "indecency" are defined by reference to vague and elastic formulae',[33] 'the courts have been unable to provide a meaningful definition of "indecent" short of "offending against recognised standards of propriety" or "shocking, disgusting and revolting ordinary people"'[34] and that the term 'pornography' is 'so vague, subjective and expansive that it could apply to all sexually oriented speech'.[35] Frederick Schauer in *The Law of Obscenity* commented that the definition and meaning of 'hard-core pornography' has been 'elusive for many years'[36] while Harry White observed that 'vague wording and the absence of clear standards has been such a persistent characteristic of censorship statutes for so long'. [37] The US Supreme Court was also in troubled waters, finding it difficult to arrive at a precise or workable definition of the terms. For example, in *Roth v United States*,[38] Justice Brennan observed that 'many decisions have recognized that these terms of obscenity statutes are not precise'.[39] Six years later, in his dissenting judgment in *Paris Adult Theatre v Slaton*,[40] the learned judge noted that the Supreme Court had 'failed to formulate a standard that distinguished protected from unprotected speech' and that a vague standard of obscenity would chill speech protected under the First Amendment.[41] In *Ginzburg v United States*, Justice Black remarked that 'not even the most learned judge, much less a layman, is capable of knowing in advance ... whether certain material comes within the area of "obscenity" as that term is confused by the Court today'.[42] Perhaps the clearest illustration of the Supreme Court's struggle with the 'elusive definition' comes from Justice Stewart in *Jacobellis v Ohio* – a case concerning the exhibition of the French film *Les Amants* (Louis Malle, 1958) – where the judge conceded that the term 'obscenity' may be 'indefinable' and that he 'could never succeed in intelligibly' defining it. However, the judge sought to assure us that 'I know it when I see it'.[43]

In the United Kingdom, the Committee on Obscenity and Film Censorship (the Williams Committee) acknowledged in the late 1970s the problems of defining terms like 'obscenity' and 'indecency' and proposed that these terms be abandoned 'as having outlived their usefulness'. In its report, the Committee noted:

> The question of definition occupied a central position in our review ... it is the definitions of the existing law which contribute very largely to dissatisfaction with it and it is the problem of drawing lines for the future with which a good deal of our evidence was concerned. .... it became clear to us that the success of any new system would depend very heavily on the effectiveness of any legal definition we proposed and also that there were very considerable difficulties in formulating a test of the right kind.
>
> ... The 'tendency to deprave and corrupt' and the words 'obscene' and 'indecent' were, we concluded, now useless. The charges of vagueness and confusion were so widespread that it was clear to us that we should break with the past completely.[44]

The courts in Canada are also unable to formulate precise definitions for these terms, prompting commentators to conclude that 'the definitive definition of obscenity' has not yet been formulated by the Canadian courts.[45] Some Australian writers, including Gordon Hawkins, have, in summarizing existing debates on this issue, noted that 'the nature of the subject matter is such that attempts at clarification or definition are inevitably doomed to frustration and must always end in an impasse'.[46]

It is noteworthy that imprecise definitions of key terms not only exist in obscenity and censorship laws but also in other branches of law.[47] The law of tort (for example, negligence and public nuisance), professional ethics and consumer protection laws are some examples where flexible terms such as 'fit and proper', 'reasonable person', 'good character' and 'necessary or expedient' are found. However, these terms (and their associated tests) raise less concern amongst commentators, litigants and judges compared to the vagueness that is apparent in obscenity and censorship laws. This may be attributable to at least two factors. The first factor is the dichotomy between criminal law and civil law with concepts of obscenity linked historically to obscene libel, a criminal offence carrying penal sanction. Therefore, clear definition of the key terms and applicable tests have been deemed necessary in the interests of justice and to comply with the rule of law. Equally, there is a long standing criminal law principle known as the principle of maximum certainty in defining offences.[48] The second factor can be found in Chief Justice Warren's judgment in *Jacobellis v Ohio*[49] where the judge observed that:

> In other areas of law, terms like 'negligence', although in common use for centuries, have been difficult to define except in the most general manner. Yet the courts have been able to function in such areas with a reasonable degree of efficiency. The obscenity problem, however, is *aggravated* by the fact that it involves the area of public expression, an area in which a broad range of freedom is vital to our society and is constitutionally protected.[50]

That is, the particular social and legal value of free speech makes vagueness in definitions especially problematic. While the value of free speech in the US context may well be exceptional, the literature and case law of many countries makes clear that free speech has a particular and high value.

The evolution of the obscenity test (as formulated by courts and legislatures in the Anglo-American common law world) is also considered at length by many legal scholars.[51] When the English Obscene Publications Act was enacted in 1857, it did not define 'obscenity' and it was not until a decade later that Lord Chief Justice Cockburn came up with a formulation that influenced the subject matter for many years in common law jurisdictions: 'I think the test of obscenity is this, whether the tendency of the matter charged as obscenity is to deprave and corrupt those whose minds are open to such immoral influences, and into whose hands a publication of this sort may fall.'[52] The Hicklin test, as it is commonly referred to, is based on the concept of morality[53] and has numerous weaknesses including the determination of whose moral code is to be set as the benchmark.[54] The test is also criticized for its focus on the effect of the article on the most vulnerable members of the society, whether or not they are likely to read or view it.[55] A new test was introduced in 1959 when the Obscene Publications Act was amended, with section 1 providing that a work is obscene if, taken as a whole, it is 'such as to tend to deprave and corrupt persons who are likely, in all the circumstances, to read, see or hear the matter contained or embodied in it'. This statutory test goes beyond the Hicklin test in looking at the article as a whole and at all the relevant circumstances when assessing its likely effects on its primary audience,[56] that is, those people who, the evidence suggests, would be likely to seek it out and pay for it, or else be sufficiently interested to borrow it or attend a viewing.[57] The test requires the jury to consider the effect of the work on a significant proportion of the likely audience. The fact that the article may corrupt a few vulnerable people who gain access to it is to be ignored.[58] Barendt observed that English law emphasizes that there is no absolute test to determine 'obscenity' but rather there is a variable standard, the application of which depends on the probable readership or audience and the way in which harm is assessed by reference to these particular people, not ordinary people in general.[59] The 1959 amendments to the Obscene Publications Act also introduced the 'public good' defence under section 4[60] with the view to prevent works of artistic or literary merits from being stifled.[61] This amendment in effect sets up a two-stage procedure where the jury must first rule whether the article is obscene and then determine whether on balance, publication of the work is for the public good if it has literary or other merits.[62] Barendt criticized this approach because 'the jury must balance the literary or other merits of a work against its obscene character and determine whether publication is justified'.[63] He is of the opinion that the US approach is more coherent in that it requires the court to consider literary and other merits of the article in the course of determining whether it is obscene.[64] Under the US law, the current formulation is found in the leading case of *Miller v California*[65] where 'obscenity' is limited to works which, taken as a whole, appeal to the prurient interest in sex; which portray sexual conduct in a patently offensive way; and which taken as a whole, do not have serious literary, artistic, political or scientific value.[66]

The US approach in considering literary and other merits of the work in the course of determining whether it is obscene appears the more sensible because if an article has serious artistic, literary or other merits, it will not (or rather, should not) be regarded as obscene in the first place. As explained in Chapters 3 and 4, under the Hong Kong and Australian film censorship systems – but not the Malaysian system – the artistic or other merits of a film are considered in the course of classifying the film, not after a decision to ban the film or to restrict it is made.

The question of what features a censorship system ought to have for it to be reconcilable with the free speech principle is a fourth theme that can be seen in the legal literature on freedom of expression. Although not always expressly discussed as an independent topic, legal writers who discuss censorship or prior restraint tend to offer views about the features that they consider ought to be introduced, after criticisms of the existing censorship system have been made.

Schauer, for example, suggested that the question of who decides what material or content is to be made available to the public is as important as the question of what material or content is to be made available. He argued that due emphasis should be placed on the entity that makes the decision and that 'in many contexts there are choices that are not about whether content should be determined, but are rather about which people and which institutions should be involved in the determination'.[67] According to this leading free speech theorist, there are ways in which 'censorship is inevitable, necessary and desirable – but it is less inevitable, necessary, or desirable that this group rather than that group do it'.[68] This point highlights the importance of entrusting the right entity to be the 'decision-maker' and in terms of film censorship, it raises the pertinent issue of competence, suitability and independence of censors, an issue considered at length in Chapters 4, 5 and 7.

Another example on this fourth theme is Barendt who has identified a number of 'disturbing features' of administrative censorship or 'the characteristic vices of prior restraints'.[69] These 'disturbing features' include the observation that an administrative censor is likely to adopt 'an unsympathetic attitude' to the materials he or she is censoring; the likelihood of bias where government officials may be keen to censor materials critical of the government; the fact that the censorship entity may be anxious about public criticism if it allows controversial material to be released; and the infringement of the principles of separation of powers when decisions about the right to publish are taken by the executive or its agents.[70] Barendt then proceeded to suggest a number of approaches where these 'vices' may be cured:

> Arrangements might be made for 'censorship' decisions to be taken by an impartial tribunal (appointed by an independent commission rather than by the government), which would be required to apply detailed and precise standards and to conduct an open hearing at which the publisher is legally represented. The initial decision might be made subject to full and prompt review. Such arrangements would meet many of the objections to censorship systems...[71]

The above quoted paragraph highlights five key features of a censorship system that will be considered in detail in later chapters of the book. They are the decision-making entities (this is also the key point raised by Schauer, as mentioned above), the censorship guidelines applied by film censors, the right to make representations to censors, the right to, and process of, an appeal against initial censorship decision, and the right to apply for judicial review challenging film censorship decisions in court. These key features along with several further issues which emerged as relevant through fieldwork will be discussed in the Malaysian, Hong Kong and Australian context. Many of these further issues are of a more detailed or operational nature. They concern the types of film subject to censorship, the constitution and composition of *ad hoc* censorship panels, the matters to be taken into consideration by censors in the course of making censorship decisions, the alteration of films before approval is granted, the provision of reasons for censorship decisions and the reclassification of films. Before reaching those matters, Chapter 2 outlines the film industries in Malaysia, Hong Kong and Australia in their respective socio-legal context.

2 The film industries in Malaysia, Hong Kong and Australia in their socio-legal context

Introduction

This chapter outlines the historical background, current setting and governmental involvement in the Malaysian, Hong Kong and Australian film industries in their respective socio-legal contexts. It provides an overview of the three film industries and relevant aspects of the political, legal and social settings of each of the jurisdictions to serve as a 'backdrop' to the discussions that follow in the book. It is also intended to position censorship within the wider framework of the industries and the jurisdictions in which they operate.

Under the 'Overview of the jurisdiction' sub-heading, the brief history, model of government and legal system of each jurisdiction are examined, along with a brief description of population according to ethnicity, language and religion. Thereafter the Gross Domestic Product (GDP) and per capita income figures will be highlighted to indicate the national standard of living. The 'Overview of the industry' section then charts the background and development of the three film industries, highlighting in particular, the timeline of major events in the industries (such as the time when film production began and the golden eras that the industries experienced) as well as the key entities that drove the development of the industries. Thereafter, the current setting of the industries is discussed, focusing on the operational arrangement of the three sectors of the industry – production, distribution and exhibition of films. At present, there is no oligopolistic control of the industry as these three sectors are now largely separated, although historically this was the case in all three jurisdictions. Data on the number of local films produced each year, the number of cinemas (and seating capacity), cinema admissions per year and the annual box office revenues are provided to point to the size of these film industries over the last decade. In general, Hong Kong produces the highest number of films per year, while Australia leads with the highest number of cinemas (and the largest seating capacity as a result of an expansion of multi-screen theatres) and the biggest annual box office receipts. Besides statistics to indicate the commercial scale of the industries, the achievements of Malaysian, Hong Kong and Australian films at prestigious film festivals are also noted as an indicator of their artistic and critical success. The government's involvement in the industry will then be discussed, focusing in particular on two aspects – first, the purpose or intention behind the governments' involvement and second, the initiatives undertaken by key government agencies in view of developing the film industries. The purpose of governmental involvement in Malaysia and Australia is chiefly cultural and social in nature while it is more commercially oriented in the case of Hong Kong. The incentives and supports provided by the governments are various in kind but are principally financial in form.

It must be noted that because the history of these film industries, their current operations and the governmental involvement are not the primary focus of this book, detailed extrapolation and analysis give way to a broad overview.[1] The discussion that follows draws upon existing literature but the analysis extends these accounts by comparing the three film industries in terms of their background, current setting and their respective governments' involvement.

Malaysia

An overview of the jurisdiction

Malaysia, a constitutional democracy,[2] is a federation comprising thirteen states and three federal territories. The states in Peninsular Malaysia gained independence from the British on 31 August 1957,[3] (forming the independent Federation of Malaya) and Malaysia was formed on 16 September 1963 when Singapore[4] and the states of Sabah and Sarawak joined the Federation.[5]

The Federal Constitution, which according to article 4 is the supreme law of the country, provides for the Malaysian system of government.[6] It establishes Malaysia as a federation with legislative and executive powers divided between the Federal and State governments.[7] A Westminster model of parliamentary government was set up with the three branches of government – legislature, executive and judiciary – each exercising separate functions.[8] The federal legislature consists of a bicameral Parliament – an elected lower house (the House of Representatives or *Dewan Rakyat*) and a non-elected upper house (the Senate or *Dewan Negara*). The *Dewan Rakyat* follows a multi-party system and, since independence, Malaysia has been governed by a coalition (of mostly ethnically based political parties) known from 1974 as the *Barisan Nasional,* led by the dominant United Malays National Organisation (UMNO). The executive power is vested in the Cabinet led by the Prime Minister while judicial powers rest with the judiciary headed by the Chief Justice.

Fundamental liberties[9] are guaranteed in Part II of the Federal Constitution. Of particular relevance to the book is article 10 which provides that 'every citizen has the right to freedom of speech and expression' but Parliament may by law impose on the right:

> … such restrictions as it deems necessary or expedient in the interest of the security of the Federation or any part thereof, friendly relations with other countries, public order or morality and restrictions designed to protect the privileges of Parliament or of any Legislative Assembly or to provide against contempt of court, defamation or incitement to any offence.

Restrictions on expression and speech were built into the constitutional provision and tensions often exist between the proponents of this fundamental liberty and the increasingly authoritarian executive.

Malaysia has a plural legal system.[10] The common law system, a legacy of British colonial rule, and the Islamic legal system which applies *Syariah* law to Muslims in regard to family and religious matters, operate concurrently.[11] The civil courts (common law courts) consist of the Federal Court (formerly known as the Supreme Court) which is the apex court of the country, the Court of Appeal, the High Courts, the Sessions Courts and the Magistrates' Courts. Judges of the higher courts are appointed by the King, acting on the advice of the Prime Minister after consultation with the Conference of Rulers.[12] The *syariah* courts, which run in parallel with the civil courts comprises the Syariah Appeal Court, the Syariah High Court and the Syariah Subordinate Courts.[13] Since 1988, there have been concerns about the administration of justice in Malaysia. In May 2008 a Commission of Enquiry found that 'ample evidence has emerged which clearly indicates that there is cause for concern about how judges in the upper echelons of the judiciary were appointed and the selection criteria employed'.[14] In addition to perception of interference in judicial appointments, there has been widespread concern about the quality of judgments.[15] As the result of the 2008 Commission of Enquiry, a Judicial Appointments Commission (JAC) was established to create greater transparency, accountability and good governance in the appointment of judges. It appears that the JAC has gone some way towards restoring public confidence in the administration of justice but it is too soon to measure its impact.

Malaysia is an ethnically and culturally diverse country. The 2010 government census tabulates a total population of 27.9 million with a breakdown based on ethnicity as follows: Malay 54.5 per cent, Chinese 25 per cent, indigenous people 11.8 per cent, Indian 7.5 per cent and other minorities 1.2 per cent.[16] The Malays and indigenous peoples are collectively known as *bumiputra* (sons of the soil). They make up the majority of the population and enjoy privileges in relation to land, public office, places in tertiary education, scholarship and trade.[17] Many of the non-*bumiputra* population are descendants of migrant workers (mainly from China and India) who came to Malaya during British colonial times. As at 2010, 72 per cent of the population are urban.[18]

Four major world religions – Hinduism, Buddhism, Christianity and Islam – are practised in the country along with a number of other beliefs such as Taoism, Sikhism and animism. The majority of the Malaysian populace are Muslims (60.4 per cent) followed by Buddhists (19.2 per cent), Christians (9.1 per cent) and Hindus (6.3 per cent).[19] Article 3 of the Federal Constitution provides that Islam is 'the religion of the federation' but it is pertinent to note that Malaysia is not an Islamic but a secular state,[20] although this legal definition is now contested politically by proponents of an Islamic state and other pressure groups. The increased 'Islamization' over the past two decades, which is traceable to the political competition between UMNO, the main governing party, and the opposition Pan-Malaysian Islamic Party (PAS, a conservative Islamic party) to claim higher 'Islamic credentials' to secure the majority Malay votes, has seen the introduction and implementation of Islamic policies both at the federal and state levels (such as the *Islam Hadhari* or Civilizational Islam policy), prohibition of practices such as yoga (by the influential National Fatwa Council of the Department of Islamic Development) and the banning of *wayang kulit* (shadow puppet theatre) in Kelantan, a state under the PAS administration. As noted in Chapter 7, the political contesting around the secular status of Malaysia may increase concerns about some of the weaknesses found in the censorship system, particularly the vagueness that appears in the censorship guidelines.[21] The Malay language (or *Bahasa Melayu*) is designated as the national language[22] and is widely used along with English, a variety of Chinese and Indian dialects as well as the indigenous languages. Malay is the official language of law, however English is still commonly used in the courts and the majority of judgments are written in English.

Malaysia is a middle-income country based on a multi-sector economy consisting of, amongst others, agriculture, mining, manufacturing and service industries.[23] In 2010, the country's GDP (purchasing power parity) stood at USD 424.8 billion, with a GDP per capita of USD 15,000 – ranking seventy-sixth in the world.[24]

An overview of the Malaysian film industry

The background

It has been said that the Malaysian film industry was founded on Chinese investments, Indian imagination and Malay labour.[25] Film exhibition began as early as 1910 with films coming in from France, Britain, America, China and India.[26] One of the earliest film exhibitors was Shaw Brothers,[27] which has, since the 1920s, expanded its cinema chains in Singapore and Malaya.[28] The beginning of commercial film-making is attributed to the production of the first local film, entitled *Laila Majnun*, which was produced in 1933 by S.M. Chisty and directed by B.S. Rajhans from India.[29]

In the late 1930s, the Shaw Brothers established a production company in Singapore and produced numerous Malay language films with Chinese directors and technical crews brought in from Shanghai. There were about 13 feature films produced during the fledging stage of the film industry before the Japanese occupation of Malaya.[30]

Film production came to a halt during World War Two and the Japanese occupation but it had picked up again by the late 1940s when Shaw Brothers re-entered the industry by setting up Malay Film Productions (MFP) in 1947.[31] Besides MFP, the other major force that played a crucial role in developing the industry was Cathay-Keris which was formed in 1953. The era in which these two film studios reigned supreme[32] (from the mid-1950s to the late 1960s) has often been dubbed the Golden Era of the film industry.[33] Shaw Brothers under its own banner (1937 to 1941) and as MFP (1947 to 1969) produced 170 films while Cathay-Keris (1953 to 1972) made 123 films.[34] These two studios, owned and run by Chinese entrepreneurs, forged an oligopolistic market structure whereby they took control of the three sectors of the industry – production, distribution and exhibition of films.[35] Classic films from this era include *Penarik Becha* (*The Rickshaw Man*, P Ramlee, 1955) and *Anakku Sazali* (*My Son Sazali*, Phani Majumdar, 1956) which were produced by MFP as well as *Hang Jebat* (Hussain Haniff, 1961) and *Istana Berdarah* (*Palace of Blood*, Hussain Haniff, 1964) which were produced by Cathay-Keris.

In the early 1960s, another studio by the name of Merdeka Studio was set up in the capital Kuala Lumpur, and was active for about 20 years, producing 89 films from 1960 to 1981.[36] Film production in Malaysia peaked in the early 1960s where the combined output of the three studios contributed to the release of 23 films in 1963 alone,[37] a figure which was only surpassed four decades later. The film industry began to decline in the late 1960s due to the rise of production costs (which made it more commercially viable to import films than to produce them locally) and the introduction of television in 1963.[38] Additionally, local films started to lose their appeal to audiences which, increasingly, became more attracted to American, Hong Kong and Indian films.[39] MFP stopped producing films in 1967 followed by Cathay-Keris in 1972. The closure of Merdeka Studio in 1981 marks the end of the studio era in the Malaysian film industry.[40]

After the collapse of the studio system, a new independent phase began in the mid-1970s with the formation of independently owned production companies. Most of these companies were headed by Malays and the films were made by Malay talent[41] for the Malay populace.[42] The inadequate grasp of production, marketing and distribution expertise led to the eventual closure of many of these production companies, which had sprung up only a few years earlier.[43] The 1980s and 1990s saw the emergence of new filmmakers, many of whom had trained abroad. Those who made an impact on the film industry include Othman Hafsham (*Mekanik* (*Mechanic*) 1983), Rahim Razali (*Matinya Seorang Patriot* (*Death of a Patriot*) 1984), Aziz M. Osman (*XX Ray*, 1992) and U-Wei Haji Saari (*Perempuan, Isteri & Jalang* (*Woman, Wife & Whore*), 1993). These filmmakers pioneered what is referred to as the 'Malaysian New Wave' movement.[44]

The advent of digital film-making technology in the new millennium paved the way for the emergence of yet another group of filmmakers, operating on relatively smaller production budgets in parallel with the mainstream-commercial film practitioners, like Aziz M. Osman, Shuhaimi Baba (*Pontianak Harum Sundal Malam* (*Pontianak: A Scent of Tuberose*) 2004), Yusof Haslam (*Gerak Khas: The Movie*, 2001) and Saw Teong Hin (*Puteri Gunung Ledang* (*Princess of Mount Ledang*), 2004). This group of independent filmmakers, which includes Yasmin Ahmad (*Sepet* (*Chinese Eye*), 2004 and *Mukhsin*, 2007), Amir Muhammad (*Lelaki Komunis Terakhir* (*The Last Communist*), 2006), Ho Yuhang (*Rain Dogs*, 2006 and *At the End of Daybreak*, 2009) and Khoo Eng Yow (*The Bird House*, 2006) produce works that are more successful in terms of critical recognition abroad compared to the commercial productions churned out by the mainstream practitioners.[45]

The current setting

Until 1981, a person or company could engage in all three sectors of the industry – production, distribution and exhibition of films – at the same time. This, as noted above, was the 'practice' during the studio era when Shaw Brothers/MFP and Cathay-Keris basically controlled the whole operation of the film industry.[46] The oligopolistic control of the industry became illegal (in 1981) as section 21(1) of the National Film Development Corporation of Malaysia Act 1981 (Act 244) prohibits the engagement of all three sectors by the same person or company.

A licence issued by the National Film Development Corporation of Malaysia or FINAS, a statutory body under the purview of the Ministry of Information, Communication and Culture, is required in order to engage in film production, distribution or exhibition. Licences issued may be subject to such conditions as FINAS imposes. FINAS is also empowered to refuse to issue a licence 'without assigning any reason' and such refusal 'shall be final and conclusive and shall not be challenged, appealed against, reviewed, quashed or questioned in any court'.[47]

The number of feature films produced, the total production costs and the gross box office takings of Malaysian films for the period of 2000 to 2010 are summarized in Table 2.1.[48]

Most of the local films released in the past decade were produced by key production companies including Grand Brilliance (renamed as Primeworks Studio in 2008), Tayangan Unggul, Pesona Pictures, Nizarman Malaysia, Skop Productions and Da Huang Pictures with exhibition and distribution works handled by other entities. As of 2010, there are 19 film exhibition companies operating in Malaysia, owning 100 cinemas, consisting of 571 screens and a total seating capacity of 110,424.[49] The exhibition sector is concentrated in the cities and dominated by two cinema chains – Golden Screen Cinemas and Tanjong Golden Village Cinemas. Distribution of films in DVD and VCD formats are led by two other companies – Speedy Video Distributors and Berjaya HVN Malaysia. Foreign films account for the vast majority of the distribution and exhibition sectors. For example, 78 per cent of the total box office revenue in 2005 was generated by foreign films, mainly from Hollywood.[50]

Table 2.1 The Malaysian film production sector in figures, 2000–2010

Year	*Number of feature films produced*	*Total production costs (in Malaysian Ringgit)*	*Gross domestic box office collections (in Malaysian Ringgit)*
2000	7	9.1 million	10.6 million
2001	11	13.3 million	13.4 million
2002	10	15.0 million	18.6 million
2003	16	23.8 million	23.4 million
2004	21	43.2 million	27.2 million
2005	20	29.8 million	26.7 million
2006	20	38.9 million	29.7 million
2007	21	36.4 million	29.6 million
2008	28	38.7 million	43.9 million
2009	27	40.5 million	50.8 million
2010	38	46.6 million	81.8 million

Table 2.2 highlights the industry's exhibition sector statistics for the years 2005 to 2010.[51]

The government's involvement in the industry

Until the 1980s, the Malaysian film industry remained a 'private undertaking' and received neither assistance nor incentives directly from the government. It was only in 1974 that a committee was set up by the government to identify problems faced by the industry and to recommend measures to overcome them.[52] The committee proposed the formation of a film development body which eventually materialized in 1981 in the form of the National Film Development Corporation of Malaysia. Since then, a number of initiatives have been introduced to spur the development of the film industry.

THE NATIONAL FILM DEVELOPMENT CORPORATION OF MALAYSIA (FINAS)

FINAS was established under the National Film Development Corporation of Malaysia Act 1981 to promote, nurture and facilitate the development of the country's film industry.[53] On a broader basis, FINAS aims to ensure the creation and availability of screen content to enrich the national identity of the country by making it available to local and international audiences.[54] In line with these objectives, FINAS provides financial assistance, production facilities and equipment and training to local film practitioners. In addition, FINAS also funds select film projects, for example *Embun* (Erma Fatima, 2002), *Paloh* (Adman Salleh, 2003) and *1957: Hati Malaya* (Shuhaimi Baba, 2007).

The establishment of FINAS reflects the government's awareness of the film industry as an enterprise with wide social, cultural and economic implications.[55] This is apparent as one of the six functions of FINAS is to '*regulate and control* the production, distribution and exhibition of films in Malaysia'.[56] This regulatory function is carried out by way of controlling the issuing of licenses for film production, distribution and exhibition.

Table 2.2 The Malaysian film exhibition sector in figures, 2005–2010

	2005	*2006*	*2007*	*2008*	*2009*	*2010*
Number of cinema admissions	25.9 million	27.9 million	33.6 million	43.9 million	44.1 million	54.3 million
Gross box office receipts	RM 217.4 million	RM 235.0 million	RM 289.3 million	RM 380.7 million	RM 403.3 million	RM 518.2 million
Number of cinemas	66	68	76	91	93	100
Number of screens	265	287	353	453	485	571
Total seating capacity	61,482	66,822	78,496	92,642	101,165	110,424

Since the introduction of the National Film Policy in 2005 (with the objectives 'to support the national film industry to be more progressive and internationally competitive' and to be the 'catalyst' in making Malaysia the film-making hub of the region), FINAS has carried out a number of measures to develop the industry. One of the main efforts is the implementation of projects focusing on infrastructure development and upgrading of film facilities which has included the setting up of a new soundstage and the acquisition of high technology film production equipment for the benefit of film practitioners. In recent years, FINAS has also facilitated the marketing and promotion of Malaysian films to overseas film buyers at international film festivals' film market sidebars. Additionally, FINAS also manages a number of incentive schemes aimed at increasing the number of film productions and these schemes are discussed below.

THE COMPULSORY SCREENING SCHEME

The Compulsory Screening Scheme (*Syarat Wajib Tayang*) was introduced in 2005 under the National Film Development Corporation of Malaysia (Compulsory Screening Scheme) Regulations 2005. Under this scheme, FINAS may certify a Malaysian or co-produced film which must then be screened at local cinemas. If a film is certified as eligible under the scheme, cinema operators are bound to exhibit the film as scheduled by FINAS[57] therefore guaranteeing the film a certain number of days of screening in the cinemas. Failure to do so is a breach of the Film Exhibition Licence conditions whereby the exhibitor may be liable to a fine or revocation of the licence. Exhibitors must screen an eligible film for 14 consecutive days in the biggest hall of their cinemas. However, the film may be moved to a smaller hall if the audience in the initial hall is less than 30 per cent of seating capacity during the first four consecutive days of the run, or where the audience is less than 15 per cent of seating capacity after the first three days of screening.[58] Exhibitors are allowed to withdraw the film from further screening if the latter situation occurs.[59] Exhibitors are also required to submit a report pertaining to changes of cinema hall or withdrawal of any certified film to FINAS.

FINANCIAL ASSISTANCE AND INCENTIVE SCHEMES

The two main forms of financial scheme are the Feature Film Loan Scheme and the Entertainment Duty Incentive Scheme. The Feature Film Loan Scheme was launched in 2006 with a RM50 million fund to assist production companies by providing them with loans to produce feature films. This scheme is managed by FINAS and the Small and Medium Enterprises Bank. To be eligible, the applicant must be a production company owned by a Malaysian citizen with a valid film production licence, a good track record in film production and the capacity to repay the loan. The maximum amount of loan obtainable under this scheme for a film project is RM1.5 million or 90 per cent of the estimated production cost, whichever is lower, and the interest rate is charged at 4 per cent per annum.[60]

The Entertainment Duty Incentive Scheme enables Malaysian film producers or production companies to claim the rebate of entertainment duties collected by local authorities from the sales of admission tickets at cinemas. At present, 25 per cent of a ticket price is charged as entertainment duty. From 1989 to 2008, a total of RM43.5 million in the form of entertainment duty rebates was channelled back to the respective producers as a form of incentive to encourage more film productions.[61]

Other forms of financial assistances available to film practitioners include the National and Cultural Film Fund (a fund of RM15 million for the production of films with historical and cultural themes); the CGI Fund (a fund to assist local film practitioners in producing films with computer-generated imagery contents); and the Film in Malaysia Incentive (a scheme providing cash rebate on Qualifying Malaysian Production Expenditure to encourage film production in Malaysia).

Hong Kong

An overview of the jurisdiction

Hong Kong, a British colony ceded by China in 1841,[62] became a special administrative region of the People's Republic of China (PRC) on 1 July 1997.[63] On the same day, the Basic Law of the Hong Kong Special Administrative Region – a constitutional document – came into effect, outlining the system of governance of the Hong Kong Special Administrative Region (HKSAR).[64] The principle of 'one country, two systems' was introduced to keep Hong Kong autonomous (except in the matters of defence and foreign affairs) and to continue the existing capitalist economic system and social life for 50 years after reunification with China.[65] The Basic Law guarantees the HKSAR 'a high degree of autonomy, enjoying executive, legislative and independent judicial power, including that of final adjudication'.[66] The fundamental rights of Hong Kong residents are also guaranteed by the Basic Law.[67] Two particularly relevant provisions to this book are article 27, which provides that Hong Kong residents 'shall have the freedom of speech, of the press and of publication' and article 4, which provides that the HKSAR shall safeguard the rights and freedoms of the residents in accordance with the law.

The executive branch of the government, known as the Executive Council and presided over by the Chief Executive (who is the head of the government), has the main responsibilities of formulating and implementing government policies, introducing bills to the legislature and drafting subordinate legislation.[68] The HKSAR has a unicameral legislature known as the Legislative Council which comprises 60 members, with 30 of them elected by popular vote and the remaining 30 indirectly elected by functional constituencies.[69] The Legislative Council's main functions, besides enacting, amending and repealing laws, include examining and approving budgets introduced by the Executive Council, debating issues of public interest and handling complaints made by residents.

Like Malaysia, Hong Kong also inherited the common law system from the British. The 1984 Sino-British Joint Declaration and the Basic Law ensure the continuance of this legal system in Hong Kong after 'the handover' of British rule to Chinese sovereignty.[70] The common law principles, rules of equity and almost all of the legislation in force before 1 July 1997 – including the Film Censorship Ordinance – continue to apply.[71] The HKSAR judiciary has final adjudication power with the Court of Final Appeal (lead by the Chief Justice, who is the head of the judicial branch) being the highest appellate court.[72] The Court of Final Appeal is followed in rank by the High Court (comprising the Court of Appeal and the Court of First Instance), the District Court, the Magistrates' Courts and Juvenile Courts.[73]

The HKSAR had a population of 7.15 million in 2010,[74] overwhelmingly located in urban areas.[75] According to the most recent by-census conducted by the Census and Statistics Department, 95 per cent of the population are ethnic Chinese, 1.6 per cent are Filipinos, 1.3 per cent are Indonesians and 2.1 per cent are of various other ethnicities.[76] The US Department of State reported that approximately 43 per cent of the population practices some form of religion and the two most prevalent religions are Buddhism and Taoism. It is estimated that there are approximately 1.5 million Buddhists and Taoists; 550,000 Protestant Christians; over 400,000 Roman Catholics; 20,000 Mormons; over 100,000 Muslims; over 40,000 Hindus; over 2,000 Sikhs; and over 3,000 Jews.[77] The Basic Law does not provide for an official religion but guarantees the residents freedom of conscience.[78] Chinese and English are the two official languages in the HKSAR and the Cantonese dialect is the most widely spoken.[79] All government public documents and legislation have to be published in Chinese and English.[80]

The special administrative region has a free-market economy driven by service-based industries. The four key sectors of the economy are financial services (including banking, insurance and stock brokerage), trading and logistics, tourism and professional services (for example, legal, accounting and information technology related services).[81] It is a developed capitalist economy with a GDP (purchasing power parity) of USD 337.1 billion in 2010.[82] The GDP per capita in the same year was USD 46,900, ranking tenth internationally.[83]

An overview of the Hong Kong film industry

The background

Film exhibition began in Hong Kong in 1897[84] while film-making is commonly believed[85] to have started in 1909 with the birth of the first known film entitled *Stealing a Roast Duck* directed by Liang Shaobo.[86] Film production, in its commercial sense, started in 1923 when Li Min-wei (generally seen as the founder of the Hong Kong film industry) established Min Xin, the first Chinese-owned film company in Hong Kong.[87] In 1925, Min Xin produced *Rogue*, Hong Kong's first feature-length film and by the mid-1930s, hundreds of films had already been produced in the territory.[88]

During the Sino-Japanese War (which broke out in 1937) and the Civil War (between Nationalists and Communists) many filmmakers in Shanghai moved their operations to Hong Kong. The influx of talent and investment from Shanghai contributed to the development of the Hong Kong film industry[89] and later to the bifurcation of the industry into two parallel cinemas – Mandarin cinema (transplanted in Hong Kong from Shanghai) and indigenous Cantonese cinema.[90] When Hong Kong fell under Japanese occupation in 1941, film production was 'suspended' for more than three years[91] and not a single Hong Kong film was made during this period.

Film production resumed after the Second World War. New production companies began to spring up, the important ones being Yung Hwa Studio and Union Film Enterprise Limited. Throughout the 1950s, about 50 to 70 production companies were set up each year resulting in a steady output of 150 to 170 films annually.[92] However, only about 20 to 25 of them stayed in business for more than a year and the surviving ones produced an average of six to eight films per year.[93]

In the 1960s and 1970s, martial arts films became very popular. This genre catapulted Hong Kong films into the international arena and skyrocketed the territory's box office revenues to unprecedented figures. It was noted that:[94]

> In the mid-1970s, Hong Kong films started to out-gross imports, and by the early 1980s they enjoyed total dominance over foreign products, including those from Hollywood. In the late 1980s and early 1990s, the income ratio of Hong Kong films to foreign films hovered around seven to three.

Besides martial arts, Cantonese operas, melodrama, comedy and romance were also popular genres with Hong Kong audiences.[95]

The Shaw Brothers Studio and Cathay Organisation are two of the most important entities in the Hong Kong film history. They dominated the industry in the 1950s and 1960s by becoming the major film producers. The sustained output is attributable to the studios' set-up – well equipped soundstages, film processing labs, a star system and a developed distribution and exhibition network that saw their films reaching local audiences and the diasporic Chinese audiences across Asia.[96] In addition to distributing and exhibiting their own productions, they also exhibited films by American studios.[97] The Cathay Organisation and Shaw Brothers' dominance began to wane in the 1970s, the former ceased film production in 1972 while the latter finally switched to television productions in 1986.[98]

After the decline of the two giant studios, the film industry was rejuvenated by two events. The first was the arrival of the 'New Wave' filmmakers in the late 1970s led by directors such as Patrick Tam (*The Sword*, 1980), Ann Hui (*The Story of Woo Viet*, 1981) and Tsui Hark (*Zu: Warriors from the Magic Mountain*, 1983). These filmmakers introduced new technical, visual and presentation styles and explored aspects of contemporary social realities in their films.[99] In the late 1980s, a second wave of filmmakers emerged, the prominent ones including Stanley Kwan (*Rouge*, 1987) and Wong Kar Wai (*Days of Being Wild*, 1990). These filmmakers drove Hong Kong cinema to greater artistic heights, gaining critical acclaim at prestigious film festivals such as the Festival de Cannes, the Venice Film Festival and the Berlin International Film Festival.[100] The second event was the establishment of Golden Harvest, which went on to become the most prominent and successful company in the 1970s and 1980s. Founded in 1970, this powerhouse produced box office hits first with the legendary cinematic martial artist Bruce Lee in the 1970s and subsequently with Jackie Chan in the 1980s and 1990s. Besides film production, Golden Harvest also expanded into distribution and exhibition to ensure its films' access to screens and a share of the box office revenues. Operating in parallel with Golden Harvest is a number of comparatively smaller independent production companies. Cinema City Company, Film Workshop Limited, and Win's Films are some of the more successful ones, thriving on local exhibitors and overseas distributors' finances to fund their productions.[101]

Hong Kong emerged as one of the world's most vibrant and prolific cinemas from the 1980s to mid-1990s with its unique productions that held audiences captive. Hong Kong films of this era were enormously popular, filling up cinemas and video stores in Taiwan, Japan, South Korea, South East Asia and Chinatowns around the world.[102] Hong Kong films were so in demand in Asian territories that production companies were able to pre-sell their films to exhibitors and distributors even before a single scene was shot.[103] This era of phenomenal success is referred to as the Golden Age of Hong Kong cinema,[104] during which the film industry produced more than 200 films a year, making Hong Kong the world's third largest film producer (behind India and the United States of America) and the second largest film exporter.[105]

In the mid-1990s the film industry suffered a down cycle after almost two decades of creative and commercial successes. Its decline is attributable to a convergence of various factors, in particular:

1 hyper production in the late 1980s and early 1990s which escalated the quantity of films but caused their quality to plummet (resulting in audiences turning away from Hong Kong films);[106]
2 the infiltration of triads in the film industry;[107]
3 strong competition from Hollywood, South Korean and Thai productions;[108]
4 rampant piracy of Hong Kong films;[109]
5 the impact of uncertainty about Hong Kong's reunification with China;[110]
6 the 1997/1998 Asian financial crisis (which not only affected the box office receipts but also caused investors to bail out of film productions).[111]

It ought to be noted that censorship is not one of the factors that caused the industry's downturn. While the number of productions decreased by the late 1990s, the film industry nevertheless still produced remarkable films during this period and well into the new millennium. There have been many films that enjoyed critical and/or commercial success like Wong Kar Wai's *In the Mood for Love* (2000), Andrew Lau and Alan Mak's *Infernal Affairs* (2002), Benny Chan's *New Police Story* (2004) and Johnnie To's *Election* (2005). In 2004, the Closer Economic Partnership Agreement (CEPA) was signed between the PRC and HKSAR allowing Hong Kong film companies preferential access to the Chinese market by removing import quotas and fostering co-production opportunities.[112]

Throughout its history, a diverse variety of films have flourished in Hong Kong, most notably after the arrival of the 'New Wave' filmmakers. Films exploring social issues (for example, Ann Hui's *The Boat People*, 1982, Fruit Chan's *Made in Hong Kong*, 1997), hyperbolic action films (John Woo's *The Killer*, 1989, Benny Chan's *Big Bullet*, 1996), social and political commentaries (Jacob Cheung's *Cageman*, 1992, Mabel Cheung's *The Soong Sisters*, 1997), exploitation films and risqué erotica (Michael Mak's *Sex and Zen*, 1991 and Wong Jing's *Naked Killers*, 1992), horror films (the Pang Brothers' *The Eye*, 2002), and gay cinema (Stanley Kwan's *Lan Yu*, 2001) are amongst those that suggest how the Hong Kong film censorship system neither restricts nor hinders creative expressions in film.

The current setting

Hong Kong is one of Asia's most prolific film producers and exporters. However, unlike the situation in Malaysia and Australia, where quite detailed statistics on the film industries are available to researchers,[113] in Hong Kong such information could not be obtained for this book. Over the last decade, its film industry has produced an average of 55 films a year. As there is no longer any major production studio dominating the film industry, most of the films released in the past decade were produced by these key entities – Media Asia Film, Emperor Motion Pictures, China Star Entertainment, Film Workshop Limited and Milkyway Image. In 2010, the Hong Kong film industry produced 54 feature films with a total investment amount of USD104 million.[114] With regard to the exhibition sector, there were 49 cinemas, consisting of 208 screens as at December 2010.[115] The sector is dominated by cinema chains such as Golden Harvest Cinema, Broadway Circuit and UA Cinemas. Hong Kong films are usually distributed through Newport Circuit and Gala Film Distribution while foreign films' distribution is handled mainly by Edko Circuit, Golden Scene Company Limited, United Artists, AMC Circuit and Pan Asia Circuit.[116] Distribution of films in the DVD and VCD formats is led by companies like Fortune Star, Joy Sales Films and Videos Distributor and Mei Ah Film Company.

The government's involvement in the industry

Since the establishment of the HKSAR in 1997, the government has set up a number of institutions and launched numerous initiatives to further develop the film industry. The key institutions and initiatives are discussed below.

THE FILM SERVICES OFFICE

The Film Services Office (FSO) was set up in 1998 to create and maintain an environment that is conducive to the long term development of the film industry, to promote local films abroad, to maintain Hong Kong's status as a major film producing centre and to enhance Hong Kong's position as a film trading and service hub in the Asia-Pacific region.[117] The FSO (which operates under the Commerce and Economic Development Bureau of the HKSAR) co-ordinates and facilitates film production and on-location filming in the territory. All the services provided by the FSO are free of charge and they include applications for filming permits (from the relevant government agencies), liaising with owners or managements to make available their premises for filming and regulating the use of pyrotechnics and dangerous materials for producing special effects in film production. The FSO also streamlines the various application procedures to establish a 'production-friendly' environment (in terms of convenience and lower filming costs) for film practitioners.

THE HONG KONG FILM DEVELOPMENT COUNCIL

The Hong Kong Film Development Council (HKFDC), which comprises members of the film fraternity and government agencies, was established in 2007 to advise the government on the overall policy, strategy and institutional arrangement for both short and long term development of the film industry.[118] The recent major initiative undertaken by the HKFDC is the Hong Kong Film New Action project whereby large scale promotions have been carried out with a view to redeveloping markets for Hong Kong productions. Under this project, the HKFDC facilitates direct negotiations between foreign distributors, exhibitors and investors and Hong Kong film practitioners, commissions extensive market surveys (with the aim of providing film practitioners with data and analysis to better understand recent market trends in other countries), generates publicity for new film-making talents, and sends delegations to targeted new markets to promote Hong Kong films.[119]

FINANCIAL ASSISTANCE SCHEMES

There are two financial schemes put in place by the HKSAR government to support the film industry. First, the Film Development Fund was set up in 1999 to support film or film-related projects.[120] A total of HKD 300 million was injected into this fund in 2007 to expand its scope into financing small and medium budget film productions.[121] In addition to financing film productions, the fund is also utilized to finance projects aimed at promoting Hong Kong films abroad, to train local talent in film production and distribution as well as to enhance the appreciation of Hong Kong films by local audiences. Second, the Film Guarantee Fund was introduced in 2003 to assist production companies in obtaining loans (for the purpose of film production) from financial institutions and to create conducive film financing infrastructure in Hong Kong.[122] Loan guarantees are provided to applicants who fulfil the criteria irrespective of the theme and content of the film to be made. The scheme guarantees the repayment of 50 per cent of the loan amount provided by the lending institution to the applicant-production company. At any one time, a production company may be eligible for a loan guarantee for one film project only and that film must be intended for commercial theatrical release in Hong Kong.[123]

Other initiatives include the Hong Kong International Film and TV Market (FILMART), organized by the Hong Kong Trade Development Council to promote cross-media and cross-industry co-operation in financing, distribution and broadcasting; and the Hong Kong-Asia Financing Forum, a platform to facilitate co-production ventures between Asian film practitioners and investors.

Australia

An overview of the jurisdiction

The Commonwealth of Australia was established on 1 January 1901 (from the federation of British colonies)[124] with the adoption of the Australian Constitution.[125]

Being a federal constitutional democracy,[126] the country comprises six states and three territories with legislative, executive and judicial powers shared between the federal, state and territory institutions.[127] Within each of these political units, there is a parliament elected by the people, an executive and an independent judiciary, exemplifying the doctrine of separation of powers between the three branches of government. The federal legislature is bicameral, comprising the Queen (represented by the Governor-General), the Senate (the upper house) and the House of Representatives (the lower house).[128] The executive branch is headed by the Prime Minister, who is the leader of the party with majority support in the lower house, while the judiciary is led by the Chief Justice.

In common with Malaysia and Hong Kong, Australia has a common law legal system.[129] At the federal level, there are four principal courts (known as the Commonwealth courts) and they are the High Court (the highest court and hence final court of appeal with both original and appellate jurisdiction), the Federal Court (which sits in each State and in the Australian Capital Territory and the Northern Territory when necessary),[130] the Family Court (a specialist court dealing with family disputes) and the Federal Magistrates Court (established to handle less complex disputes under Commonwealth laws). There are also state and territory courts established to decide on cases brought under state or territory laws as well as cases arising under federal laws where jurisdiction is conferred on them.[131] The Supreme Courts are the highest state and territory courts and they deal with both civil and criminal cases.

Interestingly, the Australian Constitution does not contain a bill of rights. Therefore, free speech is not expressly guaranteed in a constitutional document, unlike the situation in Malaysia and the HKSAR. It was observed that 'unlike the basic laws of most nations, the Australian Constitution does not contain an express guarantee of freedom of expression... Nor has legislation providing such a guarantee been enacted at a federal or state level in Australia'.[132] However, there is an implied freedom of political communication in Australia. The High Court in *Lange v Australian Broadcasting Corporation* held:[133]

> '... the freedom of communication which the Constitution protects is not absolute. It is limited to what is necessary for the effective operation of the system of representative and responsible government provided for by the Constitution.'

Lange v Australian Broadcasting Corporation and the subsequent case of *Coleman v Power*[134] set out a test to determine whether a law is invalid due to the implied freedom of political communication. The 'reasonably appropriate and adapted test', as it is called, poses two questions for the determination of the validity of a law.[135] First, does the law effectively burden freedom of communication about government or political matters either in its terms, operation or effect? Second, if the law effectively burdens that freedom, is the law reasonably appropriate and adapted to serve a legitimate end [in a manner][136] which is compatible with the maintenance of the constitutionally prescribed system of representative and responsible government and the procedure prescribed by s 128 for submitting a proposed amendment of the Constitution to the informed decision of the people? If the first question is answered 'yes' and the second is answered 'no', then the law in question is invalid. The High Court in *Lange v Australian Broadcasting Corporation* also observed that:

> Unlike the First Amendment [to the US Constitution]... which has been interpreted to confer private rights, our Constitution contains no express right of freedom of communication or expression. Within our legal system, communications are free only to the extent that they are left unburdened by laws that comply with the Constitution.[137]

Australia is a culturally diverse society. The Australian Bureau of Statistics tabulated a total population of 22.1 million in 2010.[138] About 89 per cent of the population is urban and the ethnicity breakdown is as follows: white 92 per cent (population of European descent), Asian 7 per cent and Aboriginal and others 1 per cent.[139] Australia has no state religion.[140] In the most recent census, 25.8 per cent of the population identified themselves as Catholics, making it the largest religious community in the country. This is followed by Anglican (18.7 per cent), Uniting Church (5.7 per cent), Presbyterian and Reformed (3 per cent), Orthodox (2.7 per cent), other Christian (7.9 per cent), Buddhist (2.1 per cent), Muslim (1.7 per cent) and others (2.4 per cent). Approximately 11.3 per cent of the respondents did not specify their religious belief while 18.7 per cent of them cited 'No religion' in the census.[141] English is the most widely used language (by 78.5 per cent of the population) and is the *de facto* national language of Australia.[142] Other major languages used in the country include Chinese, Italian, Greek and Vietnamese.

The country has a free-market economy with a large service sector.[143] It is also an exporter of natural resources, energy and agricultural products. Australia's GDP (purchasing power parity) totalled USD 901.5 billion in 2010, with a GDP per capita of USD 40,600 – ranking 19th internationally.[144]

An overview of the Australian film industry

The background

Film exhibition began as early as the late 1890s in Australia (which was not yet a single nation at that time, but a collection of British colonies).[145] The earliest

Australian films were made in 1896 in the documentary genre and in 1906, *The Story of the Kelly Gang* (Charles Tait), which is claimed to be the world's first feature-length film, was produced.[146] In the period of 1906 to 1911, Australia became the world's largest film producing country where more than 150 feature films were made.[147] In 1913, Australasian Films – a merger of nearly all the major Australian film companies – was established to produce, distribute and exhibit films. Australasian Films' oligopolistic approach controlled the marketplace at that time by limiting its own productions and at the same time refusing to exhibit films made by others.[148]

The film industry's development stalled in the late 1920s due to the effects of the Great Depression and in the subsequent four decades due to the dominance of Hollywood productions and the arrival of television.[149] This downward spiral continued until the 1960s, with only a handful of films being produced sporadically. Film productions during this era were primarily carried out by two companies, FT Films and Cinesound Productions, and very seldom were there more than three films made in a single year.[150] It was during this 'down period' that Charles Chauvel made the breakthrough *Jedda* (1955), the first feature film produced in colour by an Australian company and the first featuring Aborigines in leading roles.[151]

The 1960s saw social and cultural change in Australia where its populace, with an increased sense of nationalism, felt the need for an Australian identity. The government began to intervene actively in the arts and 're-establish' the film industry to produce films that defined and presented Australia and its culture to itself and to the world.[152] The Australia Council for the Arts was set up in 1967 and in the following year, it announced plans for the film industry which resulted in the establishment of the Australian Film Development Corporation in 1970 (subsequently re-established as the Australian Film Commission, AFC).[153] The AFC played a key role in encouraging film production in the 1970s, primarily by providing direct funding and investment. State-funded film agencies were also established to provide assistance and support to the film fraternity.

The 1970s was the era of the Australian film revival (also referred to as the 'emergence of the New Australian Cinema' by film scholars)[154] when the AFC along with state film agencies were the major players in the industry, investing in 90 per cent of the films made during that period and contributing more than 60 per cent of the overall funds.[155] The films produced in the 1970s have unique and distinctive 'Australian traits', for example, the 'ocker comedy' genre with films such as *Stork* (Tim Burstall, 1971) and *The Adventures of Barry McKenzie* (Bruce Beresford, 1972). The decade also saw the birth of highly acclaimed films that placed Australia on the world's film-making map like *Walkabout* (Nicholas Roeg, 1971), *Picnic at Hanging Rock* (Peter Weir, 1975) and *The Devil's Playground* (Fred Schepisi, 1976).[156]

In the 1980s, the Australian government provided further assistance to the industry in the form of tax incentives and concessions for capital expenditure on film production. A tax incentive commonly known as the Division 10BA scheme was introduced in 1981 to attract private investment in film productions.[157] As a result of this scheme, 900 film projects were launched within eight years (1981 to 1988) leading to a boom in film production.[158] One of the most commercially successful films produced was *Crocodile Dundee* (Peter Faiman, 1986) which became the highest grossing Australian film released domestically and the highest grossing film in the world in 1986.[159] In 1988, the Film Finance Corporation Australia (FFC) was established to act as the principal entity in film financing and investment. The FFC then became the major government investor in Australian films and some of the more successful titles financed in part by the FFC in the 1990s and 2000s include *Strictly Ballroom* (Baz Luhrmann, 1992), *Shine* (Scott Hicks, 1996), *Lantana* (Ray Lawrence, 2001) and *The Home Song Stories* (Tony Ayres, 2007). These films, in addition to being commercially successful[160] were also critically acclaimed.[161] There were also successful films produced outside of the FFC funding mechanism. The most remarkable being Philip Noyce's *Rabbit Proof Fence* (2002), a film prompted by the Bringing Them Home report – the national inquiry into the thousands of Aboriginal children forcibly removed from their families by state authorities.

Besides commercial successes domestically and increasing sales in international markets, Australian films (like those produced in Hong Kong) also feature prominently at international film festivals, garnering accolades and critical acclaim. For example, in 1993, *The Piano* (Jane Campion) won the Palm D'Or (at the Festival de Cannes) and three Academy Awards while *Bad Boy Bubby* (Rolf de Heer, 1993) won four awards at the Venice Film Festival. In 1997, *Shine* (Scott Hicks) garnered seven Academy Awards nominations and in 2006, Rolf de Heer's *Ten Canoes* won the Prix Special du Jury at the Festival de Cannes.

The productions that have emerged since the 1970s also illustrate the variety of films produced by the Australian film industry – from 'outback' films to fantasy-horror films, from exploitation films to critical commentaries on social issues, as well as other film genres. Film scholar Jonathan Rayner succinctly summed it up: 'After thirty years the Australian cinema has largely accomplished its commercial and artistic filmmaking objectives, and created a recognisable local and global identity as well as markets and consumers for its productions.'[162]

The current setting

The Australian film industry produced an average of 30 feature films and two international co-production features a year.[163] Table 2.3 shows the number of feature films produced annually, their total production costs as well as the domestic box office receipts of Australian films from 2000 to 2010.[164]

In Australia, all production companies operating outside television networks are described as 'independent production companies' and unlike the major studios in the United States, none of these companies dominate the film industry. Australian production companies usually raise funding with film investors and film agencies on a project by project basis.[165]

Table 2.3 The Australian film production sector in figures, 2000–2010

Year	*Number of feature films produced*	*Total production costs (in Australian Dollar)*	*Gross domestic box office collections (in Australian Dollars)*
2000	27	142 million	54.2 million
2001	25	162 million	63.4 million
2002	27	170 million	41.8 million
2003	19	71 million	30.3 million
2004	22	224 million	11.9 million
2005	29	112 million	23.1 million
2006	32	122 million	40.0 million
2007	30	272 million	36.0 million
2008	34	223 million	35.5 million
2009	32	393 million	54.8 million
2010	41	NA	50.6 million

* NA – Data not available

Film exhibition in the country is dominated by three companies – Hoyts, Village Roadshow and Greater Union, Birch Carroll & Coyle.[166] Table 2.4 provides the number of cinema admissions, the gross box office revenues, the number of cinemas and screens as well as their total seating capacity from 2005 to 2010.[167]

As in many countries, the Australian domestic box office is dominated by blockbusters from Hollywood. Australian feature films accounted for, on average, 5.5 per cent of the total gross takings at the box office in the past ten years. In 2010, for example, Australian films earned AUD 50.6 million or 4.5 per cent of the total grosses.[168] The distribution sector of the industry is led by affiliates of the major American film studios. The five main distributors are United International Pictures, Twentieth Century Fox, Columbia, Buena Vista and Warner Brothers (via Village Roadshow). Other key distributors in Australia include Icon Film Distribution and Madman Entertainment. Most of these distributors do not own cinemas but have some sort of an 'exclusive agreement' with exhibitors to supply their films to be screened in their respective cinema chains.[169]

Table 2.4 The Australian film exhibition sector in figures, 2005–2010

	2005	*2006*	*2007*	*2008*	*2009*	*2010*
Number of cinema admissions	82.2 million	83.6 million	84.7 million	84.6 million	90.7 million	92.4 million
Gross box office receipts	AUD 817.5 million	AUD 866.6 million	AUD 895.4 million	AUD 945.4 million	AUD 1,087.5 million	AUD 1,130.0 million
Number of cinemas	519	494	485	493	492	474
Number of screens	1943	1964	1941	1980	1989	1994
Total seating capacity	473,000	467,000	457,000	462,000	463,000	453,000

The government's involvement in the industry

Significant involvement by the Australian government in the film industry began in the 1960s.[170] The government's involvement is mainly through direct film funding, tax incentives and concessions as well as establishing film agencies with the aim of fostering film production and film culture.[171]

The major film agencies established by the federal government include Screen Australia (which is a merger of the AFC, the FFC and Film Australia Limited), Ausfilm and the National Film and Sound Archive. State governments also set up their own film agencies and they are Film Victoria, Northern Territory Film Office, New South Wales Film and Television Office, Pacific Film and Television Commission (Queensland), South Australian Film Corporation, Screen Tasmania, Screen West (Western Australia) and Screen ACT (Australian Capital Territory). These state-based agencies along with Ausfilm provide location services to film practitioners, encourage local film productions through financial incentives,[172] and support local film culture initiatives. They also provide film development and production support to projects originating from, or intending to have some production or post-production works in the agency's particular state. The types of incentive and support vary from state to state. For example, Film Victoria invests in film projects, promotes the state as a centre for production and provides film practitioners with assistance on locations, permits, taxation and unions matters while the Pacific Film and Television Commission assists film practitioners to create, develop, finance and market their projects through its 15 assistance schemes.

For the purpose of this book, only Screen Australia, being the principal federal-based agency, and the Australian Screen Production Incentive, being the main set of the federal government's initiatives, will be discussed.

SCREEN AUSTRALIA

Screen Australia was established in 2008 under the Screen Australia Act 2008. It brings together the functions of the FFC and Film Australia as well as most of the functions of the AFC. Acting as the key federal government direct funding body for the Australian screen production industry, the primary roles of Screen Australia are:

1. to act as a centralized funding body, providing production financing for a range of screen productions including feature films and documentaries;[173]
2. to encourage private investment in Australian screen production;
3. to support Australian screen practitioners including providing development support for feature film and documentary projects as well as assisting practitioners in increasing the visibility and marketability of their projects both domestically and internationally;[174]
4. to administer the Producer Offset incentive and the Australia International Co-production Program;[175]
5. to support the development of screen culture in Australia; and
6. to provide authoritative data and research to the film industry and government.

THE AUSTRALIAN SCREEN PRODUCTION INCENTIVE

In addition to providing funds via Screen Australia, the government also provides tax incentives to film practitioners. There are three types of tax incentive under the Australian Screen Production Incentive – the Producer Offset, Location Offset and Post, Digital and VFX Offset – introduced in 2007 with the aim of increasing production and assisting the industry to grow by developing sustainable businesses.[176] These three mutually exclusive incentives, replaced the government's earlier schemes – the Division 10BA scheme[177] and the Film Licensed Investment Company (FLIC) scheme.[178]

The Producer Offset is a refundable tax offset for producers of qualified screen productions. For feature films, this incentive offers a 40 per cent tax rebate of the Qualifying Australian Production Expenditure (QAPE, which is defined as production expenditure reasonably attributable to goods, services and property provided by or used in Australia) incurred on the project.[179] In addition to increasing local productions, the offset also encourages co-productions by providing an avenue to attract overseas investment in Australian projects. In order to be qualified for the offset, a feature film must fulfil the following criteria:[180]

1. it must be completed;
2. it must have a sufficient level of significant Australian content or it must be an official co-production;
3. its QAPE must meet or exceed the relevant threshold (that is, AUD 500,000 for a feature film);
4. the applicant must be an Australian company or a foreign company with a permanent establishment in Australia;
5. the applicant must have either carried out, or made arrangements for carrying out, all the activities necessary for the making of the film;
6. the film must be produced for theatrical release in commercial cinemas.

The offset is applied against the taxable income of the applicant for the year, with any remainder being refunded in cash. Access to the Producer Offset will not bar a producer or production company from accessing other tax incentives provided by state film agencies.[181]

The Refundable Film Tax Offset (RFTO) was introduced in 2001 to encourage foreign productions to use Australian locations, cast, crews and service providers in producing their films.[182] The RFTO was renamed the Location Offset in 2007 and at present, it provides for a 16.5 per cent offset on a minimum of AUD 15 million expenditure. This 16.5 per cent offset, which is calculated from a production's QAPE, may represent between a 10 per cent to 15 per cent cash subsidy on the total budget of an eligible production.[183] The Post, Digital and VFX Offset was introduced to assist the Australian visual effects, post-production and animation sector. Under this incentive, a 30 per cent offset is available for projects that spend at least AUD 500,000 in qualifying post, digital and visual effects expenditures in Australia.[184] These would include expenditures on visual effects, audio and visual editing and green-screen photography tasks and the offset would apply irrespective of whether or not the production was shot in Australia.

Summary

Film production started at different points of time in the three jurisdictions covered in this book. The first to commence film production was Australia, where films were produced as early as 1906, followed by Hong Kong in 1923 and Malaysia in 1933. Over the years, the film industries have undergone cycles of 'success' and 'failure', and each has enjoyed a 'golden era' where the number of local productions soared and local films enjoyed popularity amongst domestic audiences in the face of strong competition from foreign films. The Malaysian film industry experienced this in the 1960s, the Australian film industry in the 1970s and the Hong Kong film industry in the 1980s.

At present, the production sectors of the film industries in Malaysia, Hong Kong and Australia are made up of independent production companies. There are no dominating studios or enterprises in the industries like there once were. The three sectors of the industry – production, distribution and exhibition – are now largely separated (although some prudent exhibitors also double as distributors) and therefore there is no oligopolistic control of the film markets. The Hong Kong film industry produces the highest number of films amongst the three industries under study. It produces, on average, 55 films a year, while the Australian and Malaysian film industries produce, on average, 31 and 30 films per year respectively. There are higher numbers of co-productions with foreign investors in the Hong Kong and Australian film industries compared to the Malaysian film industry, where the number of joint-production projects is negligible.

Malaysian films are made primarily for the domestic market. Overseas markets are very limited and the occasions of foreign distribution and exhibition are rare.[185] The market for Australian films is comparatively wider, partly because of the language of the films, covering in particular the United States and the United Kingdom. Amongst the three film industries, Hong Kong has the biggest market size where their films are distributed and exhibited in China, the United States, the United Kingdom, Australia, Japan, Korea, and South East Asian countries. The Hong Kong and Australian film industries have also produced a far greater number of films of acknowledged critical and aesthetic standing over the last 30 years. Those films are not only remarkable in terms of artistic achievement and commercial success but also encompass more genres and wider subject matters than Malaysian films. Hong Kong and Australian films are featured more prominently at prestigious international film festivals, winning accolades and critical admiration.

In terms of distribution and exhibition, the Malaysian, Hong Kong and Australian marketplaces are, at present, dominated by Hollywood productions. Domestic films' share of the total national box office did not exceed 50 per cent of the gross receipts over the past decade. Hong Kong films accounted for, on average in the ten years up to 2010, 30.8 per cent of the total gross takings at the domestic box office, followed by Malaysian films with 16.3 per cent and Australian films with 4.7 per cent.[186] The total box office receipts of these three industries also differ where Australia has the highest gross receipts with an average of AUD 740 million annually in the five years up to 2010.[187] Cinema admissions were also the highest in Australia with an average of 85.2 million per year in the five years up to 2010, followed by Malaysia and Hong Kong.[188]

The Malaysian, Hong Kong and Australian governments are involved in their respective film industries through agencies set up to promote the development of the industries and to provide assistance to film practitioners. However, each government entered the scene at a different time – the Australian government started its active participation in the 1970s, the Malaysian government began in the 1980s and the HKSAR government got involved in the late 1990s. The governments' intention or purpose in being involved in the industry also differs. The Malaysian and Australian governments aim to foster a national identity through films as well as to ensure the creation and availability of screen content for local and international audiences while the Hong Kong government's involvement appears to be more inclined towards commerciality rather than social or cultural reasons. The types of incentive and support introduced also differ, although they are principally financial in form. In Malaysia and Australia, tax incentives or rebates are provided. Malaysian producers may claim the refund of entertainment duties levied on cinema ticket sales while Australian production companies may apply for various kinds of tax offset or concession at the federal and state levels. Neither entertainment nor production tax incentives are offered in Hong Kong but the government has introduced a scheme to guarantee loans provided by financial institutions to film practitioners, an effort to create conducive film financing infrastructure.

Each of the three governments has also introduced a form of incentive or scheme that is unique to their respective film industry. In Malaysia, there is the Compulsory Screening Scheme where qualified local films will enjoy guaranteed public exhibition in major cinemas across the country for a period of time. In Hong Kong, major events such as film festivals and film markets are held annually to promote local films, to enhance Hong Kong's position as a film trading and service hub and to serve as platforms for joint ventures with foreign distributors, exhibitors and investors. Large scale efforts have also been carried out to develop new markets for local productions. In Australia, comprehensive support and assistance are available to potential projects – from script development to production, and finally the marketing of the completed film both locally and internationally.[189]

Government agencies – FINAS in Malaysia, the FSO and HKFDC in Hong Kong and Screen Australia and state government bodies in Australia – also invest in or fund film productions. The HKFDC finances small and medium budget productions through the Film Development Fund that it administers, the Australian agencies provide direct funding and investment in select film projects, whereas FINAS funds certain 'nationalistic' productions.[190] The purpose of film investment and project funding again appears to differ. Where FINAS and Screen Australia aim to ensure the creation of national screen content, FSO and HKFDC appear to do so more for commercial considerations.

3 Film censorship systems in Malaysia, Hong Kong and Australia

The laws, guidelines and processes

Introduction

There are three types of censorship system in which films are regulated. The first can be termed a state-based regulation system where entities are officially established under legislative instruments to examine films prior to their availability to the public. Such entities operate under the purview of a government ministry or department and exert formal powers to censor films. This system is the most common of the three and it is adopted in Malaysia, Hong Kong and Australia. The second system can be termed an industry self-regulation system as exemplified by the Motion Picture Association of America (MPAA) in the United States of America where the entity responsible to rate productions was set up by the film industry itself. The third system is regulation by an independent body as represented by the British Board of Film Classification (BBFC) in the United Kingdom. The BBFC was established by the cinema industry in 1912 to provide centralized and consistent film classification.[1] In the 1940s, it became an independent body funded by the fees charged for film classification. The BBFC is independent of both the British government and the film industry.[2]

The film censorship systems in Malaysia, Hong Kong and Australia are made up of their respective film censorship laws, guidelines and processes. This chapter discusses the main features of the laws and guidelines and describes the censorship processes. Each piece of legislation forming the legal basis for film censorship in the three jurisdictions under study came into force at different times and each has its distinctive features for the censorship processes. In addition to legislation, each jurisdiction also has a set of guidelines to assist censors in making their decisions. All three sets of guidelines contain a list of prohibited types of film and content, some of which are peculiar to each set of guidelines.[3] There is no absolute freedom of expression for film practitioners and no absolute freedom of choice for adults in these jurisdictions. Malaysia, Hong Kong and Australia have systematic film censorship processes in place and the structure of each process is, to a large extent, similar: films are censored and classified prior to their availability to the public; censorship is carried out based on legislative provisions and guidelines; and decisions made at the first instance may be reviewed by appealing to a higher-ranking decision-making entity.

The Malaysian system

The law: Film Censorship Act 2002 (Act 620)

The legislation regulating film censorship in Malaysia is the Film Censorship Act 2002 (Act 620). It came into force on 1 April 2002, repealing and replacing the Film (Censorship) Act 1952 (Act 35).[4] When the Film Censorship Bill 2001 was tabled for its second reading, the then Deputy Minister of Home Affairs stated that because film has strong effects on the behaviour, attitude and lifestyle of the people, it was the responsibility of the government to enact laws to ensure that the noble values of Malaysians were not eroded by the presence of undesirable content in films.[5]

The Film Censorship Act 2002 is divided into eight parts. Part I deals with preliminary matters,[6] Part II provides for the establishment of the Board of Censors while Part III makes provisions for the control of films and film publicity materials by setting out the mechanics of submitting films and film publicity materials for censorship.[7] Part III also provides for the making of alterations to films as required by the Board of Censors,[8] the issuance of censorship certificates,[9] as well as the requirement to display the mark of approval, censorship certificate, classification and the name and address of the person who exhibits, distributes, displays or sells the film.[10] Part IV establishes the Appeal Committee and provides a mechanism enabling film practitioners who are dissatisfied with the decision of the Board of Censors to appeal to the Appeal Committee.[11] Part V contains provisions conferring powers on the Home Minister to issue directions,[12] prohibitions[13] and exemptions[14] as well as to make regulations under the Act.[15] Part VI then deals with powers relating to the enforcement of the Act and includes powers to investigate, search, seize and arrest. Penalties are also prescribed for specific offences under the legislation.[16] Part VII contains miscellaneous matters, including prosecution of censorship offences.[17] The final part of the Act, Part VIII, deals with repeal, transitional and saving provisions.[18] The Schedule to the Act provides for the administration and the conduct of meetings of the Board and the Committee.

The guidelines: Film Censorship Guidelines 1993

The censorship guidelines applied by the Board of Censors are known as the *Garis Panduan Lembaga Penapis Filem 1993* or Film Censorship Guidelines 1993 which were issued in the Malay language by the Prime Minister's Department and approved by Cabinet on 17 November 1993.[19] The Guidelines have since been applied as a guide for making censorship decisions until 15 March 2010 where they were replaced by a new set of guidelines known as the *Garis Panduan Penapisan Filem* or Film Censorship Guidelines.[20] As is explained in Chapter 7, only minor changes and few improvements have been made and it may well be argued that the 2010 Guidelines are even more vague and convoluted than the 1993 ones. Since the 2010 Guidelines are relatively new, it is unclear how they will be applied by censors and a more substantial amount of time would be needed to observe emerging patterns of application and their consequent effects.

Additionally, on 21 December 2011 the Home Ministry announced that it will gradually cease censoring films and is considering substituting the current censorship arrangement with some form of industry regulation scheme. However, as of 1 June 2012, no changes have been made to the law and overall censorship scheme[21] and it appears very unlikely that a new scheme will be enforced in the near future.[22] Therefore, the initial focus remains on the 1993 Guidelines which have been in use for 17 years and clearly informed practitioners' views during the fieldwork. The 2010 Guidelines will be textually examined and commented on in Chapter 7 in light of the fieldwork, when proposals for the reform of the Malaysian film censorship system are made.

Unlike in Hong Kong and Australia, there is no specific provision in the Malaysian film censorship law that expressly provides for the power to make censorship guidelines. However, sections 19C and 28(2)(c) of the repealed Film (Censorship) Act 1952 (Act 35) may have empowered the relevant minister to draw up the guidelines.[23] In any event, no challenge was ever made to the 1993 Guidelines, and the 2002 Act does give the Home Minister power, as noted above, to issue directions as to the process to be followed in censorship.

The Film Censorship Guidelines 1993 comprises six parts.[24] Part A of the Guidelines lays down the general principles of film censorship in the following terms:

1 to protect Malaysian society from the possibility of negative influences resulting from watching films which may drive them to engage in immoral acts or to sympathize with ideologies that are inconsistent with the *Rukunegara*;[25]
2 to prevent the exhibition and distribution of anti-government films and films that may offend other countries, especially ASEAN and Islamic countries or their leaders;
3 to prevent the exhibition and distribution of films that propagate false teachings, deviations, criticisms or insults against any religion;
4 to safeguard racial harmony;
5 to serve as a code of conduct to promote the noble values of Malaysian society;
6 to prevent the good name of individuals or organizations from being tarnished due to the screening of a film.

Part B of the Guidelines deals with the definition of 'film', Part C provides for the steps to be followed by censors in censoring films and Part D sets out the eight questions that censors must consider before making a censorship decision. Parts C and D are examined further below, where the film censorship process in Malaysia is discussed. Under Part E, the types of film, content and portrayal that are not allowed to be exhibited and distributed in Malaysia are categorized into four broad headings referred to as 'censorship elements': 'Ideology and Politics', 'Religion', 'Socio-culture' and 'Order and Decorum'. Brief particulars of the prohibited types of film, content and portrayal are stated under each of these elements. Part F, the concluding part of the Guidelines, states that they are to be applied responsibly and that censors should be mindful of the aspiration of the government to create a Malaysian race that is culturally advanced and morally honourable. The appendix to the Guidelines entitled '*Garis Panduan Terperinci Bagi Panduan Lembaga Penapis Filem Dalam Tontontapis Sesebuah Filem*' (Detailed Guidelines for the Guidance of the Board of Film Censors in Censoring Films)[26] provides additional descriptions to some of the particulars mentioned under the four censorship elements stated in Part E.

The Guidelines are not published in the *Gazette* but copies are made available to film practitioners upon request purportedly to assist them in making production decisions as well as decisions in relation to acquiring exhibition and distribution rights to foreign films. However, many film practitioners have commented that the Guidelines are vague, inconclusive and confusing.[27] Persistent calls have been made by film practitioners for a clearer set of guidelines to be introduced for the benefit of the film industry. The *Dasar Perfileman Negara* (National Film Policy) which was approved by the Cabinet on 23 February 2005 had highlighted this issue by pointing out that the Guidelines lacked clarity and, therefore, its application had caused significant problems to film practitioners.

The process

Section 9 of the Film Censorship Act 2002 requires films to be submitted to the Board of Censors for censorship purposes before they can be exhibited and distributed to the public. The censorship process of a foreign film is similar to that of a local film. After a film is received for censorship purposes, the Chairman of the Board of Censors will appoint three or more members from the Board to form a panel to examine the film. A larger panel may be formed if the Chairman is of the opinion that the film to be examined is controversial or that there may be difficult issues that would arise from the film.[28] After viewing the film, the panel will then determine whether there is any scene, dialogue, sound or subtitle that should be altered based on the censorship guidelines. If alteration to the film is necessary, the panel will consider a set of eight questions stated in Part D of the Guidelines in order to determine the extent of alteration that should be made. These questions are:

1. What is the genre of the film?
2. What is the theme of the film?
3. What is the message of the film?
4. Are there any lessons to be learned from the film?
5. Does the film have the possibility of influencing a particular age group?
6. Does the film over-revere or venerate any particular race, religion, country or ideology?
7. Does the film have the possibility of offending any particular race, religion or country?
8. Is the film compatible with the nation's aspiration?

Under section 10(1) of the Film Censorship Act 2002, there are three types of decision that the Board of Censors can make after examining a film and they are:

1 approve the film for exhibition without any alteration;
2 approve the film for exhibition with such alteration as the Board may require;
3 refuse to approve the film for exhibition.[29]

After a decision is made, a censorship report will be prepared and submitted to the Chairman of the Board of Censors for approval. If the Chairman disagrees with the decision, he may request further viewing and deliberation by a larger panel.

The censorship decision is to be communicated to the owner of the film in writing.[30] If a film is approved for exhibition subject to alteration or if a film is refused approval, the Board must provide reasons for its decision.[31] If a film is approved subject to alteration being made, the Board will seek the film owner's consent to make such alteration. If consent is withheld, the film will be refused approval for exhibition and will be returned to its owner. It is provided under section 11(1) of the Act that alteration to a film may be made either by the Board or by the owner of the film.[32]

Films that are approved for exhibition and distribution will be classified under section 15 of the Act. There were five classification categories applicable in Malaysia prior to the introduction of the Film Censorship Guidelines on 15 March 2010 and they are summarized in Table 3.1. It is noteworthy that films that are classified in restricted categories – 18SG; 18SX; 18PA and 18PL – may still be subject to alteration and not released in their entirety.[33]

In January 2012, these classification categories were replaced with a new and simplified set of categories and they are: 'U' (for general audience, suitable for viewing by all levels of society); 'P13' (not recommended for viewing by persons under 13 years of age without guidance from parents or guardians); and '18' (restricted to persons of 18 years of age and over only). After a film is classified, a censorship certificate will be issued[34] and it is an offence if the classification mark is not displayed or if the film owner displays a classification which is different from that given by the Board.[35]

Table 3.1 Film classification categories applicable in Malaysia

Classification category	*Description*
U: For general audience	Suitable for viewing by all levels of society.
18SG: For 18 and above	Contains elements of violence or horror that are not excessive. Suitable for viewing by those who are 18 years old and above only.
18SX: For 18 and above	Contains elements of sex that are not excessive. Suitable for viewing by those who are 18 years old and above only.
18PA: For 18 and above	Contains religious, social or political elements. Suitable for viewing by those who are 18 years old and above only.
18PL: For 18 and above	Contains a combination of two or more elements of violence, horror or sex that are not excessive or contains religious, social or political elements. Suitable for viewing by those who are 18 years old and above only.

In addition to submitting a film for censorship purposes, film practitioners are also required to submit every film's publicity material[36] to the Board for its approval before such material can be displayed, distributed or circulated.[37] The Board may approve the material without alteration, or approve it with such alteration as the Board may require, or refuse to approve it.[38] If the Board approves publicity material subject to alteration being made or refuses to approve it, reasons for the decision must be provided.[39] In addition, the Home Minister has absolute discretion to prohibit the display, distribution, possession or circulation of a film's publicity material, if the Minister is of the opinion that it would be contrary to public interest.

In the event a film owner is dissatisfied with the censorship decision made by the Board of Censors, the owner may appeal to the Appeal Committee under section 21(1) by submitting a notice of appeal within 30 days from when the owner is notified of the Board's decision. The notice of appeal may contain the film owner's representation[40] and an appeal may be made in relation to a decision that the film is not approved for exhibition, in regard to alteration that is required to be made to the film, or in regard to the classification category given to the film. After an appeal is filed, the Appeal Committee, with a quorum of six members, will examine the film again and review the decision in question.[41] The Committee may confirm, vary or reverse the decision of the Board. The Committee's decision is said to be final and not to be challenged in court.[42] The Home Minister has the power, under sections 26 and 28, to override censorship decisions made by the Board and the Committee. With section 48 providing that 'no decision of the Minister, the Board or the Committee under this Act or any regulations made under this Act shall be subject to appeal or review by any court on any ground', the final censorship decision appears to rest with the Minister and that ministerial power appears to be unfettered.[43]

The Hong Kong system

The law: Film Censorship Ordinance (Cap. 392)

The legislation constituting the legal basis for film censorship in Hong Kong is the Film Censorship Ordinance (Cap. 392), which came into force on 10 November 1988.[44] The Ordinance attempts to preserve the features of the earlier approach to censorship and to achieve two other objectives: first, to introduce a three-tier film classification scheme and second, to remove any ambiguity in the legal legitimacy of film censorship in the territory.[45] The enactment of the Ordinance can be directly linked to the embarrassing 'leak' of the Executive Council's confidential documents by the Asian Wall Street Journal in March 1987.[46] According to those documents, the Hong Kong Government was well aware as early as 1972 that the censorship of films might be illegal because the principles of censorship were stated in internal guidelines and not in the regulations made under the Places of Public Entertainment Ordinance (Cap.172).[47] The International Covenant on Civil and Political Rights (ICCPR) was invoked during the consultative process and debates on the Film Censorship Bill.[48] The main argument canvassed during the debates was whether section 10(2)(c) of the proposed bill was compatible with the principle of freedom of expression as provided for in Article 19 of the ICCPR.[49] Subsequently, Article 19 was referred to in section 10(3)(d) of the Ordinance where censors are required to take into account the article when determining the suitability of a film for exhibition. The inclusion of Article 19 was a historic event in Hong Kong, being the first incident where a provision of an international covenant has found its way into the domestic law.[50]

The Film Censorship Ordinance contains ten parts. Part I deals with preliminary matters[51] while Part II provides for the establishment of the Film Censorship Authority,[52] the Panel of Censors[53] and the Panel of Advisers.[54] Part III makes it an offence to exhibit a film unless the film has been issued with either a certificate of exemption or a certificate of approval by the Film Censorship Authority. Part IV[55] sets up the mechanism for submission of films for censorship purposes. Part V[56] then deals with film classification[57] and the issuance of certificates of approval, notice of refusal to approve and notice concerning excision of a film.[58] Part VI provides that the certificate of exemption or certificate of approval issued must be displayed in a conspicuous position where the film is to be exhibited. Part VIA is of particular importance to film distributors as it deals with publication (release) of films in videotape and disc formats.[59] Part VIB in turn deals with submission for approval of film advertising materials.[60] Part VII establishes the Board of Review,[61] sets out the functions of the Board and the procedures of review.[62] The final part of the legislation, Part VIII, deals with enforcement and miscellaneous matters.[63] This part provides for offences in relation to exhibition or distribution of Category III films[64] as well as offences in relation to contravention of conditions endorsed on censorship certificates and the revocation of censorship certificates.[65] The power to make regulations under the Ordinance is provided under section 29 and the power to make censorship guidelines is provided under section 30.

The guidelines: Film Censorship Guidelines for Censors

The censorship guidelines applied in Hong Kong are the Film Censorship Guidelines for Censors, which came into effect on 3 December 1999 and are available in both Chinese and English language versions. The Guidelines were made under section 30 of the Film Censorship Ordinance, which provides that the Secretary for Commerce and Economic Development may from time to time cause to be prepared and published in the *Gazette*, guidelines not inconsistent with the Ordinance, indicating the manner in which it is proposed that censors exercise their functions. In addition to film censorship, the Guidelines, which are divided into 11 parts, also deal with other incidental matters such as film advertising materials.

Part I states that the Guidelines should be read in conjunction with the Film Censorship Ordinance; that each film must be considered on its own merits; and that the aim of censors should be ‘to reflect contemporary public attitudes towards censorship standards’.[66] The first part also acknowledges that the results of public opinion surveys on film censorship standards and advice provided by the Panel of Advisers are of assistance to censors in making censorship decisions. The legal principles of film censorship are stated in Part II by reproducing sections 10(2) and (3) of the Ordinance.[67] Part III then explains the rationale and functions of the three-tier classification scheme as well as describing the film classification categories applicable in Hong Kong. Paragraph 6 of the Guidelines states the rationale as follows:

> The classification of films into a three-tier system gives adults the opportunity to see a wider range of films dealing with the realities of the adult world, but at the same time, restricts children and youth from viewing what could be harmful to them in a way or another.

The two functions of the scheme are to lay down 'a set of legally enforceable rules to restrict admission and access to adult films by minors' and to offer parents 'some advance information about the suitability of the film' to enable them to decide whether their children should be allowed to watch the film or not.[68] Part IV then stipulates that the person who submits a film for censorship purposes is required to state the classification category that is being sought for the film, and the censor assigned to examine the film should attempt to accommodate this wish, but may indicate any other classification he or she would be prepared to give, or refuse approval.[69] Part V, entitled 'Approaches in Classification', constitutes the bulk of the Guidelines. This part provides for the approaches to be taken in censoring films by setting the limits of six censorship elements; 'Cruelty, Torture or Violence', 'Horror and Shock', 'Disability', 'Sex and Nudity', 'Language' and 'Offensive Behaviour and Criminality'. It is interesting to note that the Guidelines expressly acknowledged that, apart from the 'Disability' and 'Offensive Behaviour and Criminality' elements, the rest of the elements are either established art forms or the reality of life in Hong Kong. For example, under the 'Sex and Nudity' element, it is stated that: 'The depiction of nudity is an established art form'.[70] Part V also provides for a list of content that is prohibited in any film to be exhibited and distributed in Hong Kong.[71]

Part VI deals with exemption of films where the classes and descriptions of films suitable to be exempted from censorship are stated.[72] Part VII then deals with film titles where the Film Censorship Authority 'may refuse to issue a certificate of approval if he is of the opinion that the proposed title of a film is unsuitable for exhibition, publication or display to the public'.[73] Part VIII deals with film advertising materials and film packaging where all advertising materials for, and packaging of, Category III films must be submitted for approval before they can be publicly exhibited, displayed or distributed.[74] Parts IX and X of the Guidelines are not relevant for the purposes of the book as they provide for films submitted by clubs and cultural organizations and the exemption of slides of non-commercial nature from censorship requirement, respectively. The final part of the Guidelines, Part XI, provides for advisory services where censors may be called upon to provide advice to film producers on the suitability or otherwise of a particular scene, language or theme, but such pre-production advice is not binding on the censor.[75] Non-binding advice may also be given by censors in respect of choosing a classification category for a film submitted for censorship purposes and the possibility of changing a film's classification category.[76]

The process

Section 8(1) of the Film Censorship Ordinance provides that a film intended for exhibition must be submitted to the Film Censorship Authority (hereinafter referred to as 'the Authority') in order to be dealt with either under section 9, which provides for exemption of films,[77] or under section 10 which provides for censorship of films. Section 8(2) then provides that when a film is submitted, it must be accompanied by a statement as to the classification category that is being sought for the film and a declaration as to whether the film has been classified under the Control of Obscene and Indecent Articles Ordinance (Cap. 390).[78]

The censorship procedure is the same for foreign and local films. After a film is accepted under section 8 of the Ordinance and that film is not exempted, section 10(1) provides that the Authority shall assign a censor to examine the film. In addition, the Authority may also assign not less than two advisers (from the Panel of Advisers) to provide advice to the assigned censor.[79] The censor is required to view the film as soon as practicable and to consider the matters stated under section 10(2) as well as take into account the matters stated under section 10(3) of the Ordinance.[80] The two provisions read as follows:

> (2) The censor shall as soon as practicable view the film and consider the following matters for the purpose of making his decision under subsection (4):
> (a) whether the film portrays, depicts or treats cruelty, torture, violence, crime, horror, disability, sexuality or indecent or offensive language or behaviour; and
> (b) whether the film denigrates or insults any particular class of the public by reference to the colour, race, religious belief or ethnic or national origins or the sex of the members of that class.
> (3) The censor shall, in viewing the film and considering the matters referred to in subsection (2), also take into account the following matters:
> (a) the effect of the film as a whole and its likely effect on the persons likely to view the film;
> (b) the artistic, educational, literary or scientific merit of the film and its importance or value for cultural or social reasons; and
> (c) in relation to the intended exhibition of the film, the circumstances of such exhibition.

Thereafter, the censor is obliged to consult the advisers (if any) assigned to the film.[81] The censor may also consult the Authority[82] or, with the approval of the Authority, consult any other person.[83] However, such consultations are not binding on the censor.[84] The censor may then proceed to make his or her decision.

In making censorship decisions, censors are guided by the Film Censorship Guidelines for Censors. Section 10(4) of the Ordinance provides for the three types of censorship decision that a censor can make and the subsequent actions that must follow the decision:

(a) if he [the censor] is of the opinion that the film is suitable for exhibition, approve the film for exhibition, give it a classification under section 12(1) and record in writing by reference to the matter referred to in subsection (2) or (3) a statement of the reasons for his decision;
(b) if he [the censor] is of the opinion that the film is not suitable for exhibition because of a matter referred to in subsection (2), refuse to approve the film for exhibition and record in writing by reference to the relevant matter referred to in subsection (2) a statement of the reasons for his decision; or
(c) if he [the censor] is of the opinion, by reason of a specified piece or specified pieces of the film, that the film is not suitable for exhibition because of a matter referred to in subsection (2), or that he is unable to give the film an appropriate classification under section 12(1), record in writing –
  (i) the classification under section 12(1) he would be prepared to give to the film if such specified piece or pieces were excised from the film; and
  (ii) by reference to the relevant matter referred to in subsection (2), a statement of the reasons for his decision, or the reasons why he is unable to give the film an appropriate classification under section 12(1), as the case may be.

If a film is approved for exhibition, the censor will classify it under section 12. The applicable classification categories are summarized in Table 3.2.

Table 3.2 Film classification categories applicable in Hong Kong

Classification category	*Description*
Category I	Approved for exhibition to persons of any age.
Category IIA	Approved for exhibition to persons of any age subject to the condition that any advertising material which relates to the film shall contain the following notice in block letters and Chinese characters prominently and legibly displayed – 'NOT SUITABLE FOR CHILDREN'
Category IIB	Approved for exhibition to persons of any age subject to the condition that any advertising material which relates to the film shall contain the following notice in block letters and Chinese characters prominently and legibly displayed – 'NOT SUITABLE FOR YOUNG PERSONS AND CHILDREN'
Category III	Approved for exhibition only to persons who have attained the age of 18 years subject to the condition that any advertising material which relates to the film shall contain the following notice in block letters and Chinese characters prominently and legibly displayed – 'APPROVED FOR EXHIBITION ONLY TO PERSONS WHO HAVE ATTAINED THE AGE OF 18 YEARS'

Categories I, IIA and IIB are advisory in nature. There is no restriction on access to films so classified whereas films classified Category III are legally restricted to persons of 18 years of age and above.

After classifying the film, a certificate of approval will be issued under section 13(1) in respect of that film. Where a film is refused approval for exhibition, the Authority will issue a notice of refusal which states the censor's reasons for the decision to the person who submitted the film.[85] In the situation where a censor decides that a film is not suitable for exhibition, or that an appropriate classification could not be given due to a specified piece or pieces of the film, the Authority will issue a notice of the censor's decision to the person who submitted the film specifying the piece or pieces of the film that require excision and the reasons for the censor's decision.[86] The Authority will return the film to the person who submitted it in order for the required excision to be made or, upon that person's request, the Authority may arrange for the excision to be done.[87] After the excision is made, the film will be approved with the classification category previously stated by the censor to be appropriate subject to the excision being made. The issuance of a certificate of approval will follow and unless a condition to the contrary is imposed, the certificate also operates as an approval for the release of the film in videotape and disc formats.[88]

Besides films, certain film advertising materials[89] also need to be approved by the Authority. Whether a piece of film advertising material is subject to censorship would depend on the classification category the film receives. The relevant provision is section 15K which provides that if a film is classified under section 12(1)(c) (that is, the Category III classification), any advertising material of that film must be submitted for approval. If a film is classified under section 12(1)(a) or (b) (Category I, Category IIA or Category IIB classifications), it is not mandatory for the film's advertising material to be submitted for approval. Where advertising material is submitted, the Authority may approve or refuse to approve it.[90] In making its decision, the Authority must consider the matters set out under section 10(2), take into account the matters stated in section 10(3)[91] and have regard to the following matters:[92]

(a) the standards of morality, decency and propriety that are generally accepted by reasonable members of the community;
(b) the dominant effect of the material as a whole;
(c) the location where the material is likely to be displayed and the persons likely to view it; and
(d) any artistic, educational, literary or scientific merit it may possess.

Advertising materials will be refused approval if they contain contents that are offensive to 'public morality, decency and ordinary good taste'.[93]

Censorship decisions are reviewable by the Board of Review when there is an appeal or request to do so. In a meeting to review a censorship decision, the attendance of six members of the Board shall form a quorum,[94] but in the event that after 30 minutes have elapsed since the time fixed for the meeting and less than six members are in attendance, then four members are sufficient to form a quorum.[95] Therefore, at least four individuals will be reviewing the appealed censorship decision.

There are three categories of person who may request the Board to review a decision and they are:

1 the person who submitted the film;
2 the Authority; and
3 the person who is aggrieved by the exhibition of a film or the release of videotapes or discs of a film.

Section 17(1) of the Ordinance provides that where a person who submits a film is aggrieved by the censorship decision, he or she may, not later than 28 days after the day on which he or she is notified of the decision, request the Board of Review to review the decision in question. Section 17(2)(c) then provides that after a date to review the decision is fixed, a notice will be served on the person who made that request (the affected person), the Authority, and on any other person whom the Chairman of the Board considers to be a person who has an interest in the review or who can assist the Board in the review (the interested person), informing them that they and their representatives may attend and make representations before the Board. At the review meeting, the Board will view the film, consider the notice of request to review and the decision to which the request relates, consider the representations made under section 17(2)(c) and where appropriate, consider the matters stated under section 10(2) as well as take into account the matters stated under section 10(3) of the Ordinance.[96]

Section 18(1) of the Ordinance provides that when the Authority is of the opinion that a decision to approve a film for exhibition was not, or is no longer, an appropriate decision, the Authority may request the Board of Review to review the decision. In making the request, the Authority must serve on the person whose film was so approved for exhibition (the affected person), a copy of the notice of request and a statement informing the affected person that he or she may make written representation regarding the matter to the Board.[97] Section 18(3)(c) then provides that after a date is fixed for a meeting to review the decision, notice must be served on the affected person, the Authority, and any interested person, informing them that they and their representatives may attend the meeting and make representations. The affected person will be required to produce the film to which the request relates[98] and if he or she fails to do so, the earlier decision to approve the film for exhibition is deemed to be revoked.[99] At the meeting, the Board will view the film, consider the notice of request, the decision to which the request relates and the affected person's written representation, consider the representations made under section 18(3)(c) and, where appropriate, consider the matters stated under section 10(2) as well as take into account the matters stated under section 10(3) of the Ordinance.[100]

Section 19(1) of the Ordinance provides that a person or persons aggrieved on moral, religious, educational or other grounds by the exhibition of a film or the release of a film in videotape or disc formats, may request the Board of Review to review the decision. Such a request may be declined if it is made in a frivolous and vexatious manner.[101] If a request is accepted, section 19(3) provides that the affected and interested persons and the Authority will be served with a copy of the notice of request and a statement informing them that they may make written representation to the Board in respect of that request. Section 19(4)(c) then provides that after a date is fixed for a meeting to review the decision, a notice must be served on every concerned person and the Authority, informing them that they and their representatives may attend the meeting and make representations. At the meeting, the Board will view the film, consider the notice of request for review, the decision to which the request relates and any written representation made under section 19(3), consider the representations made under section 19(4)(c) and, where appropriate, consider the matters stated under section 10(2) as well as take into account the matters stated under section 10(3) of the Ordinance.

At the end of a review, the Board of Review will give its directions to the Authority or censor 'with respect to the exercise by him of any of his functions' under the Ordinance and the Authority or censor must comply with such directions.[102] A copy of the Board's decision will then be served on the affected person, the Authority and the interested person.[103]

The Australian system

The law: Classification (Publications, Films and Computer Games) Act 1995 (Act No.7 of 1995)

The principal legislation governing film censorship (or classification) in Australia is the Classification (Publications, Films and Computer Games) Act 1995 (Act No.7 of 1995), which was enacted by the Commonwealth Parliament and came into operation on 1 January 1996. Complementary state and territory enforcement legislation was enacted to support the Act by adopting the classification decisions made thereunder and creating an offence regime in each of the states and territories.[104] The Act recognizes that the Commonwealth, states and territories are equal partners in the National Classification Scheme and that the policy on classification matters is derived from agreement between all jurisdictions.[105] The philosophy underlying the Act and carried out through the scheme is to protect members of the community from exposure to unsolicited offensive material and minors from material that may harm or disturb them, but otherwise permitting adults to view (in relation to films) whatever they wish to.

For almost a century before the Act was passed, film censorship was governed by regulations made under the Customs Act 1901.[106] For example, the Customs (Cinematograph Films) Regulations were enacted to control the importation of films.[107] Once a film was imported, the circumstances in which the film could be exhibited and distributed were determined by the states and territories. Each state and territory had its own legislation governing film censorship and this 'piecemeal' regulating-style created an unnecessarily complex and unsatisfactory situation as the entire system lacked uniformity. In the words of the former Attorney-General, Daryl Williams, 'It is a mess!'[108] A reference was finally made to the Australian Law Reform Commission in 1990 and the Commission recommended that:

> There should be a federal Act, based on the Constitution s 122, establishing the classification bodies and setting out the procedure for classification... There will be a single procedure, avoiding the overlaps and duplications that presently exist, and that classifiers will derive their powers from a single source, removing the difficulty that they sometimes face now of conflicting legislation from different jurisdiction. [109]

When the Classification (Publications, Films and Computer Games) Bill was tabled for its second reading, Michael Lavarch, the then Attorney-General noted that the agreement of the states and territories to the Bill provided an opportunity to make Australia's censorship laws 'more uniform and simple, with consequential benefits to the industry and the public'.[110] The passing of the Act thus established a uniform National Classification Scheme.

As its title suggest, the Classification (Publications, Films and Computer Games) Act 1995 provides for the classification of publications, films and computer games. For the purpose of this book, the provisions of the Act will only be discussed in regard to films. The Act contains ten parts. Part 1 provides for the preliminary matters[111] while Part 2 deals with the classification of films where it sets out the categories of classifications[112] as well as laying down the procedural steps relating to submission of films for classification purposes.[113] Part 3 provides for the application for approval of film advertisements[114] whereas Part 4 deals with reclassification of films.[115] Part 5 is of particular importance to film practitioners as it provides for review of classification decisions.[116] This part sets out the persons who may apply for a review of a classification decision,[117] the procedure of an application for review[118] as well as the approach in which applications for review will be dealt with.[119] The Classification Board is established under Part 6[120] while the Classification Review Board is established under Part 7.[121] Part 8 deals with miscellaneous matters such as the time frame within which the Classification Board and the Classification Review Board must make their decisions[122] and the power of the Governor-General to make regulations under the Act.[123] Part 9 in turn deals with transitional provisions and repeals.[124] Part 10, which is the final part of the Act, is not relevant for the purpose of this book.

On 24 March 2011, the Australian Law Reform Commission (ALRC) was asked to undertake a review of censorship and classification and report on the framework for the classification of media content in Australia. The review considered issues including the effectiveness of the National Classification Scheme, the options for reform, the extent existing classification laws continue to provide an effective framework for the classification of media, the current classification categories, the rapid pace of technological change and the effect of media on children. The ALRC's report, entitled Classification – Content

Regulation and Convergent Media, was tabled in Parliament on 1 March 2012. Its central recommendation is the establishment of a new National Classification Scheme regulating the classification of media content through the enactment of a new legislation – the Classification of Media Content Act – to replace the existing classification cooperative scheme for the classification of publications, films and computer games. Recognizing that it is not possible to classify all media content in a digital age, the report made 57 recommendations for a new scheme that applies consistent rules to media content on all platforms – in cinemas, on television, on DVDs, and on the internet.[125] The key recommendations made by the ALRC that are relevant to the film industry are:[126]

1 a new Australian Government scheme that replaces the current cooperative scheme with enforcement under Commonwealth law and the establishment of a single agency responsible for this scheme;[127]
2 a platform-neutral regulation with one set of laws establishing obligations to classify or restrict access to content across media platforms;[128]
3 a clear scope of what must be classified (feature films that are both made and distributed on a commercial basis and likely to have a significant Australian audience must be classified prior to their availability to the public);[129]
4 a single set of classification categories that apply to all media content in order to ensure that the same categories and criteria are applied to the classification of all media content. The recommended new classification categories are: G, PG, M, MA15+, R18+, X18+ and Prohibited. It is recommended that the RC (Refused Classification) category be renamed as Prohibited and its scope framed more narrowly;[130]
5 a shift in regulatory forms to restricting access to adult content (content that has been, or is likely to be, classified R18+ or X18+) where content providers must take reasonable steps to restrict access to adult content consistent with the principle that children should be protected from material likely to harm them; and
6 the abolition of the Classification Review Board.[131]

The report is still under the federal, state and territory governments' consideration at the time this book went to press. Therefore, it is not certain as to whether all, or which particular, recommendations will be adopted. If the key recommendations noted above are translated into legislation and policies, it could potentially lead to the end of any single state having the power to override film classification decisions made by the Classification Board as the South Australian Classification Council has on occasion done. Another likely effect of the recommendations would be the availability of more contentious content in film as it is proposed that the scope of the new Prohibited category be narrowed down, therefore necessarily entailing fewer restrictions on film content allowable for exhibition and distribution. This will give Australian film practitioners a greater freedom of expression and the audience a wider choice of materials to watch. On the other hand, the recommendation to abolish the Classification Review Board raises concerns that the Classification Board would not be able to review its own decision completely free from bias and there would be the potential for conflict of interest.

As the recommendations have yet to materialize in the form of enforceable legislation, scheme and policies, the focus of the book remains on the classification system as it existed on 1 June 2012.

The guidelines: Guidelines for the Classification of Films and Computer Games

The classification guidelines applied in Australia are known as Guidelines for the Classification of Films and Computer Games. This set of guidelines was introduced on 30 March 2003 and subsequently revised in May 2005. Prior to the introduction of the Guidelines, there were two separate sets of guidelines – one for films (the Classification Guidelines for Films and Videotapes) and one for computer games (the Classification Guidelines for Computer Games) – each having separate classification categories and different applicable standards. The Guidelines serve to assist the Classification Board and the Classification Review Board by providing the details of what material falls within each classification category for the Boards to determine the most appropriate classification of a film.

The Guidelines were made under section 12 of the Classification (Publications, Films and Computer Games) Act 1995 which also stipulates that the guidelines made must be agreed between the Commonwealth, states and territories and must be published in the *Gazette*. If the ministers agree to amend the guidelines, the guidelines are taken to be amended accordingly.[132] Classification guidelines are to be reviewed from time to time and revised, if necessary, to ensure that they stay relevant. According to Des Clark, the then Director of the Office of Film and Literature Classifications (OFLC),[133] the Australian Government is committed to a classification system that 'is clear, simple and which works for the community and industry'.

The Guidelines are divided into four parts. The introductory part states that the Guidelines are a 'tool' for classifying films and it explains 'the different classification categories, and the scope and limits of material suitable for each category'.[134] The introductory part also explains the legal context in which the Australian film classification system works as well as the applicable classification principles where section 11 of the Act (which provides for the matters to be taken into account in making classification decisions) and the preamble to the National Classification Code (which sets out the classification principles) were reproduced in full. The second part then explains the three essential principles underlying the use of the Guidelines. These interrelated principles are 'the importance of context', 'assessing impact' and 'the six classifiable elements', and are discussed further in Chapter 4. The third part of the Guidelines prescribes the limits of content suitable for each classification category (for example, under the MA15+ category, '*strong* coarse language may be used', however '*aggressive or very strong* coarse language should be *infrequent*')[135] while the final part lists the meaning of the key terms used in the Guidelines.

The process

Non-exempted films[136] have to be submitted to the Classification Board to be classified before they can be legally made available to the public. There is no difference in terms of procedure or standards in classifying Australian films and foreign films. Section 14 of the Classification (Publications, Films and Computer Games) Act 1995 provides for the procedure of making an application for classification of a film.[137] When making classification decisions, the Board operates in panels where at least three members of the Board will be assigned to examine a film. A larger panel may be formed in respect of a film if there are indications that there may be difficult questions that would arise from the film.[138] In the event that members of the panel are divided in opinion, the decision of the majority prevails.[139]

In classifying a film, the Classification Board must assume that the film will only be released in the form in which it is considered for classification.[140] Subject to section 9A (which provides that film that advocates the committing of a terrorist act must be refused classification), films are to be classified in accordance with the National Classification Code and the classification guidelines.[141] The National Classification Code sets out the principles of classification in Australia as follows:[142]

> Classification decisions are to give effect, as far as possible, to the following principles:
> (a) adults should be able to read, hear and see what they want;[143]
> (b) minors should be protected from material likely to harm or disturb them;
> (c) everyone should be protected from exposure to unsolicited material that they find offensive; and
> (d) the need to take into account of community concerns about:
>   (i) depictions that condone or incite violence, particularly sexual violence; and
>   (ii) the portrayal of persons in a demeaning manner.

In making classification decisions, the Board must also take into account the matters stated under section 11 of the Act which are the standards of morality, decency and propriety generally accepted by reasonable adults; the literary, artistic or educational merit of the film; the general character of the film including whether it is of a medical, legal or scientific character; and the persons or class of persons to or amongst whom the film is released or is likely to be released.

After having viewed the film and taken the matters stated under section 11 into account, the panel may then proceed to classify the film with an appropriate classification based on the Guidelines. In the classification process, the Classification Board neither requires nor recommends alteration to be made to film. The Board only determines the classification category and consumer advice that should be given to the film. Classification categories are provided under section 7(2) and they may be described in ascending order as in Table 3.3.

Table 3.3 Film classification categories applicable in Australia

Classification category	*Description*
G (General)	For general audience. Suitable for all ages.
PG (Parental Guidance)	Not recommended for viewing by persons under 15 years of age without guidance from parents or guardians.
M (Mature)	Not recommended for persons under 15 years of age.
MA15+ (Mature Accompanied)	Not suitable for persons under 15 years of age. Under 15s must be accompanied by a parent or adult guardian.
R18+ (Restricted)	Restricted to persons of 18 years of age and over only. May be offensive to sections of the adult community.
X18+ (Restricted)	Restricted to persons of 18 years of age and over only. Contains only sexually explicit material with depictions of actual sexual intercourse and other sexual activity between consenting adults.
RC (Refused Classification)	Banned

There is no restriction on access to films classified G, PG or M whereas films classified MA15+, R18+ or X18+ are legally restricted. Films that exceed the R18+ or X18+ classification limits will be refused classification (RC), which means they are banned.[144] While section 7(2) determines the classification categories, the criteria for differentiating between those classifications are found in the National Classification Code and the Guidelines for the Classification of Films and Computer Games and section 9 clearly states that films are to be classified in accordance with the Code and the Guidelines. If the Classification Board classifies a film PG, M, MA15+, R18+ or X18+, it must also determine the consumer advice which gives information about the content of the film.[145] After classifying and determining the consumer advice of the film, the Director of the Board will issue a classification certificate in respect of that film[146] and the certificate must include the following matters:[147]

1 the determined markings for the classification given to the film;[148]
2 the consumer advice for the film; and
3 the applicant's obligations about the display of the determined markings and consumer advice.

An applicant for classification may ask for a copy of the Board's reasons for its decision.[149]

As is the case in Malaysia and Hong Kong, film advertising materials are also regulated in Australia where the relevant provisions are found under Part 3 of the Classification (Publications, Films and Computer Games) Act 1995.[150] The Classification Board is empowered under section 29 to approve or refuse to approve an advertisement for a film either on an application for its approval or on its own initiative. In making its decision, the Board must take into account the matters set out under section 11 (which provides for the matters to be taken into account in classifying a film) and the Guidelines.[151] The Board must refuse to approve an advertisement if it is of the opinion that the advertisement:

1 describes, depicts or otherwise deals with matters of sex, drug misuse or addiction, crime, cruelty, violence or revolting or abhorrent phenomena in such a way that it offends against the standard of morality, decency and propriety generally accepted by reasonable adults to the extent that it should not be approved; or
2 depicts or describes, in a way likely to cause offence to a reasonable adult, a person who is, or appears to be, a child under 18 (whether the person is engaged in sexual activity or not); or
3 promotes crime or violence, or incites or instructs in matters of crime or violence; or
4 is used, or is likely to be used, in a way that is offensive to a reasonable adult.

The Board must also refuse to approve an advertisement for a film classified RC or a film that has not been classified.[152] However, in relation to film yet to be classified, the person who intends to distribute or exhibit the film may apply to the Board for a certificate of exemption in relation to the film for advertising purposes.[153] If a film is advertised ahead of it being classified, there must be a marking on the advertisement stating 'This film is yet to be classified' and the marking must be replaced by the classification marking when the film is subsequently classified. Additionally, film trailers must then be only screened with films of the same or higher classification.

Decisions made by the Classification Board are reviewable by the Classification Review Board and section 42(1) provides that the following persons may apply for a review:

1 the Commonwealth Minister;[154]
2 the applicant for classification of the film concerned (the original applicant);
3 the publisher of the film concerned; and
4 a person aggrieved by the decision.

The procedure to apply for a review is provided under section 43. An application may be made by the Minister at any time,[155] whereas application by the rest of the persons mentioned under section 42(1) must be made within 30 days after the receipt of the notice of the Classification Board's decision[156] or within such longer period as the Classification Review Board may allow.[157] If an application for review is made by a person other than the original applicant, the Convenor of the Review Board is under a statutory duty to notify the original applicant in writing of the application and of the day on which the application will be considered.[158]

The manner in which the Classification Review Board must deal with an application for review of a decision is the same as that of the manner in which the

Classification Board deals with an application for classification of film, which means that the decision will be made *de novo*.[159] When the Review Board is convened to review a decision, it will hear submissions from the person who made the application for review as well as other parties with an interest in the decision.[160] The Review Board will make the classification decision afresh and provide the consumer advice of the film. In reviewing a decision, the Review Board is to be constituted of at least three members who are nominated for the purpose by the Convenor.[161] In the event the members are divided in opinion, the decision of the majority will prevail.[162] The Convener must give written notice of the Review Board's decision to the applicant and to the persons who in the Convener's opinion have an interest in the matter.[163]

The Convenor will thereafter issue a classification certificate in respect of the film.[164] The earlier classification certificate issued by the Director of the Classification Board is taken to be revoked when the Convener of the Review Board issues the subsequent certificate in respect of that film.[165]

Conclusion

The Malaysian, Hong Kong and Australian film censorship systems are set up by the means of legislation and complemented by guidelines. Together, these documents inform, to a large extent, the censorship process in each of the three jurisdictions. From the examination of the documents, it is apparent that the systems displayed marked differences in several areas. These key differences, which give rise to issues and concerns, are analysed in the following chapter.

4 Film censorship systems in Malaysia, Hong Kong and Australia

The key issues

Introduction

Although the film censorship systems in Malaysia, Hong Kong and Australia share broad similarities, on close examination, there are numerous distinctive features between them. On paper, these features appear to give rise to concerns and issues that may adversely affect film practitioners and the film industries. There are eight key issues identified in the Malaysian film censorship system when the documents about the law, guidelines and process are analysed and compared with the Hong Kong and Australian systems. These key issues are in regard to:

1 the decision-making entities;
2 the exemption of films from censorship;
3 the matters to be taken into account by censors;
4 censorship guidelines;
5 alteration to films and determination of classification category;
6 provision of reasons for decisions;
7 appeal against censorship decisions; and
8 the availability of judicial review.

In this chapter, the discussion of these eight key issues will be presented in the context of each jurisdiction and arranged in the typical sequence a film would go through in a censorship process. It begins with identifying the entities responsible for making censorship decisions and the determination of whether a film is subject to censorship and continues until the point where a film practitioner challenges a censorship decision in court by way of judicial review. The chapter will highlight the differences in regard to the key issues between the Malaysian, Hong Kong and Australian systems and analyse the weaknesses that are apparent in the printed materials pertaining to their laws, guidelines and processes. This analysis then sets the basis for further investigation and evaluation, through fieldwork, of how the systems operate and affect the film industries.

The Malaysian system

Decision-making entities

There are three entities empowered by law to make film censorship decisions in Malaysia: the Board of Censors, the Appeal Committee and the Home Minister. The Board of Censors and the Appeal Committee are established under section 4(1) and section 22(1) of the Film Censorship Act 2002 respectively and operate under the purview of the Film Control Division of the Home Ministry.[1] The Board consists of 60 members, appointed by the Home Minister, who are retired senior government officers[2] and the Committee consists of 20 members,[3] 16 of which are appointed by the Home Minister, the rest being *ex-officio* members.[4] Retired senior government officers are appointed as film censors because of their knowledge of, and familiarity with, government policies.[5]

Two provisions in the Schedule to the Film Censorship Act 2002 may impair the independence of the Board and the Committee in discharging their duties. The first is paragraph 4 which provides that members of the Board and the Committee (except the *ex-officio* members) are appointed for a term of three years or such shorter term as the Minister specifies. After the term of office has expired, such members are eligible for reappointment. The second is paragraph 6 which reads: 'The Minister may revoke the appointment of a member of the Board or a member of the Appeal Committee other than an *ex-officio* member *without assigning any reason* for the revocation.'[6] These provisions raise the possibility that film censorship decisions will be made by members of the Board or Committee with a view to securing their tenure of office.

The Home Minister holds three particularly notable powers under the Film Censorship Act 2002. The Minister is empowered under section 25 to issue to the Board or the Committee directions as to government policy relating to exhibition and distribution of films and such directions must be given effect to by the Board and Committee.[7] Under section 26, the Minister is conferred the power, which is exercisable with absolute discretion, to prohibit the exhibition, display, distribution, possession, circulation or sale of any film or film publicity material, if the Minister is of the opinion that it would be contrary to public interest. Under section 28, the Minister can exempt any film or class of films, any film publicity materials or any person from the application of any provisions of the Act or any regulations made thereunder. It is also important to highlight that section 48 provides that decisions made by the Minister are not subject to appeal or review by any court on any ground.

Section 26 in particular, is questionable as it confers a very wide power on the Minister to prohibit the exhibition, distribution, possession, circulation or sale of a film, all of which are vital activities in a film industry. Because of section 48, the prohibition order made under section 26 appears not to be subject to appeal or review. Once the Minister forms the opinion that the exhibition, distribution, possession, circulation or sale of a film would be contrary to public interest, the Minister is empowered to ban the film. What matters would be contrary to public interest are not stated in the Act and thus are left open to the judgment of the Minister. This far reaching power also enables the Minister to ban a film even if the film was initially approved for exhibition by the Board under section 10 or by the Committee under section 23. The first Malaysian film to 'suffer' under this veto power was *Lelaki Komunis Terakhir* (*The Last Communist*, Amir Muhammad, 2006) which was initially approved for exhibition without any alteration and classified as suitable for general viewing by all levels of society by the Board. The film was banned by the Minister 13 days before it was to begin its theatrical release in Malaysia.[8]

The exemption of films from censorship

Not every film is subject to censorship in Malaysia.[9] There are numerous exceptions to the general rule that films must be approved by the Board of Censors before they can be made available to the public. One of the exceptions is found in section 8(3) of the Film Censorship Act 2002 which empowers the Board to issue a certificate of exemption in respect of any film imported into Malaysia which the owner does not intend to exhibit or distribute in the country or which it is intended for private use only.[10] The other exception is found in section 2(2)(a) which reads: 'This Act shall not apply to any film sponsored by the Federal Government or the Government of any State.' Section 2(2)(a) created a situation where a number of 'privileged' Malaysian films are not subject to censorship whereas other films will have to undergo the censorship process. This provision created a double-standard in the system where films funded by the government are allowed to be exhibited and distributed without being censored. In addition, the Home Minister is empowered under section 28 to exempt any film from censorship.

Matters to be taken into account by censors

Unlike the Hong Kong Film Censorship Ordinance and the Australian Classification (Publications, Films and Computer Games) Act 1995, the Malaysian Film Censorship Act 2002 does not stipulate the matters that censors must consider or take into account in the course of making film censorship decisions. This omission means two important factors – the artistic merit of a film and the contemporary community standards – which may have substantial impact on decisions to be made, are not taken into account by the Board of Censors and the Appeal Committee during the censorship process.

It is noteworthy that there is no formal and systematic effort being undertaken in Malaysia to ensure that the censorship decisions made are reflective of current community standards. It is apparent from the marked inconsistencies of the decisions that film censorship is carried out subjectively and not based on the standards generally accepted by reasonable adults in the society.

Censorship guidelines

The Film Censorship Guidelines 1993 were issued on 17 November 1993 and were applied for 17 years without any form of revision. As noted in Chapter 3, a new set of guidelines was introduced by the Home Ministry on 15 March 2010 to replace the 1993 Guidelines. In general, the majority of the provisions contained in the new Film Censorship Guidelines are similar to those in the 1993 version. There is little improvement to the quality of the guidelines being achieved by the 2010 revision exercise. The 2010 Guidelines will be discussed in Chapter 7.

The Film Censorship Guidelines 1993 do not contain provisions relating to classification categories[11] and, consequently, the types of content allowable under each applicable classification category are not spelt out. Upon careful examination, it is apparent that the majority of provisions in the Guidelines lack clarity and there are neither definitions nor explanations for most of the key terms and phrases used therein. A simple example illustrates the point: 'films that may retard national resilience are not to be allowed'.[12] There are many more instances like this, as explored below.

The Guidelines categorize films and content that are deemed not suitable for exhibition and distribution into four censorship elements, which are 'Ideology and Politics', 'Religion', 'Socio-culture' and 'Order and Decorum'.[13] Under the 'Ideology and Politics' element, it is provided that the following are not to be allowed:

1. films containing ideological propaganda that is inconsistent with the principles of the *Rukunegara*;
2. films praising or spreading the teachings of communism that will arouse the sympathy of audiences towards communism;
3. films that are detrimental to the political climate of the country;
4. films that are detrimental to the image of the country; and
5. films that may incite social tension.

From these provisions, it appears that there is the potential for political censorship in Malaysia. Under the second censorship element, 'Religion', it is provided that any film which gives an anti-God or anti-religion message that may affect the religious faith of its adherers or contains insults to any religion is prohibited. Under the 'Socio-culture' element, 'films that may corrupt the morality and good conduct of the society' and 'films that may encourage the development of a culture that is incompatible with the Malaysian way of life' are not allowed while under the 'Order and Decorum' element, the guidelines provide that the following content is not to be allowed in films exhibited and distributed in Malaysia:

1. portrayal of criminal acts which include detailed depiction of the *modus operandi* of such acts that may be imitable;
2. portrayal of victory of wickedness over justice and truth;
3. portrayal of excessive violence;
4. portrayal of explicit sex;
5. portrayal that raises racial, religious, ethnic or class sentiments;
6. portrayal of misuse or enjoyment of drugs; and
7. portrayal which may incite the doing of unlawful acts.

The appendix to the Guidelines then provides descriptions to some of the above mentioned particulars of the four censorship elements. Out of the four elements, 'Ideology and Politics' is the most vaguely described whereas 'Religion' is the most detailed, with primary focus on films dealing with the Islamic faith where a total of 54 descriptions can be found. In addition, the Guidelines do not provide that censors should consider the degree, intensity and realism of the way a censorship element is presented. The provisions merely spell out in very general terms the types of film (in terms of their possible effects on the audience) and the portrayals in film that are not to be allowed.

The Guidelines are silent as to whether censors must take into account the context of the film in making their censorship decision. Therefore, even if a scene or a line of dialogue is justifiable in the context of the film as a whole (or is necessary for the narrative or the aesthetics), it may not survive the censors' 'scissors' if that particular scene or dialogue contains an element that is prohibited by the Guidelines. This is in contrast with the film censorship guidelines applied in Hong Kong and Australia where contentious content may be allowed by censors if it is contextually justified in the film as a whole. Equally, it will be seen below that the descriptions used in Hong Kong and Australia are not as wide ranging and vague as those in Malaysia.

The Film Censorship Guidelines 1993, on the face of it, appear to have five substantial defects. They are in relation to the non-provision of the types of content allowable under each classification category; a lack of clarity in most of the provisions; the many types of film, content and portrayal which are prohibited; the lack of provision ensuring that the context of a film is to be taken into account by censors; and the absence of a requirement to consider the degree, intensity and realism of the way a censorship element is presented in film.

Alteration to films and determination of classification category

Films submitted for censorship purposes may be subjected to alteration,[14] as one of the three types of decision that censors can make under section 10 of the Film Censorship Act 2002 is to 'approve the film for exhibition with such alteration as it may require'.[15] However, the film owner's consent must be obtained before any alteration can be made to the film by the censorship authority. If consent to alter is given, the required alteration will be made and the film subsequently approved, whereas if consent is withheld, the film will be refused approval for exhibition and distribution. It is important to note that alteration may be required by censors even when a film is classified in a restricted classification category.

Closely linked to the issue of alteration, the film censorship law and guidelines do not provide that film practitioners may indicate and discuss (if necessary) with censors the classification category to be given to their films. Therefore, unlike the Hong Kong censorship system, there is no formal channel within the Malaysian system to seek a particular classification category, which could play a crucial role in the commercial viability of a film in the market.

The provision of reasons for decisions

Section 10(3) of the Film Censorship Act 2002 provides that when the Board of Censors approves a film for exhibition subject to alteration being made to the film, or refuses to approve a film for exhibition, the Board must furnish in writing to the owner of the film, its reasons for requiring such alteration or for the refusal. Besides these two types of decision, the Board is not statutorily bound to furnish its reasons for decisions. For example, the Board is not bound to furnish reasons why it classifies a film with a particular classification category. In addition, there is no provision in the law or the Guidelines requiring the Appeal Committee and the Home Minister to provide reasons for their decisions. Under the common law applied in Malaysia, in the absence of a statutory requirement to provide reasons, there is no general duty or obligation on the part of the decision-maker to furnish reasons for its decisions.[16]

Appeal against censorship decisions

Section 21(1) of the Film Censorship Act 2002 provides that the owner of a film who is aggrieved by the decision of the Board of Censors may within 30 days from the date on which the owner is notified of the decision, appeal to the Appeal Committee by lodging a notice of appeal. The word 'owner' is defined under section 3 as follows:

> 'owner', in relation to a film or film publicity material, means –
> a. a person who is entitled to the possession of the film or film publicity material whether it is made or produced in Malaysia or imported from outside Malaysia; or
> b. any person who has the film or film publicity material in his control, possession or ownership at the time in question.

Therefore, sections 21(1) and 3 enable film directors, producers, exhibitors and distributors who are aggrieved by the Board's decision to appeal to the Appeal Committee for a review of the censorship decision in question. There is no provision in the law that confers members of the public with the right to appeal against censorship decisions.

In appealing for review of a censorship decision, the film owner must lodge a written notice of appeal[17] and that notice may contain his or her representations.[18] The only representation allowed is the written notice of appeal; the law does not provide film practitioners with the right to make oral representations before the Committee.

Availability of judicial review

There are two ouster clauses in the Film Censorship Act 2002. The first is section 23(2) which reads: 'The decision of the Appeal Committee shall be final and shall not be questioned in any court of law' and the second is section 48 which reads: 'No decision of the Minister, the Board or the Appeal Committee under this Act or any regulations made under this Act shall be subject to appeal or review by any court on any ground'. When the Film Censorship Bill 2001 was tabled for its second reading, the then Deputy Home Minister defended the need for section 48 by stating that it is imperative that there be a final decision in film censorship matters and that 'trivial problems should not be brought to courts for adjudication'.[19] However, censorship not only encroaches on the right to freedom of expression but also affects the right to livelihood of film practitioners and these fundamental rights are enshrined under articles 10 and 5 of the Federal Constitution respectively.[20] It is not clear that censorship matters would necessarily be trivial.

If the ouster clauses are given their intended effect of completely shutting out the possibility of judicial review, film practitioners in Malaysia will not be able to challenge censorship decisions and seek legal remedies at all. As the decision-making process and the decision itself are not subject to scrutiny by courts, there appears to be a real danger for film practitioners that their films may be censored on the whims and fancies of the decision-making entities.

The Hong Kong system

Decision-making entities

There are four entities involved in making film censorship decisions in Hong Kong: the Film Censorship Authority, the Panel of Censors, the Panel of Advisers and the Board of Review. These entities are constituted under the Film Censorship Ordinance and operated within the Television and Entertainment Licensing Authority of the Government of the Hong Kong Special Administrative Region (hereinafter referred to as 'TELA') until 1 April 2012, when TELA was abolished and its functions taken over by the Office for Film, Newspaper and Article Administration of the Government of the Hong Kong Special Administrative Region.

Section 3 of the Film Censorship Ordinance established the Film Censorship Authority 'who shall be a public officer appointed by the Secretary for Commerce and Economic Development'. The Panel of Censors is established under section 4 and its members (censors) are appointed by the Chief Executive of Hong Kong through open recruitment exercises where members of the public are invited to apply for a position.[21] Appointments of censors are notified in the *Gazette*[22] and in 2010, there were 40 gazetted censors working at TELA. The Panel of Advisers is established under section 6 and its members (referred to as 'adviser' in the Ordinance) are appointed by the Film Censorship Authority. They are responsible for advising censors in the process of forming their opinions on which censorship decisions will be based.[23] The establishment of the Panel of Advisers allows for wider public participation in film censorship as it comprises about 300 members drawn from the Hong Kong community, representing people of different age, sex and profession.[24] The Board of Review is established under section 16 and it consists of the Secretary for Commerce and Economic Development and nine other members *not being public officers*,[25] appointed by the Chief Executive.[26] Hong Kong censors are appointed under the terms of civil service and their tenure of office lasts until the age of retirement (that is, 55 years old) if there is no resignation.[27] Being a part of the civil service, film censors are subject to the same code of conduct and disciplinary requirements as officers of other government departments and, therefore, the same criteria for termination of service applies.[28]

Unlike the Malaysian Film Censorship Act 2002, the Ordinance does not confer absolute discretionary power on any of the decision-making entities to prohibit the exhibition, distribution, circulation or sale of film.

The exemption of films from censorship

In Hong Kong, it is an offence to exhibit a film[29] which is not issued with either a certificate of exemption under section 9 or a certificate of approval under section 13 of the Film Censorship Ordinance.[30] Section 8(1) of the Ordinance provides that a film intended for exhibition must be submitted for censorship purposes. The Film Censorship Authority may exercise its power under section 9 to exempt certain classes of film from censorship, in which case, a certificate of exemption will be issued with or without conditions.[31]

Section 29 then empowers the Secretary for Commerce and Economic Development to make regulations to provide for 'the classes or descriptions of films that are suitable to be exempted under section 9'.[32] These classes are set out in the second schedule to the Film Censorship Regulations (Cap. 392A) as cultural, educational, instructional, promotional, sporting, travelogue, musical and religious films. These classes of film are relatively innocuous and therefore, can be exempted from the censorship process.

Matters to be taken into account by censors

The artistic merit of a film is one of the matters that censors must take into account in the process of making censorship decisions. The relevant provision is section 10(3)(b) of the Film Censorship Ordinance which reads:

> The censor shall, in viewing the film and considering the matters referred to in subsection (2), also take into account the following matters:.... (b) the artistic, educational, literary or scientific merit of the film and its importance or value for cultural or social reasons.

It appears that such consideration is able to 'off-set' the effects of the matters stipulated under section 10(2)[33] which may cause the film to be otherwise banned or classified with a restricted classification category.

In addition to 'artistic merit', censors are also required to take into account current community standards and attitudes towards film censorship. Two of TELA's missions in regard to film censorship are stated as follows:[34]

> 'We are committed to – Following closely standards of taste and decency accepted by the community and reflecting them in our decision making; and Maintaining the relevance of our regulatory framework with regard to community needs, technological development and international practices.'

Paragraph 2 of the Film Censorship Guidelines for Censors declares that 'the aim of the censors should be to reflect contemporary public attitudes towards censorship standards'. In order to ensure that decisions are reflective of current community standards, TELA commissions surveys of community views on a regular basis.[35] In addition to surveys, which are reported as Public Opinion Survey on Film Classification System, censors are also able to gauge community standards by consulting members of the Panel of Advisers for their views on the appropriate classification to be given to films. Film censorship in Hong Kong appears to be implemented comparatively objectively and not based on censors' personal standards.

Censorship guidelines

Section 30 of the Film Censorship Ordinance provides that the Secretary for Commerce and Economic Development may 'from time to time' prepare censorship guidelines for the guidance of censors. The Film Censorship Guidelines for Censors were introduced in 1999 after a lengthy period of public consultation and discussion with all major representative bodies of the film industry.[36] The way in which the Guidelines are to be applied is stated in paragraph 2. It provides that the guidelines are to be read in conjunction with the Film Censorship Ordinance and censors should aim to reflect contemporary public attitudes towards censorship standards in their decisions. A more liberal standard is to be applied to films to be classified Category III as censors ought to assume that only adults get to watch such films.[37] In applying the Guidelines, censors should also take into account the prevailing public view and be aware of the changes of public opinion brought to light by public opinion surveys on film censorship standards.[38]

In addition to section 12 of the Ordinance, the film classification categories are also described in the Guidelines and the limits of each censorship element under every classification category are set out clearly, based on the degree, intensity and realism with which such elements are presented in a film.[39] For example, under the 'Language' element, it is stated in paragraph 33 that: 'For Category IIA films, *mild* expletives with sexual connotations or coarse language may be used but only *infrequently* and are justified in context'.[40] Thus, in carrying out their censorship duties, censors will consider the duration and frequency of the depictions of censorship elements, the presentation of the elements (for example, whether the contentious scenes are made up of close-up shots and whether the depictions are detailed and realistic) and whether the portrayals were contextually justified. The provisions in the Hong Kong guidelines are much clearer and more precise than those of the Malaysian guidelines. Additionally, the guidelines applied in Hong Kong are systematically structured and presented in a straightforward manner.

This can be illustrated by the following provision, among many others: 'Scenes showing triad ceremonies, rituals, hand signs and paraphernalia including cryptic poems and icons should only be permitted in Category III films'.[41]

The Film Censorship Guidelines for Censors provide for six censorship elements, which are 'Cruelty, Torture or Violence', 'Horror and Shock', 'Disability', 'Sex and Nudity', 'Language' and 'Offensive Behaviour and Criminality,' and contain a list of content that is prohibited in films to be exhibited and distributed in Hong Kong. Paragraph 36 provides that:

> The following materials should not be permitted in any film:
>
> a. detailed or gratuitous depiction of a child who is, or who is apparently, under the age of 16 years engaging in sexual activity or crime;
> b. explicit or gratuitous depiction of extreme violence or cruelty;
> c. detailed instruction or encouragement in dangerous or criminal techniques which are imitable;
> d. detailed promotion, incitement or instruction on the use of dangerous drugs; and
> e. depiction of bestiality, necrophilia, sexual acts accompanied by offensive perversion (such as sadism or masochism) or exploitative incestuous behaviours.

Paragraph 37 then provides that if a depiction of the activities referred to in paragraph 36 is neither detailed nor explicit, it may be allowed to be classified Category IIB or Category III provided it is contextually justified. In addition, there are four types of film that will be refused approval in Hong Kong; namely, films which 'encourage public hatred or fear of the physically or mentally handicapped',[42] hard core pornography,[43] films which glorify the power of triads and membership in a triad society[44] and films made 'with the intention of inciting hatred or denigration on racial, religious, national or sexual differences'.[45] The latter is subject to paragraph 42 where 'films which seek, without obviously distorting facts, to depict existing or historical cases of racial or religious hatred should not give rise to objection' and paragraph 44 where 'censors should be prepared to accept films with a humorous but irreverent attitude to race, religion or sex, and those which, without malice, raise fair comment or practices in Hong Kong or overseas'. It is clear from the provisions of the Guidelines that not many types of film, content or portrayal are strictly and absolutely prohibited in Hong Kong, which is in marked contrast with the provisions in the Malaysian Film Censorship Guidelines 1993.

It is important to note that there are numerous provisions in the Hong Kong Guidelines allowing censors to approve films containing contentious elements if such content is justifiable in the context of the film concerned. For example, paragraph 19 provides that violence may be allowed by censors even though it is 'depicted in a way which might terrorize, hurt or seriously unsettle' if 'there are sufficient other elements in the film which make such an effect *justifiable*'. Another provision which may be highlighted here is paragraph 37 which, as discussed above, allows the five prohibited types of content listed under paragraph

36 to be approved if they are neither detailed nor explicit and they are 'justified in the context of the film as a whole'.

Alteration to films and determination of classification category

Hong Kong film censors are empowered under section 10(4)(c) of the Film Censorship Ordinance to refuse to approve a film for exhibition unless certain footage (that is prohibited by the censorship law or guidelines) is excised from the film.[46] Although censors have the power to require excision to be made to film, in practice, this power has been very rarely exercised.[47]

When a film is submitted for censorship purposes, it is to be accompanied by a statement as to the classification category which is sought for the film.[48] The person who submits the film is thus given an opportunity to indicate to the censor the classification category that is desired for the film and, according to paragraphs 10 and 60 of the Film Censorship Guidelines for Censors, the assigned censor should, as far as possible, accommodate the classification sought. In the event that the classification sought cannot be accommodated, the censor can advise the person who submits the film as to the minimum excision that can be made to the film to secure the desired classification. These provisions provide a channel for film practitioners to interact with censors over the issue of classification category to be given to film.

The provision of reasons for decisions

By virtue of section 10(4) of the Film Censorship Ordinance, censors are required to provide reasons for all the types of censorship decision they make under the provision. Censors are not only required to provide their reasons for refusing to approve a film for exhibition, they are also required to provide reasons even if a film is approved for exhibition. Censors must also provide reasons when they are unable to give a film an appropriate classification or when they require excision to be made to the film. In addition, section 13 provides that where the censor refuses to approve a film or requires excision to be made to the film, or where the censor is unable to give an appropriate classification, the Film Censorship Authority shall forthwith give written notice of the censor's decision and the reasons for the decision to the person who submitted the film. Although the censors' duty to provide reasons for their decisions is expressly provided in the Ordinance, there is no statutory provision requiring the Board of Review members to do the same.

Appeal against censorship decisions

There are three categories of person who may appeal against a censorship decision:

1 the person who submits the film;[49]
2 the Film Censorship Authority;[50] and
3 the person who is aggrieved by the exhibition of a film or the release of a film in video tape or disc formats.[51]

Therefore, depending on which type of film practitioner submits the film for censorship purposes, film directors, producers, exhibitors and distributors may appeal against a censorship decision. It is noteworthy that a member of the public who is aggrieved by a censorship decision also has the right to appeal against it.

When a censorship decision is appealed to the Board of Review, the film practitioner concerned has the right to make both oral and written representations to the Board. Written representations can be made under sections 17(1), 18(2) or 19(3) while oral representations can be made under sections 17(2)(c), 18(3)(c) or 19(4)(c) of the Film Censorship Ordinance. A right to be heard is therefore afforded to film practitioners by these statutory provisions.

Availability of judicial review

As there is no ouster clause in the Film Censorship Ordinance, film censorship decisions are open to challenge in court by way of judicial review. It is therefore possible for judicial review to be sought by film practitioners as an extension to the censorship process.

The Australian system

Decision-making entities

In Australia, film 'censorship' is generally known by the label 'classification', and there are two entities responsible for making film classification decisions: the Classification Board and the Classification Review Board. The Classification Branch of the Australian Government Attorney-General's Department provides administrative support to the Boards and has overall responsibility for Australian classification policy.

The Classification Board (hereinafter referred to as 'the Board') is established under section 45 of the Classification (Publications, Films and Computer Games) Act 1995 and its Director, Deputy Director and Senior Classifiers are appointed as full-time members.[52] Regulation 17A of the Classification (Publications, Films and Computer Games) Regulations 2005 provides that the maximum number of members of the Board is 30 and in 2011 the Board had 12 full-time members.[53] Members of the Board (except temporary members)[54] are appointed by the Governor-General[55] and in doing so, regard is given to 'the desirability of ensuring that the membership of the Board is broadly representative of the Australian community'.[56] Before recommending the appointment of a member (selected through a competitive merit selection process via open recruitment exercises) to the Governor-General, the Commonwealth Minister must consult with the state and territory ministers in regard to the recommendation.[57] A full-time member is to be appointed for a period specified in the instrument of appointment and such period shall not be longer than five years. A member is also eligible for reappointment[58] but must not hold office for a total of more than seven years.[59]

The circumstances under which the appointment of a member of the Board could be terminated are expressly provided under section 65 of the Act. For example, an appointment can be terminated because of the member's mental incapacity[60] or where the member is absent from duty, except on leave of absence, for 28 days in any 12 months.[61]

The Classification Review Board (hereinafter referred to as 'the Review Board') is established under section 72 of the Act and it consists of a Convenor, a Deputy Convenor and at least three, but not more than eight, other members.[62] Members of the Review Board are appointed by the Governor-General[63] and in doing so, section 74(2) requires that regard is to be given to the desirability of ensuring that its membership is broadly representative of the community.[64] Before recommending the appointment of a member, the Commonwealth Minister must consult with the state and territory ministers.[65] Members of the Review Board are also recruited through a competitive merit selection process and they are to be appointed as part-time members[66] for a time period as specified in the instrument of appointment but such period shall not be longer than five years.[67] Members are eligible for reappointment but cannot hold office for a total of more than seven years.[68] The Review Board meets as needed[69] and its Convenor is empowered to give directions regarding the constitution of the Review Board for the purpose of considering a matter.[70] In 2011, the Review Board operated with six members.[71] The circumstances under which the appointment of a member can be terminated are stated under section 83. For example, an appointment can be terminated because of the member's mental incapacity[72] or where the member fails, without reasonable excuse, to disclose his or her interest in relation to matters under consideration.[73]

There is no provision in the Act that confers absolute discretionary power on the Minister, the Board, the Review Board or any of their members in carrying out their duties. The Board's decision-making processes are expected to reflect sound administrative law practices and they are required to prepare annual reports.[74] The Boards' activities are also subject to parliamentary scrutiny.[75]

The exemption of films from classification

As in both Malaysia and Hong Kong, not every film is subject to censorship in Australia.[76] Section 5B(1) of the Classification (Publications, Films and Computer Games) Act 1995 lists 13 types of film as exempt films and provides that, subject to section 5B(3),[77] application for classification of exempt films is not necessary. The 13 types of exempt films are business, accounting, professional, scientific, educational, current affairs, hobbyist, sporting, family, live performance, musical presentation, religious and community or cultural films.[78] Section 28A then provides that application may be made to the Board that an unclassified film is an exempt film and the Board may grant a certificate under section 28B certifying that the film is an exempt film. In the event the Board decides that a film that has earlier been granted a certificate under section 28B contains material that was not brought to the Board's attention before the certificate was granted and such material would have caused the film to be classified M or a higher classification, the Board must revoke the certificate granted.[79]

Matters to be taken into account by classifiers

Section 11 of the Classification (Publications, Films and Computer Games) Act 1995 provides for the matters to be taken into account by classifiers in the course of making their decisions. These matters are 'the standards of morality, decency and propriety generally accepted by reasonable adults'; 'the literary, artistic or educational merit' of the film; the 'general character' of the film including 'whether it is of a medical, legal or scientific character'; and 'the persons or class of persons to or amongst whom it is published or is intended or likely to be published'. This provision recognizes the importance of freedom of artistic expression and current community standards by requiring classifiers to take into account the artistic merit of the film as well as the standards of morality, decency and propriety accepted by the community when making their decisions.

To ensure classification decisions are reflective of the community's standards, the Act provides that the Board and Review Board should, as far as possible, be constituted by members who are broadly representative of the Australian community.[80] In addition, the Community Assessment Panel (CAP) scheme was introduced to 'test the extent to which the decisions made by the Board reflected current Australian community standards'.[81] Members of the CAP (randomly selected from a cross-section of the society) are given basic classification training before being asked to make classification recommendations for films shown to them. The classifications recommended by the CAP will then be compared to those given by the Board to gauge how accurately the Board's decisions reflect current community standards.[82] Besides the CAP scheme, research and surveys into community standards and attitudes towards film classification are also carried out periodically.[83]

Classification guidelines

Public consultations were carried out to obtain community feedback before the Guidelines for the Classification of Films and Computer Games were drawn up and introduced in 2003. The consultative process was widely advertised to call for submissions and discussion papers were also sent to stakeholders.[84] The Guidelines expressly state that they are to be revised from time to time with 'extensive community input' and since 2003 the Guidelines have been revised twice to keep the provisions up to date and relevant.

The method of applying the Guidelines is stated in the 'Using the Guidelines: Essential Principles' section where three inter-related principles – 'context', 'impact' and 'classifiable elements' – are explained. It is provided that the 'context' principle is to be used to determine whether a 'classifiable element' is justified by a film's storyline or themes and the 'impact' of a film will have to be assessed in view of the 'classifiable elements' that appear in the film. The Guidelines employ the hierarchy as stated in Table 4.1 in assessing the 'impact' of a film:

Table 4.1 Levels of impact and the Australian classification categories

Level of impact	*Classification category*
Very mild	G
Mild	PG
Moderate	M
Strong	MA15+
High	R18+
Very high	RC

The Guidelines then went on to provide that in assessing the impact of a film, the classifiers are required to consider the treatment of individual classifiable elements, the cumulative effect of those elements, and the purpose and tone of the scenes containing such elements. The impact of a scene may be higher if, for example, it contains greater detail, is prolonged or is realistic rather than stylized.

The scope and limit of contents suitable for each classification category are also described in the Guidelines. With the exception of X18+ and RC, all the classification categories are presented in a similar format. They begin with the 'Impact Test' section which determines the threshold for the classification category and then this is followed by a list of the classifiable elements with descriptions limiting the content for each element in the category.[85]

There are six classifiable elements provided in the Guidelines and they are themes,[86] violence, sex, language, drug use and nudity. In summary, the Board will take into account:

1 whether these classifiable elements (as they appear in a film) are justified in the context of the film;
2 the impact of each of the classifiable elements, including their frequency, intensity and cumulative effect;
3 the purpose and tone of scenes containing classifiable elements; and
4 the manner in which the classifiable elements are treated, before classifying a film in an appropriate classification category.

Films will be refused classification (banned) if they contain any of the following content:[87]

1 detailed instruction or promotion in matters of crime or violence;
2 the promotion or provision of instruction in paedophile activity;
3 depictions of child sexual abuse or any other exploitative or offensive depictions involving a person who is, or appears to be, a child under 18 years;
4 gratuitous, exploitative or offensive depictions of:
   a. violence with a very high degree of impact or which are excessively frequent, prolonged or detailed;

   b. cruelty or real violence which are very detailed or which have a high impact;
   c. sexual violence;
5 depictions of practices such as bestiality;
6 gratuitous, exploitative or offensive depictions of:
   a. sexual activity accompanied by fetishes or practices which are offensive or abhorrent;
   b. incest fantasies or other fantasies which are offensive or abhorrent;
7 detailed instruction in the use of proscribed drugs; or
8 material promoting or encouraging proscribed drug use.

The Guidelines are drafted in a comparatively precise and simple manner and the key terms employed therein are clear and detailed in comparison with the Malaysian guidelines.

Alteration to films and determination of classification category

The Board is not empowered under the law to require alteration to be made to films. It only determines the classification of a film and decides the consumer advice that should be given about the film.[88] Similarly, the Review Board in reviewing a decision does not have the power to require alteration to be made to films.

Unlike the Hong Kong film censorship system, the Australian system does not provide for film practitioners to indicate and discuss with classifiers the classification category sought for their films. Neither does the Board provide film practitioners with advice as to alterations that can be made to a submitted film in order for it to be classified under a particular category.[89]

The provision of reasons for decisions

There is no provision in the Classification (Publications, Films and Computer Games) Act 1995 requiring either the Board or the Review Board to provide reasons for their decisions. Although section 26 of the Act deals with notices of decision, it does not confer on film practitioners the right to reasoned decisions. The provision merely states that the Director of the Board and the Convenor of the Review Board must give written notice of the decision they made to the applicant and to persons who have an interest in the matter.

In Australia, there is no general common law right to reasoned decisions.[90] However, section 13 of the Administrative Decisions (Judicial Review) Act 1977 provides that any person who is entitled to apply to the court for review of any decision reviewable under section 5 may request the decision-maker for a statement of reasons for the decision.[91] Where a request is made, the decision-maker must furnish, as soon as practicable and in any event within 28 days after receiving the request, the said statement of reasons in writing.[92] Therefore, film practitioners may request a statement of reasons from the Board and the Review Board.[93] It is noteworthy that the Review Board does publish the reasons for its decisions on the Australian Government Classification website.[94]

Appeal against classification decisions

Section 42(1) of the Classification (Publications, Films and Computer Games) Act 1995 provides for four categories of person who may appeal against a Board's decision to the Review Board, and they are the Commonwealth Minister,[95] the original applicant for classification, the publisher of the film and a person aggrieved by the decision. The word 'publisher' is not defined in the Act but with reference to the definition of 'publish' under section 5,[96] 'the publisher of the film' would include film directors, producers, distributors and exhibitors. As regards a 'person aggrieved by the decision', the Review Board may refuse to deal with an application made by this category of person if it is satisfied that the application is frivolous or vexatious and not made in good faith.[97] Section 42(3) further provides that if the decision in question is a restricted decision – that is, a decision to classify a film MA15+, R18+, X18+ or RC – a person who has engaged in activities or research into the contentious aspects of the theme or subject matter of the film concerned, or an organization whose purposes or activities are related to the contentious aspects of the theme or subject matter of the film, are to be taken as persons aggrieved by the decision.[98]

The applicant for a review may be present at the screening of the film in question before the Review Board[99] but it is not provided in the Act that the applicant has the right to make representations. However, online material suggests that, in the process of reviewing a decision, the Review Board will hear submissions from the applicant and from parties with an interest in the decision.[100]

Availability of judicial review

The Classification (Publications, Films and Computer Games) Act 1995 does not contain an ouster clause purporting to bar film practitioners from challenging the decisions made by the Board and the Review Board by way of judicial review. In fact, there have been numerous judicial review applications being made to challenge decisions of the Review Board, which is further discussed in Chapter 6.

Summary: an evaluation of the key issues

On the face of it, the Malaysian film censorship system appears to suffer in the eight key areas discussed above. The issues raised by analysing the systems on paper may be summarized as follows.

Decision-making entities

The Malaysian Board of Censors can be filled with retired senior government officers by the Home Minister and unlike in Hong Kong and Australia, no open recruitment exercise is carried out in Malaysia to locate suitable and competent candidates to be appointed as members of the Board. The appointment of members of the Board and the Appeal Committee may be revoked by the Minister at any time without having to provide any reason for the revocation. The discretionary power to reappoint these members after their terms of service have expired also rests with the Minister. Since tenure of office lies in the hands of the Minister, members of these two entities could be inhibited by concerns over their tenure and influenced to make decisions that conform to the Minister's (or the Executive's) wishes or directives. Film censorship decisions could thus be overly influenced by government policies or personal instructions and not by the merits or content of the film itself or by the provisions of the law and guidelines. An example is the banning of *Lelaki Komunis Terakhir* (*The Last Communist*, Amir Muhammad, 2006) discussed in Chapter 5 below. This is in stark contrast with the position in Australia where the law spells out clearly the circumstances under which the appointment of members of the Board and the Review Board could be terminated. By expressly laying down the circumstances of termination of appointment, arbitrary termination appears to be very unlikely. Consequently, members of the public can expect that these decision-making entities will be more independent in making their decisions.

In addition, the Malaysian Home Minister has considerable power, exercisable at his absolute discretion, to prohibit the exhibition, distribution, possession or sale of any film in the country. No decision-making entity is afforded such power under the Hong Kong and Australian film censorship systems.

Free speech scholars, including Schauer and Barendt, have often discussed in their writings the importance of having competent and impartial decision-makers in censorship matters.[101] The former, for example, noted that the determination of who decides what material or content is to be made available to the populace is of equal importance to the determination of what type of material or content is to be made available,[102] while the latter described the likelihood of bias, where officials appointed by the government may be keen to censor materials that are critical of the government, as one of the 'disturbing features' of administrative censorship.[103]

The exemption of films from censorship

The appearance of a double-standard exists in the treatment of films in Malaysia because the Film Censorship Act 2002 provides that films funded by the government are not subject to the censorship process. Additionally, the Home Minister is empowered to exempt any film from censorship at his sole discretion. If this power is exercised, it would appear to undermine the censorship system as a whole. Apart from exempting certain types of film that are stipulated in the legislation, no decision-making entity in Hong Kong or Australia is given *carte blanche* power to exempt films from the censorship process.

Matters to be taken into account by censors

Unlike the Hong Kong Film Censorship Ordinance and the Australian Classification (Publications, Films and Computer Games) Act 1995, the Malaysian Film Censorship Act 2002 does not stipulate the matters that censors must consider or take into account when making censorship decisions. Quite apart from the undesirable lack of clarity this gives the Malaysian system, it is not at all clear whether the artistic merit of the film under examination is taken into account in practice at all.

Additionally (and again, in contrast with the situation in the Hong Kong and Australian models), film censors in Malaysia are not required to take into account contemporary community standards. There appears to be no effort made in Malaysia to ensure that the censorship decisions are reflective of current community standards. Therefore, Malaysian censors appear to carry out their duties more subjectively when compared with the approach adopted by their Hong Kong and Australian counterparts who aim to achieve a level of objectivity.[104] Malaysian censors may be imposing their personal standards within the system and ignoring the standards of reasonable adults in the community. As discussed in Chapter 1, artistic merit is taken into account by the English and American courts when they decide whether a work charged to be obscene is so or otherwise. The legal literature on this point indicates the importance of the consideration of artistic merit in deciding whether a 'speech' or 'expression' is to be suppressed.

Censorship guidelines

The Malaysian Film Censorship Guidelines 1993 appear to suffer from four related 'defects':

1 The provisions in the Guidelines lack clarity. They are imprecise, vaguely drafted and the key terms and phrases are not defined. This 'defect' will leave censors with wide discretion to interpret the provisions and inconsistent censorship decisions could well be made.
2 Unlike the guidelines applied in Hong Kong and Australia, the Malaysian Guidelines do not provide for contentious content to be approved for exhibition and distribution if it is justified in the context of the film as a whole. Related to this omission, there is no provision in the Guidelines requiring censors to take into account the degree and intensity with which censorship elements are presented in a film and the realism of such presentation. Therefore, if contentious material or a censorship element appears in a film, the scene containing such content must be altered or possibly, the entire film itself will be refused approval for exhibition. This 'defect' has made the Malaysian censors' job rather simplistic as they are not required, unlike their Hong Kong and Australian counterparts, to weigh considerations such as the context of the film and the degree, intensity and realism of presentation of particular content in the film.
3 The applicable film classification categories are not provided for in the Guidelines and thus the limit of each censorship element allowable under the various classification categories is not set out clearly within the censorship system.
4 Many more types of film, content and portrayals are prohibited under the guidelines applied in Malaysia when compared to the guidelines applied in

> Hong Kong and Australia. For example, political censorship is provided in the Malaysian Guidelines where films propagating or portraying political ideology such as communism are prohibited. There is no political censorship in films under the Hong Kong and Australian guidelines. Another example would be the strict regulation of films containing religious themes or content, which appears to be absent in the Hong Kong and Australian guidelines.[105]

In comparison, the Hong Kong and Australian film censorship guidelines are relatively clearly drafted, systematically presented and responsive in nature, which appears likely to make their application more coherent and the outcomes more relevant and acceptable. Both sets of guidelines were drawn up with input from film practitioners and the public and they contain:

1 clear instructions as to how they should be applied;
2 provisions allowing contentious content to be justified in the context of the film;
3 provisions requiring censors to take into account the degree, intensity and realism with which a particular censorship element is presented; and
4 descriptions of the limits of content allowed under each classification category.

Like obscenity and indecency laws, vagueness in definitions and applicable standards or tests also exists in film censorship and it can be found in the censorship guidelines applied by censors.[106] Although vagueness cannot be completely eliminated, the degree of uncertainty could, and should, be minimized. As discussed in this chapter (and confirmed in the following chapter), the Hong Kong and Australian systems are more successful in dealing with the problems of vagueness than the Malaysian system, and this is achieved primarily by drawing up clearly defined descriptions of the limits of content allowable under the systems. As raised in Chapter 1, vagueness bedevils discussion of censorship laws. However, a key factor in practice is the relative clarity of terms and how consistently they can be understood and applied.

Alteration to films and determination of classification category

Malaysian censors are empowered under the censorship law to require alteration – which includes excision, addition, erasure and reconstruction of scenes, dialogues, sound and subtitles[107] – to be made before a film is approved for exhibition and distribution. This is in contrast with the situation in Australia and Hong Kong where the former's decision-making entities do not have such power, while the latter's censors only have the power to require excision to be made and it is only exercised under extreme circumstances.[108] Alteration in whatever form, affects the artistic integrity of the film concerned and the exercise of such power raises concerns about freedom of expression particularly to the 'free speech and autonomy' rationale discussed in Chapter 1. This rationale sees speech or expression as having an inherent value and as being an integral aspect of every individual's right to self-fulfilment. Alteration to films in effect restricts and suppresses film practitioners' expression and thus inhibits their autonomy and self-fulfilment.

In addition, there appears to be no formal channel for film practitioners in Malaysia to interact with censors over the issue of classification category. The classification category a film receives has implications for its commercial viability, as a restrictive category may reduce potential audiences and therefore shrink box office revenues as discussed in Chapter 5. In Hong Kong, when a film is submitted for censorship purposes, the film practitioner concerned may indicate the classification category that is being sought for the film. The censor assigned to examine the film will have to, as far as possible, accommodate the classification sought and in the event the classification could not be accommodated, advice will be given about any excision that could be made to the film to secure the desired classification. Discussion between censors and film practitioners may occur within such a process. On paper, the Australian system also lacks a formal channel for film practitioners to indicate the classification they are seeking or discuss the classification category to be given to their film.

The provision of reasons for decisions

Under the Malaysian film censorship system, the provision of reasons for decisions is confined to only two instances: one, where the Board of Censors approves a film for exhibition subject to alteration being made to the film and two, where approval is refused. Additionally, the Appeal Committee and the Home Minister are not required under the Film Censorship Act 2002 to provide reasons for their decisions. In Hong Kong, censors are required to furnish reasons for every censorship decision they make under the Film Censorship Ordinance, while in Australia, the Administrative Decisions (Judicial Review) Act 1977 ensures that film practitioners are able to obtain reasons for the decisions made on their films.

In Malaysia and Hong Kong, reasons for censorship decisions are not made public. They are only provided to the film practitioners concerned. In Australia, reasons for film classification decisions made by the Board are also not made available to members of the public, but the Review Board's reasons for decisions are published on the Classification website.

Appeal against censorship decisions

Film practitioners in Malaysia are not afforded a statutory right to make oral representations before the Appeal Committee at the appeal stage of a censorship process. Such an omission would appear to deprive them of an opportunity to be heard to justify the contentious content or portrayals in their films that censors found objectionable. In contrast, the Hong Kong Film Censorship Ordinance confers on film practitioners the right to make oral representations before the Board of Review. In Australia, such right is not statutorily guaranteed but the Review Board has expressly stated on its official website that it will hear submissions from the person who appealed against the decision as well as from parties with an interest in the decision.

Availability of judicial review

There are two ouster clauses in the Malaysian Film Censorship Act 2002 purporting to oust the court's judicial review jurisdiction in film censorship matters. This is in stark contrast with the Hong Kong and Australian legislation where there is no provision barring film practitioners from seeking legal remedies from the judiciary. It must be noted that judicial review appears to be an important safeguard for film practitioners working in jurisdictions with a state-based censorship system, as is the case in Malaysia, Hong Kong and Australia.

The ouster clauses' effect of excluding judicial review applications may be avoided if the courts extend the ambit of jurisdictional errors to include errors of law therein. The English and Malaysian courts' approach in dealing with ouster clauses is discussed in Chapter 6 where it is argued that whenever an error of law is committed by the decision-maker, no ouster clause, however widely drafted, may exclude judicial review of the decision made. Another point to be noted in regard to the availability of judicial review is that free speech scholars argue that it is wrong for entities other than the courts to decide ultimately whether an individual has a right to free speech.[109] This suggests that film censorship authorities' decisions to ban films should not be final, conclusive or exempt from judicial scrutiny.

The film censorship laws, guidelines and processes as discussed in the preceding chapter and the key issues and concerns analysed in this chapter suggest that the Malaysian film censorship system needs to be reformed. However, many aspects of the situation set out in the documents about the laws, guidelines and processes can be further, and usefully, examined through fieldwork that investigates the operation of the system in each jurisdiction. Results from that fieldwork are reported and analysed in the following chapter.

5 Film censorship systems in Malaysia, Hong Kong and Australia

The practitioners' opinions and experiences

Introduction

As discussed in Chapter 1, interviews with Malaysian, Hong Kong and Australian film practitioners were conducted to obtain their opinions of the key issues that arise in the film censorship systems as identified and analysed in the preceding chapter. The film practitioner interviewees were also asked about their experiences in dealing with censorship authorities and about any changes to the existing system that they hoped to see take place. The key issues discussed during the interviews are closely linked to one another, forming the larger question of 'What are the effects of the film censorship laws, guidelines and processes on the film industries?', which is then used to answer the question of 'What changes, if any, to the film censorship system appear likely to promote the artistic vibrancy and commercial viability of the film industry?' Thirty six interviews were conducted with film practitioners from the three jurisdictions under study and the outcome is reported in this chapter. After a summary of the general perceptions and experiences of the interviewees in each of the systems, their opinions of the specific key issues are discussed and finally conclusions are drawn from the opinions.

The Malaysian film censorship system has been described, amongst other things, as 'restricting', 'conservative', 'outdated', 'inconsistent' and 'haphazard'. All of the Malaysian film practitioners interviewed for this book felt artistically and/or commercially constrained by the system. Tsai Ming-liang, a Malaysian-born, Taipei-based and internationally renowned film director, noted that:[1]

> One of the reasons why I chose not to return to Malaysia to make films is because it is very troublesome. You are not sure when you will encounter problems with the authorities… and after you have completed your film, you are never sure whether it will be approved for exhibition or not.

U-Wei Haji Saari, another prominent Malaysian director, pointed out that:[2]

> Sloppy censorship indicates to the outside people that we are so intolerant and that we are really way back. That scares them… because now films are going global with things such as co-productions, so it is difficult for me to get

> foreign producers to invest in my work because they know that it can be butchered, it can be censored! That is the negative effect of our censorship.

The above opinions were echoed by Lorna Tee, a Malaysian film producer and distributor now based in Hong Kong, in that 'it is hard because you don't know how your film will be censored and whether it can be released in Malaysia, or whether you have to re-edit it… that is not good commercially'.[3]

A point that is apparent from the Malaysian fieldwork is that favouritism is prevalent, in that independent film practitioners are marginalized while the more established practitioners appear to receive better treatment from censors. The preferential treatment includes easier access to censors for discussion (three of the interviewees disclosed that they can easily meet with censors to discuss the censorship decisions made on their films because they personally know the censors, as well as the Chair of the Appeal Committee) and more lenient censorship decisions on certain 'preferred' films. This made it clear that what is permissible in one film may not be so in another. Amir Muhammad, an independent film director and producer who had his two independently produced films banned, noted that the censors tend to be 'friendlier' to films financed by established production companies. In reference to *Susuk* (2008),[4] a horror film which he directed for a prominent production company, Amir noted that the two minor cuts required by the Board of Censors 'may have a lot to do with the fact that it was financed by this big company and they [the censors] don't really bother the big companies. They pick on the small ones'.[5] Yasmin Ahmad, whose films *Sepet* (*Chinese Eye*, 2004) and *Muallaf* (*The Convert*, 2008) had encountered censorship problems, noted that:

> They [the censors] will let go of a film that has a man touching a woman's breast and then they will not let go of a film that has a woman showing a little bit of leg, like in *Sepet*. They let *Remp-it* go but not *Sepet*... see, if you are a big film producer and have friends in high places, you are more likely to get things through.[6]

The award-winning film director then went on to state that:

> If a film was independently produced, it is easier for them to ban it but if it was produced by big studios like some of my films, then they are less likely to ban it and I think perhaps because they know the people who are producing them, that it was from a big studio.... Big studios seem to be able to get things through more easily than independent filmmakers. *Muallaf* was independent and it is having problems.[7]

Film directors and producers in Malaysia are inhibited by censorship concerns whenever they embark on a film project. Some quotes from the interviews will exemplify this point: 'censorship is always at the back of our minds';[8] 'there are many films which I think will never get passed if they are made';[9] 'in every film that I wanted to make, I would always think "Would the censorship board allow it to be shown to the public?"';[10] and 'we get short of ideas because we cannot do this, cannot do that'.[11] Self-censorship is common and most of the Malaysian directors and producers interviewed disclosed that they self-censor and often avoid violence, sex and other contentious content in their films because of censorship concerns even though such content may be necessary in the context of their films. Some of the interviewees pointed out that the restrictive censorship system in Malaysia has created an environment which was 'not suitable for film makers to grow',[12] caused their films to be much less appealing to cinema-goers,[13] and was the root cause of the very limited variety of films being produced locally.[14] Censorship ensures only 'safe films' are made and nothing else. Aziz M. Osman, a director and producer who was shaken by the experience that he had with the censorship authorities, admitted that 'after the experiences that I have had [with the censors], I don't want to take risks anymore… I need to play safe, I need to survive'.[15]

The standard of censorship has also become stricter than before the introduction of the Film Censorship Guidelines in 1993. Tsai Ming-liang, for example, pointed out that 'there is no improvement in terms of perception and openness to arts… at least last time, in P. Ramlee's films [in the 1950s and 1960s], there were kissing scenes or bathing scenes but now, they are not allowed at all… it is, in fact, moving backwards and has become very conservative'.[16] The Malaysian interviewees also said that freedom of expression was very important for them,[17] some even describing it as of 'the ultimate importance'.[18] It is clear from the interviews that film practitioners in Malaysia crave freedom of artistic expression, which they do not enjoy, and that they believe the censorship system adversely affects their ability to produce commercially viable films.

Some of the Malaysian interviewees also pointed out that there was double standard applied to treatment between local films and foreign films. Ruhani Abdul Rahman, a film producer, noted that Malaysian filmmakers were often reminded not to include many types of content in their films but such content was allowed in foreign films. The producer believed that this was detrimental to local producers in that their films would not be as appealing and competitive as imported ones.[19] For example, prior to 2004 Malaysian filmmakers were not permitted to make horror films (which are very popular among local audiences) but such films were imported from abroad (notably from Hong Kong, Japan, Korea and America) to be distributed and exhibited locally.[20] The pre-2004 prohibition not only obstructed creative expression but also barred local filmmakers from gaining a share of the profitable horror film market.[21]

By contrast, the interviews with Hong Kong film practitioners clearly showed the interviewees to be happy and satisfied with the existing censorship system. There is no major dissatisfaction with or complaint about the overall functioning of the system. Gordon Chan, for example, noted that 'I never had any problem at all with the Hong Kong film censorship system in my 20-odd years in filmmaking'.[22] The current President of the Hong Kong Film Directors' Guild then added 'I always think that the freedom of speech and the censorship system in Hong Kong are the main reasons why our films succeed'. The Hong Kong interviewees were generally of the opinion that the film censorship system worked very well, particularly its three-tier classification scheme which they described as 'a very good practice'.[23] Benny Chan, a commercially successful action film director and producer, noted that:

> The three-tier classification scheme is very clear and as a director, there is no problem for me at all. We know that certain scenes would push a film into the Category III classification and therefore will make it not suitable for young audiences but it does not prohibit us from making the film we wanted. As long as we are willing to accept that the film will eventually be classified Category III, we can go ahead and make it.[24]

Producer Terence Chang observed that the classification scheme is 'a good one' and that it worked very well in Hong Kong. Chang then added that since the introduction of the scheme, coarse language, nudity and sex scenes were allowed in films for exhibition and distribution.[25] Wellington Fung, a veteran film producer and co-founder of Media Asia (one of the largest and most successful film production and distribution companies in Hong Kong today) was of a similar opinion and further noted that 'the classification system gives liberty to filmmakers to make different types of film and to choose their audiences when they decide on a film project'.[26]

The Hong Kong interviewees also saw the film censorship system as 'liberal',[27] 'efficient',[28] 'very practical',[29] 'running smoothly and reasonable',[30] 'operates in a consistent manner',[31] that 'it does not affect creativity'[32] and, importantly, 'there is no government interference in it'.[33] Gordon Chan, for example, attributed the critical and commercial successes enjoyed by the Hong Kong film industry to the liberal and transparent censorship system. Chan noted that 'I do think the reason why the film industry is so successful is because of our freedom of expression and that freedom was due to the way in which our censorship system was handled'.[34] The positive responses are supported by the fact that when the interviewees were asked what reforms they would like to see to the Hong Kong film censorship system, most of them replied with confidence that change to the system is not necessary.[35] Benny Chan, for example, expressed the view that: 'I think the censorship system is really good. We have the three-tier classification scheme, we can appeal, we can discuss with censors... so it is really good. I don't see any changes or reforms are needed.' It is noteworthy that all of the Hong Kong interviewees were hard-pressed to come up with any substantial changes that they thought could make the current system better.

Additionally, in stark contrast with the perceptions and experiences of the Malaysian interviewees, all of the Hong Kong interviewees disclosed that they did not feel at all constrained by the film censorship system. The interviewees noted that they very rarely self-censored their film projects and did not avoid graphic violence, sex or other contentious content in their films because of censorship concerns in Hong Kong.[36] The interviewees were also of the opinion that the Hong Kong censors were not conferred wide discretionary powers under the law and that the film censorship standards had remained more or less the same after the reunification with China in 1997. The interviewees also expressed the opinion that freedom of expression is very important to them. Gordon Chan, for example, related the importance of the freedom to the viability of the film industry and the competitiveness of local productions. Chan was of the opinion that in order to compete with foreign films (particularly those from Hollywood) local film practitioners needed the freedom to produce creative and cutting edge films to attract audiences. In addition, Chan pointed out that freedom of expression was also crucial to filmmakers who wanted to explore sensitive social or political issues in their films.

It is not the Hong Kong film censorship system but the Chinese film censorship system that causes concerns to Hong Kong film practitioners. Benny Chan, for example, noted that:

> The biggest market for us now is in Mainland China and it does not have a three-tier classification system like the one we have here in Hong Kong... film censorship in China is very strict and our concern is with Chinese censorship, not with censorship in Hong Kong... we really need the Mainland Chinese market and the size of the box office revenue there is very attractive.

Mabel Cheung, who spent more than a year in Beijing dealing with the censorship authorities to get her film *The Soong Sisters* released without her having to excise 18 minutes of the film's footage (as required by the Chinese censors), claimed that 'a lot of Hong Kong filmmakers are looking towards China and they have to self-censor in order to get co-production projects and to get their films released there. That really restricts them!'[37] Gordon Chan, who has in the past decade worked both in China and Hong Kong, revealed that 'when I work in a co-production project in China, I feel so constrained' and, like his colleagues Benny Chan and Mable Cheung, Chan thought that China should adopt the Hong Kong three-tier classification scheme.[38]

The majority of the Australian film practitioners interviewed for this book were satisfied with the country's classification system. They were of the opinion that it was 'in good shape', 'effective', 'works well' and 'representative of the community standards'.[39] For example, Tony Ayres, a director and producer, thought that Australia had 'a healthy classification system where films get seen in the context that they were designed to be seen in';[40] Rolf de Heer, an award-winning film director and producer, noted that the classification system was 'not a restrictive' one;[41] Ray Lawrence, a film director, was of the opinion that the classifiers were doing 'a good job'[42] while James Hewison, Theatrical Distribution Manager at Madman Entertainment, found the classification process to be 'transparent' and noted that 'there are very few films that can't be released in cinemas',[43] while Joel Pearlman, Managing Director of Roadshow Films, observed that the system was 'effective in providing guidance to all the constituents who need it'.[44]

These interviewees noted that they were neither artistically nor commercially constrained by the classification system. They were of the opinion that freedom of expression is very important for them as filmmakers and agreed that they did enjoy it in Australia. The interviewees were also of the opinion that they were free to make the films they wanted to as long as there is a demand for such films in the market. Therefore, the Australian film industry is subject more to commercial pressures than censorship. As Tony Ayres puts it: 'the kind of constraints in terms of freedom of expression for us are more economic… in terms of the stories that you can tell being the kind of stories that people would want to see'. It is also apparent from the fieldwork that Australian film practitioners do not avoid graphic violence, sexual content or other contentious elements in their films (or the films they intend to distribute or exhibit) because of censorship concerns, or purely out of fear of how the films might be classified. Censorship was not viewed as an impediment in this case. Such content was avoided, if ever, because of different factors, such as on moral grounds and personal taste, commercial considerations or because such content was not necessary for their films. Peter Campbell, for example, noted that his distribution company, Accent Film Entertainment, did 'reject films that are exploitative… but that had nothing to do with the censorship system but morals';[45] while director Ray Lawrence, noted that 'I feel responsible for the amount of violence, sex and the contentious content… All my films are for mature audience but I would still self-censor in a way if I felt that something was gratuitous'.

The interviewees' opinions of the key issues that arise from the film censorship systems as identified in Chapter 4 will now be considered in turn.

Film practitioners' opinions of the key issues

Decision-making entities

There are three concerns with regard to the film censorship decision-making entities in Malaysia:

1 the suitability and competence of the appointed film censors;
2 the independence of film censors in making censorship decisions; and
3 the Home Minister's discretionary power to override censorship decisions and prohibit the exhibition and distribution of films.

All of the Malaysian interviewees expressed concerns about the suitability and competence of the film censors in carrying out their duties. As discussed in Chapter 3, the Board of Censors is made up of retired senior government officers with little, if any, knowledge or experience in film and filmmaking. U-Wei Haji Saari noted that government officers who performed well during their tenure were 'rewarded' with a position on the Board after they retired from service. The filmmaker was of the opinion that these censors were 'conservative and narrow minded' and that they censored films according to their whims and fancies. Based on his own experiences in dealing with the Board, U-Wei found that the censors approached film as something that 'challenges or threatens' them and they did not attempt to understand or appreciate films. He added: 'from what I have seen the censors do to my films, I don't think they are sensitive enough nor really have real bearing of what film is all about'. The way in which censors were appointed was also questioned by Ruhani Abdul Rahman: 'what the government is doing is just giving these retired officers something to do [after their retirement]. I think it should not be that way. It should be given to the right people to do the job'. The seasoned producer also noted that most of the censors had no experience in or knowledge of film and thus were not suitable to serve as film censors.[46] Lorna Tee was also of the opinion that the Malaysian censors had 'very little understanding of film' while Ahmad Puad Onah, a producer and distributor who heads Primeworks Studio, found the censors to be operating with the mindset that 'anything that is out of the ordinary should not be shown to the audience'. Ahmad Puad was also of the opinion that the censors did not understand the adverse effects of alteration to the film as a whole, noting that 'there are not enough people who know and understand the film industry in the censorship board… the board is filled with retired government officers who cut scenes out without understanding how it will affect the film'. Tsai Ming-liang felt that the censors' exposure to the varieties of film was very limited. Tsai noted that the censors' appreciation of film was very shallow and therefore they were not qualified to make censorship judgments.

The suitability, competence and maturity of film censors are also reflected in their decisions. Amir Muhammad noted that there were many 'stupid decisions' being made. He cited the censorship decision for *Love Conquers All* (Tan Chui Mui, 2006), a film he produced, as one example. The Board of Censors required alteration to be made to a scene where a character of Chinese ethnicity uttered the word '*assalamualaikum*'[47] to a character of Malay ethnicity. The Board required alteration to be made to the scene, citing the reason that a Chinese character is not supposed to utter that word. As a result, the dialogue had to be 'beeped' making it seem as if the Chinese character was cursing, which in effect made 'something rude out of something which wasn't'.[48] While elaborating his experiences in dealing with censors, Aziz M. Osman also suggested that the censors were ill-equipped and not intelligent enough to make censorship decisions.[49] Aziz was also of the opinion that the composition of the Board of Censors and the Appeal Committee was not representative of the Malaysian community and that the censors were out of touch with contemporary community standards, being unaware of 'what is really happening on the ground'. Commenting on her experiences in meeting with members of the Board and Committee over the censorship decision of her film *Sepet* (2004) – an interracial love story between a Chinese boy and a Malay girl – Yasmin Ahmad remarked that the censors concerned were not competent to carry out their duties, that they 'just censor indiscriminately' and that they were 'lazy, stubborn and stupid'.

The influence of the Home Minister on the Board of Censors and Appeal Committee caused concerns over independence. This could be linked to the fact that members of the Board and the Committee are appointed by the Minister[50] and their appointments may be revoked by the Minister at any time and without having to assign any reason.[51] An example is the banning of *Lelaki Komunis Terakhir* (*The Last Communist*, Amir Muhammad, 2006) – a documentary tracing the places where Chin Peng, exiled leader of the Communist Party of Malaya, had lived.[52] The film was initially approved for exhibition without any alteration and classified 'U' (suitable for general audience) by the Board of Censors but after the Home Minister exercised his discretionary power under section 26 of the Film Censorship Act 2002 to ban the film, the Board turned around and claimed that the film was not suitable to be exhibited and distributed in Malaysia. This incident suggests that, first, the Board is not independent and free from political pressure and second, the censors have no confidence in the decisions they make.[53] Khoo Eng Yow, an independent film director and producer, felt that Malaysian censors are 'too obeying' and submissive to external pressures. The independence of censors was also raised by fellow film director James Lee, who noted that 'it is their job at stake and to play safe, anything that they felt is a concern or will cause uproar, they will just censor or ban it'. Leonard Tee, a distributor, noted that the censors were not willing to bear any responsibility for the decisions they made and 'if they don't understand [the film], they will think that it is dangerous… and they will just ban it'.

Regarding the Home Minister's discretionary power under section 26, Ahmad Puad Onah was of the opinion that the Minister should not be empowered to override censorship decisions made by the Board of Censors and the Appeal Committee: 'I don't agree that the Minister [should be] given that discretionary power to ban a film after the Appeal Committee has approved it'. This opinion is echoed by other interviewees like Khoo Eng Yow who deemed the exercise of such power as 'not healthy' while Amir Muhammad, whose film *Lelaki Komunis Terakhir* became a victim under this provision, remarked that judicial review is all the more needed to counter this seemingly unfettered discretion.

In Hong Kong, censors are appointed by the Chief Executive under the terms of civil service and their tenure of office lasts until the age of retirement, if there is no resignation or disciplinary termination.[54] The fieldwork conducted suggests that the Hong Kong censors are in fact not subject to political pressure or interference. The Hong Kong interviewees found the members of the Panel of Censors and Board of Review to be 'qualified to carry out their duties',[55] 'open-minded',[56] 'effective'[57] and 'approachable for discussions'.[58] Some of the interviewees were also of the opinion that the way in which film censors were appointed was 'fine and acceptable'.[59] Gordon Chan noted that the Hong Kong film censorship system was comparatively better than others because its decision-making entities were very well balanced. Chan elaborated that there were members of the public of different background, age and experience (in the Panel of Advisers) that provided their opinions of how the community would view certain film content and whether they needed to be censored. Then, there was also the group of professionals such as cultural leaders, academics, artists and experts in various fields (in the Panel of Censors and the Board of Review) who provided their views and pointed to the direction in which Hong Kong society should be heading. Chan added:

> At times you will encounter sensitive issues or controversial content in films and you will need this professional group to spearhead the trend.… They may

> find the content to be controversial but nevertheless agree [that it should be released] because "this is the right time to bring it up and discuss about it"... or they may stop it because they think "it shouldn't be done or there should be different standards".

In addition, unlike the Malaysian Film Censorship Act 2002, the Hong Kong Film Censorship Ordinance does not confer wide discretionary power on any of the decision-making entities.

In Australia, the full time members of the Classification Board and members of the Classification Review Board are appointed by the Governor General based on the recommendation made by the Commonwealth Minister after consultation with state and territory ministers. The candidates are selected through a merit-based selection process. Before an appointment is made, regard is given to the desirability of having the membership of the Boards broadly representative of the Australian community. The appointment of a classifier is for a time period as specified in the instrument of appointment and the circumstances under which an appointment may be terminated are expressly provided for in the Classification (Publications, Films and Computer Games) Act 1995.[60] Such circumstances include physical or mental incapacity, absence from duty (except on leave of absence) for a certain period of time, or failure to disclose interest in relation to a matter under consideration.

Only two of the Australian film practitioners interviewed for this book had issues with the suitability of classifiers. Richard J. Frankland, an indigenous filmmaker, had doubts concerning the suitability of the classifiers because 'they were talking from their cultural shape and not from the cultural shape of all Australians'.[61] On the composition of the decision-making entities, Frankland commented: 'They need to go through intense cultural indigenous programs. They need to know about the variance in other cultures. I think they are utilizing their powers very much based on the Euro-centric upper-middle class perspective.' The other interviewee – Peter Campbell, a distributor – was disappointed with the members of the Classification Review Board that he had encountered during the appeal process of *9 Songs* (Michael Winterbottom, 2004), a film which contains explicit sexual content that his company distributes, because he had found them to have a 'precast judgment' on the film.[62]

Apart from Frankland and Campbell, the other Australian interviewees were satisfied with the appointment to, and composition of, the Classification Board and the Classification Review Board.[63] For example, Ray Lawrence was of the opinion that 'the censorship board should consist of intelligent people who should be able to see the difference between something that has artistic, social and cultural merits rather than just slop. And I think, in the main they do... ',[64] while Greg Denning, an executive at Icon Film Distribution Australia, thought that Australia had 'a system in place which is representative of the community. The fact that we have very few instances where there is public outrage about a classification decision says that... very rarely people feel that they [the classifiers] have got it wrong.'[65] This view is echoed by Jan Chapman, producer of the critically acclaimed film *The Piano* (Jane Campion, 1993), who noted that the Board consisted of a cross section of the people who were representative of the Australian community.[66]

It is noteworthy that there is no provision in the Classification (Publications, Films and Computer Games) Act 1995 that confers wide discretionary power on any of the entities involved in the making of classification decisions. More importantly, unlike the Malaysian Minister, the Australian Minister is not empowered to override decisions made by the classifiers.

The exemption of films from censorship

Section 2(2)(a) of the Malaysian Film Censorship Act 2002 provides that the Act shall not apply to any film sponsored by the Malaysian Government, while section 28 empowers the Home Minister to exempt any film from censorship. These provisions appear to be supporting a double standard in film censorship and were criticized by the interviewees. When referred to these provisions, U-Wei Haji Saari responded that they sounded 'dubious' and that it was 'irresponsible' for someone to be given the complete power to exempt films from censorship at his or her discretion. Amir Muhammad questioned the rationale and necessity of having such a wide power resting on a single individual. Saw Teong Hin was of the opinion that the power to exempt certain films from censorship was 'not fair' because it was akin to claiming that 'anything that I [the government] do is morally upright and good and everything others do is suspect'[67] while Khoo Eng Yow thought that every film should be subjected to the same censorship process.

In Hong Kong, the Film Censorship Authority is empowered to exempt certain classes of film from censorship.[68] However, unlike the Malaysian Home Minister, the Film Censorship Authority does not have *carte blanche* power to exempt any film from undergoing the censorship process. Only films that fall within 'the classes or description of films' as set out in the second schedule to the Film Censorship Regulations may be exempted and they include cultural, educational, instructional, promotional, sports, travelogues, musical and religious films.[69] The classes of film that may be exempted are clearly stipulated in legislation and there was no dissatisfaction or complaint at all from the Hong Kong interviewees that the power to exempt films had been abused.

In Australia, the 13 types of film entitled to exemption from classification are stipulated under section 5B(1) of the Classification (Publications, Films and Computer Games) Act 1995 and they include business, scientific, educational, current affairs, sporting, musical presentation and religious films. The decision-making entities are not empowered to exempt, at their discretion, any other types of film from classification. This is in marked contrast with the Malaysian Minister's power to exempt any film from censorship at his discretion, a power which, if exercised, poses a challenge to the overall integrity of the film censorship system in Malaysia. It is worth noting that the Australian interviewees made no comment about the exemption of films from classification.

Matters to be taken into account by censors

The Malaysian Film Censorship Act 2002 does not stipulate the matters to be considered or taken into account by censors in the course of making censorship decisions. This omission means two important considerations, the artistic merit of the film and the prevailing community standards, which may otherwise have substantial impact on censorship decisions, could be left out of the decision-making process.

Artistic merit of the film

Although most of the Malaysian interviewees agreed that the consideration of the artistic merit of a film would have substantial impact on the censorship decision, they were doubtful as to whether the censors were able to appreciate the artistic merit of the films they examined and let it influence their decisions. For example, Amir Muhammad remarked that 'the censors wouldn't recognize it [artistic merit] even if it sat on their faces. I mean films like *Brokeback Mountain* (Ang Lee, 2005) wouldn't get past' while Khoo Eng Yow thought that the decision-making process in Malaysia was 'simplistic' where censors did not think, consider or evaluate much when they were making censorship decisions.

In Hong Kong, the matters to be considered and taken into account by film censors are stipulated under section 10(2) and (3) of the Film Censorship Ordinance. One of the matters listed is 'the artistic, educational, literary or scientific merit of the film and its importance or value for cultural or social reasons'.[70] The consideration of artistic merit appears to be able to offset content or portrayal that may otherwise cause the film to be banned or approved under a higher classification category. All of the Hong Kong interviewees agreed that consideration of the artistic merit of a film had substantial impact on the censorship decision to be made. Benny Chan said: 'when a film has high artistic value, it is unlikely to be banned or subjected to excision' while Patrick Tam noted that because of this consideration, films with strong sexual content or graphic violence were still released in Hong Kong, if the films had artistic merits.[71]

Although all the interviewees agreed that the consideration of artistic merit substantially affects a film's censorship decision, not all of them agreed that artistic merit should be taken into account in the decision-making process. However, many more interviewees supported the consideration than those who did not. One of the interviewees who thought artistic merit should not affect censorship decisions was Kenneth Bi, who was of the opinion that films which were considered as artistic 'should not get away with more' compared to those which were considered to be devoid of such merit. Censors may possibly equate films with artistic merit and films made by established filmmakers. Mabel Cheung was of the opinion that 'censors could be biased to the more established or famous directors as opposed to a filmmaker from nowhere'. Lo Chi Leung, who was of a similar view, illustrated his answer by referencing two Hong Kong directors:

> If Ann Hui made a film that borders between Category IIB and Category III, it will be classified Category IIB because of the name Ann Hui, but if that film is made by Wong Jing, it will end up being classified Category III. It could be that biased.[72]

It would be unfair if censors were influenced by the reputation of the filmmakers in this way and not purely by the artistic merit of the film *per se* when making censorship decisions. The risk of that occurring is present, which underlines the importance of qualified and competent people being appointed as censors to lessen this risk.

The matters to be taken into account by Australian classifiers when making film classification decisions are provided under section 11 of the Classification (Publications, Films and Computer Games) Act 1995. One of such matters is 'the literary, artistic or educational merit of the film' and most of the Australian interviewees agreed that the taking into account of artistic merit of a film had substantial impact on the classification decision and that it should be so. Tony Ayers highlighted an example – *Shortbus* (John Cameron Mitchell, 2006) 'which has explicit sexual content got an R rating rather than an X rating which allowed it to be distributed theatrically and certainly I think it is due to its artistic merits'; Rolf de Heer remarked that 'I not only think so [that the consideration of artistic merit had substantial impact on classification decisions], I know so. Absolutely, yes!'; while Greg Denning noted that 'when something is not gratuitous and if it is there for historical accuracy or is of artistic value and not just gore for gore's sake or sex for sex's sake, I do think that is taken into account'.

An example that illustrates the effect of the artistic merit of a film on its classification decision is the classification of the critically acclaimed film *The Piano Teacher* (Michael Haneke, 2001) with an R18+ category although it contains actual sexual activity. An exception to the general rule prescribed in the classification guidelines – that films depicting actual sex are to be classified X18+ which would bar the film from exhibition and distribution in most of the states and territories in Australia – was made by classifiers due to the artistic merits of the film.[73]

Current community standards

No systematic effort is carried out in Malaysia to ensure that censorship decisions made are reflective of current community standards. Censorship decisions appear to be made subjectively, based on the personal standards of the censors. Most of the Malaysian interviewees were of the opinion that film censorship decisions should be made based on the standards currently prevailing in the community. U-Wei Haji Saari, for example, thought that it was sensible to do so because 'society and values change, meanings change and so we must also change and grow or else we will be stuck in a time capsule'.[74] The director also agreed that the Malaysian censors made censorship decisions based on their subjective views and they did not take current community standards into account:

> That is what happened to me. The person who censored my film feels that it is offensive to her, so it does not matter whether the public feels that the film is OK... They don't think of the public and I don't think there is any survey that has been done [on] what is the tolerance level or what offends the public... it is just that a few people were appointed by somebody to make decisions, important decisions on one of the most important art forms in Malaysia... it is so bizarre!

In *Reclaiming Adat: Contemporary Malaysian Film and Literature*, it was observed that 'the censorship board perceives itself to be the moral and national guardian of Malaysian society' and that the Board of Censors is 'arbitrary in its choice of targets and uneven in carrying out its goal'.[75] This view was echoed by another writer who commented that 'the trouble with censorship in Malaysia is that it is arbitrary and left to the individuals who fill our censorship board. Decisions are based on what the individual feels is right or wrong and they are not accountable for it'.[76]

The situation is different in Hong Kong as the censorship guidelines expressly provide that 'the aim of the censors should be to reflect contemporary public attitudes towards censorship standards'.[77] This aim is achieved in two ways. First, regular public opinion surveys on film censorship standards are conducted to gauge the extent their decisions reflect community standards. Second, members of the Panel of Advisers (which comprises members drawn from the community representing people of different age, gender and profession) are assigned to provide opinions to censors in the decision-making process.

The Hong Kong interviewees were satisfied with the approach in which censorship decisions were made and they agreed that film censorship decisions should be made objectively based on current community standards as opposed to the censors' subjective personal standards. As Mabel Cheung puts it, 'film censorship decisions should be made based on the current atmosphere of the society, they should be very close to the opinion that prevails in the public'. Two interviewees however, suggested that a combination of professionals' views and community standards would be ideal. Benny Chan was of the opinion that under certain circumstances, censorship decisions should not be made based solely on the community's standards because it might be important to also take into account experts or professionals' views of the effect of the film concerned – 'whether it will adversely affect young children or influence the community'.[78] Gordon Chan who shared the same opinion noted:

> While we factor in what the community thinks about film, we also need professionals and scholars to make sure that we can have it [the release of film] in a positive way and move ahead. The general audience tends to be more conservative, so for the society to evolve or for any culture to move forward, we need scholars, artists and leaders to lead the way. So I think the balance between their views is very important.

In Australia, there are two provisions that require classifiers to take into account community standards when they classify films. The first is section 11 of the

Classification (Publications, Films and Computer Games) Act 1995 which provides that classifiers must take into account, amongst other things, 'the standards of morality, decency and propriety generally accepted by reasonable adults' while the second provision is found in the National Classification Code which sets out four principles for classification, one of which reads:

> Classification decisions are to give effect, as far as possible, to the following principles:
>
> > ... (d) the need to take into account community concerns about (i) depictions that condone or incite violence, particularly sexual violence; and (ii) the portrayal of persons in a demeaning manner.

Two major efforts are being undertaken to ensure classification decisions are in line with community standards. The first effort is filling the Classification Board and Classification Review Board with members who are broadly representative of the Australian community and the second effort is the establishment of the Community Assessment Panel (CAP), a scheme introduced to gauge how accurately the classifiers' decisions reflect the prevailing community standards. Most of the Australian interviewees agreed that classification decisions should be made by taking into account the community standards as opposed to classifiers' own standards and they noted that film classification decisions in Australia were being made by taking into account such standards. Jan Chapman, for example, observed that the film classification standards in Australia had become more liberal over the years and that there was more understanding on the part of the classifiers in the standards acceptable by the society particularly on sexuality and sexual contents.

Censorship guidelines

As discussed in Chapter 4, substantial defects were found in the Malaysian Film Censorship Guidelines 1993. For ease of discussion and comparison, the interviewees' opinions of the guidelines will be discussed on a jurisdiction-by-jurisdiction basis under two subheadings: 'Clarity of provisions' and 'Context; degree, intensity and realism of presentation; and limits of the categories'.

The Malaysian Film Censorship Guidelines 1993

The Malaysian interviewees were not involved in the drafting of the Film Censorship Guidelines 1993 in that they were not invited to discuss or submit their opinions when the guidelines are being drawn up by the government.

CLARITY OF PROVISIONS

Almost every Malaysian interviewee agreed that the Film Censorship Guidelines 1993 lacked clarity. They described the Guidelines as 'ridiculous and broad enough that you can read anything into it',[79] 'outdated',[80] 'too general, does not give an idea of what can and cannot be done, vague and not descriptive'.[81] The interviewees were also of the opinion that the Guidelines were not coherently applied, resulting in inconsistent censorship decisions. Yasmin Ahmad described the application of the Guidelines as 'haphazard' and 'at the whims of whoever is in charge'. Ahmad Puad Onah felt that there was a double standard in its applications, noting 'we do get the feeling that "why is this movie allowed but not that movie?"' while Shuhaimi Baba was of the opinion that the application of the Guidelines was more lenient on foreign films compared to local films, particularly those made by Muslim filmmakers. She noted, for example, that kissing scenes are permitted in foreign films but not in films made by Malaysian filmmakers. Shuhaimi Baba's view was shared by Aziz M. Osman where he questioned why imported horror and fantasy films were allowed to be screened in Malaysia whereas local films featuring ghosts and spirits ended up being banned by censors.

The incoherence of application was not only apparent between the inconsistent decisions made on different films but also between decisions made on the same film. For example, films like *Gone in Sixty Seconds* (Dominic Sena, 2000) and *Ocean's Eleven* (Steven Soderbergh, 2001) – just to highlight a few – were not approved for exhibition in cinemas but were subsequently approved for distribution on DVD and broadcasted on television. An even more absurd censorship decision was made on the film *Kami* (Effendee Mazlan, 2008) where the Board of Censors required a line of dialogue in the film (which contains the Malay word '*palat*', meaning 'penis') to be removed before approval for exhibition was granted but the Board had earlier approved the film's publicity materials which contained exactly the same word.[82] It is puzzling how such decisions could be made by the censors.

Incoherence of application and the resulting inconsistencies in censorship decisions appear to have their root in vague guidelines which allow censors to interpret and apply them in ways that they deem fit. This has a very negative impact on the Malaysian film industry because 'it is hard for filmmakers, producers and distributors to gauge how their films will end up being censored… and that is bad for business, bad for people who invest in films as a business proposition'.[83]

CONTEXT; DEGREE, INTENSITY AND REALISM OF PRESENTATION; AND LIMITS OF THE CATEGORIES

In relation to contextual justification, the main concern amongst the Malaysian interviewees was that film censors did not consider the film under examination as a whole when they were making censorship decisions. Censors often viewed a film as 'bits and pieces' and not a connected whole. For example, if there was a shot or a scene that contained contentious content or portrayal, the shot or scene must be altered (normally by way of excision) even though it was justifiable in the context of the film as a whole, or was crucial to the story and presentation of the film. U-Wei Haji Saari noted that:[84]

> [The censors] don't see the film as a whole… they don't see it as fluid. They will just see the lines, for example they will say 'this line offended me… that

> line makes me feel uneasy, so have to be removed!' Or 'that shot of a woman sitting *berkemban*[85] taking a bath that I am uncomfortable with, take it out'.

The director added that this censorship approach caused problems to filmmakers because it affected not only the narrative, but also the aesthetic aspects of a film.[86]

In addition, unlike the guidelines applied in Hong Kong and Australia, the Malaysian Film Censorship Guidelines 1993 do not require censors to take into account the degree, intensity and realism of presentation of a censorship element. The guidelines also do not set out the limits of censorship elements under the applicable classification categories.

Compared to the Hong Kong and Australian film censorship guidelines, the Malaysian guidelines prohibit many more types of film, content and portrayal. There are four censorship elements prescribed in the guidelines – ideology and politics, religion, socio-culture and order and decorum, which are further divided into sub-categories and rules. Because of these extensive restrictions, the Malaysian interviewees felt that they were artistically and/or commercially constrained and that their freedom of expression was impeded.[87]

The Hong Kong Film Censorship Guidelines for Censors

In comparison with the Malaysian Film Censorship Guidelines 1993, the Hong Kong Film Censorship Guidelines for Censors appears to be much better on paper. This was confirmed by almost every Hong Kong film practitioner interviewed for the book.[88] They were satisfied with the provisions of the Guidelines as well as their application by censors. Gordon Chan, for example, noted that 'the reason why we did not have censorship problems is that the censors have very good guidelines and they are also open-minded'. The interviews conducted in Hong Kong also revealed that film practitioners were invited to discuss and comment on the draft guidelines before they were introduced in December 1999. Wellington Fung, for example, stated that: 'there was a very thorough discussion on where the lines are supposed to be drawn' while Gordon Chan noted that 'there were a lot of discussions... the whole censorship system that exists now was established after a series of discussions and debates and I think that is why it is acceptable to the film industry and filmmakers'.

CLARITY OF PROVISIONS

The provisions in the Film Censorship Guidelines for Censors are clear, precise and well structured. The clarity of the provisions helps film practitioners know beforehand which category his or her film will end up being classified in before they embark on the production of their film. Lo Chi Leung, for example, noted that 'I will know whether my film will be classified Category II or Category III and we [Lo and his producers] could decide before shooting began whether we want the film to go down the Category II path or the Category III path' while

Benny Chan noted that 'the guidelines are very clear, so there is no problem for me to differentiate what types of content fall within which classification categories'. Mabel Cheung, one of the leading Hong Kong female directors, also shared the same opinion: 'the censorship guidelines are clear, so I will know before I make the film whether it will fall into Category III or otherwise. I know exactly what classification I will get'.

In addition, most of the Hong Kong interviewees were of the opinion that the guidelines were coherently applied. Only two interviewees, Winnie Tsang and Lo Chi Leung, pointed out that there was incoherence in the guidelines' application in regard to the censorship element of language. Both Tsang and Lo highlighted that the censors tended to classify local Cantonese films containing coarse language with a higher classification category (Category III) compared to the foreign English language films (Category IIB) although the expletives used were of similar meaning in both types of film.[89]

CONTEXT; DEGREE, INTENSITY AND REALISM OF PRESENTATION; AND LIMITS OF THE CATEGORIES

The Hong Kong guidelines allow censors to approve films containing censorship elements or contentious content for exhibition and distribution, if such content is justifiable in the context of the film as a whole. The guidelines also prescribe the limits of each of the censorship elements under every classification category. The limits are set based on the degree, intensity and realism to which these elements are presented in a film.

There are six censorship elements prescribed in the guidelines – cruelty, torture or violence; horror and shock; disability; sex and nudity; language; and offensive behaviour and criminality. Although these six censorship elements are in the guidelines, the Hong Kong interviewees did not feel they were artistically or commercially constrained because they were not barred from producing (or acquiring the rights to) films containing those elements. The censorship elements were prescribed mainly for classification of films into appropriate categories and, as noted in Chapter 3, these censorship elements were not absolutely prohibited, unlike those prescribed in the Malaysian Film Censorship Guidelines 1993.

The Australian Guidelines for the Classification of Films and Computer Games

Most of the Australian interviewees did not have any strong opinions about the Guidelines for the Classification of Films and Computer Games which were introduced in 2003 after extensive discussions and consultations with members of the film fraternity and the public. The fieldwork revealed that the interviewees were not very familiar with the guidelines and that they only had a broad idea of what is permissible within the 'censorship boundaries'. The interviewees, particularly the directors, intimated that they rarely referred to the guidelines when they made their films.

CLARITY OF PROVISIONS

The provisions in the Guidelines are clear and the key words and phrases used therein are well defined, presumably to avoid inconsistent interpretations by classifiers that will subsequently cause problems to film practitioners in pursuing their film productions and acquisitions. There were no negative comments voiced by the Australian interviewees over the clarity of the Guidelines. Some interviewees even commended the clarity of its provisions and noted that they knew which classification category their films would be classified in.[90]

Additionally, most of the Australian interviewees were of the opinion that the guidelines were coherently applied. For example, Tony Ayres noted that the classifiers were consistent in the application of the Guidelines while Jan Chapman observed that the Guidelines were 'coherently applied' and that the films she produced 'were classified very much in the way we expected'.

CONTEXT; DEGREE, INTENSITY AND REALISM OF PRESENTATION; AND LIMITS OF THE CATEGORIES

In making a classification decision, classifiers are required to determine the overall impact of the film. The impact is to be assessed by considering the treatment of the classifiable elements; the degree, realism and intensity of their presentation; and the cumulative effect of all the elements that appear in the film. Classifiers are also required to consider whether the elements (as they appear in a film) are justified in the context of the film as a whole. The limits of contents suitable for each classification category are also clearly prescribed in the Guidelines.

There are six classifiable elements provided in the Guidelines – themes, violence, sex, language, drug use and nudity. Although apparently higher in number (of the elements) compared to those listed in the Malaysian guidelines (four censorship elements), the Australian interviewees disclosed that they did not feel artistically or commercially constrained by the provisions. This is because, similar to the situation in Hong Kong, these elements are not prohibited outright. They are provided mainly for classification purposes. It was striking that there was no concern at all about the classification guidelines expressed by the Australian interviewees unlike their Malaysian counterparts.

Alteration to films and determination of classification category

Alteration to films and restricted categories

In Malaysia, the Board of Censors is empowered to require alteration to be made before a film is approved for public exhibition[91] and the word 'alteration' is defined in the Film Censorship Act 2002 as to include excision, addition and reconstruction of scenes, dialogues, sound or subtitles.[92] Alteration will not only affect the film's artistic integrity, the exercise of the power to require alteration to be made also encroaches on filmmakers' right to freedom of expression. Although in practice the Board will seek consent from the film's owner before any alteration is made, this does not allow the film practitioner concerned any other option because, if consent to alter is withheld, approval for the film's exhibition and distribution will be refused.[93] In short, it is 'mandatory' for a film practitioner to consent to the required alteration if he or she wishes to have the film released in Malaysia. Khoo Eng Yow commented that in a situation where alteration was required by the Board 'the filmmakers are actually helpless... you cannot do anything because if you do not consent, you cannot show your film'. Shuhaimi Baba, in reference to her 1995 film *Ringgit Kasyorga* (*Dollar to Heaven*) – a film which explores the themes of corruption and abuse of power among the Malaysian elites – noted that she had to allow substantial alterations to be made so that the film could be released,[94] while Saw Teong Hin noted that 'you have to abide by it, otherwise you can't get your film into the cinemas'. This is particularly so for those whose film's market is confined to Malaysia.[95]

U-Wei Haji Saari, many of whose films have been required by the censors to be altered, was 'upset' and 'completely annoyed' with the exercise of such power. His first film *Perempuan, Isteri & ...* (*Wife, Woman & Whore*, 1993) – about a woman sold into prostitution who wanted revenge on the man responsible – had to undergo extensive excision in addition to having part of its title deleted.[96] Two scenes from his Festival de Cannes' Directors' Fortnight bound film *Kaki Bakar* (*The Arsonist*, 1995) – a film about a Javanese man in Malaysia who commits acts of arson after feeling mistreated due to social inequalities – had to be excised. And *Jogho* (*Champion*, 1997) – a film about vengeance set in a bull-fighting community – had 18 cuts made to it. U- Wei felt that the alterations 'destroyed not only the rhythm but also the overall narration and aesthetic' of his films ('it makes the film jumpy'). He was particularly upset because the censors involved had acted as if they were 'cleaning up' his films ('they try to clean it up, try to *halal* it'[97]), which suggested that his films were 'dirty', 'immoral' and 'unhealthy'. The filmmaker added:

> Who are these people? I don't know their background. I don't trust them.... Are they cultured? I don't think so.... They don't even tell you who they are and these invisible people just butchered your work. It takes you five years to do a film from thinking to finishing up and they tamper with it in the matter of two hours. That is not fair, that is wrong!

Shuhaimi Baba has also had similar experiences with the censors. She was required to excise many scenes from her film *Ringgit Kassyorga* in order to get the approval to release it: 'I had to take out so many scenes that the film didn't make sense anymore... and I didn't have enough money to do re-shoots, so whatever little that I re-shot couldn't help the film'. Ahmad Puad Onah was of the opinion that censors should not be empowered to require alteration to be made to films. The film producer appeared to have concerns for both financial and artistic considerations as he said:

> We should not, just to get an approval [for exhibition] from them, have to reshoot or do away with certain scenes or [have to] create new ones... I don't

> think they should be given that power… because it will cost us more money…. When we make a film, we have already considered all the aspects and we wanted the film to be in a certain way. Alteration will change this, so I don't think censors should be allowed to require us to make alterations.

Like many others in Malaysia, Tsai Ming-liang's *I Don't Want to Sleep Alone* (2006) – a film set in Kuala Lumpur about a migrant worker nursing an injured drifter he found on the street – also suffered the same fate of having to undergo alterations. The Appeal Committee required five scenes to be excised and some of the subtitles to be deleted[98] before approval for exhibition was granted. Tsai noted that 'they just use their power to order excisions to be made and when they do so, audiences will only get to see an incomplete work, an injured film'.

Alteration to films may also cause financial losses to film practitioners.[99] For example, *Amok* (Adman Salleh, 1995) was subjected to extensive alteration where ten scenes were required to be removed from the film. Because of the severe excisions (which the film's producer, Ruhani Abdul Rahman, described as 'horrible'), 'the story, message and appeal of the film are lost, people who watch it could not understand the film and I lost money!'[100]

All of the Malaysian interviewees were of the opinion that once a film was classified with a restricted category, alteration should not be required to be made to the film. For example, Amir Muhammad noted that 'if a film is rated 18 and above, it should be released uncut'. Ahmad Puad Onah, who also prefers films to be released intact, was of the opinion that 'when they classify a film for 18 and above but still insist that scenes are cut, then there is no point in the classification'. U-Wei Haji Saari also favoured films to be released in their entirety and preferred classification over censoring the content of films. He noted: 'I don't believe in censoring anybody's work. I don't believe in censoring whatever you want to say but I believe in "censoring" the audience'.[101]

In Hong Kong, censors are empowered to require excision to be made to a film before an approval for exhibition and distribution is granted.[102] However, it must be stressed that Hong Kong censors can only require excision to be made, not other forms of alteration as in Malaysia. It is equally important to point out that the interviews conducted in Hong Kong revealed that, in practice, censors very rarely require excision to be made to films.[103] The statutory power to do so is exercised, if ever, only in extreme cases where even the restricted classification of Category III could not accommodate the contents.[104] Gordon Chan noted that the censors would only require excision to be made 'if they think those materials cannot be shown even under Category III… for example, if it is too excessive or explicit'. Although Chan is not in favour of the exercise of such power, he saw the justification for it and pointed out that most of the time where excision was required, the decision did reflect the opinion of the public. However, Chan stressed that none of the films that he was involved in as director or producer or both (amounting to over 35 feature films) had ever been required to be excised by the Hong Kong censors and that 'I was always given the classification category that I hoped for.' Terence Chang, the producer of John Woo's films in Hong Kong and Hollywood, noted that 'I never had to do any alteration to my films in Hong Kong to secure a particular category, although we did cut out some blood-spilling shots to change *Mission: Impossible II* from R to PG in the United States.'[105] According to Patrick Tam, what normally happens in Hong Kong where a film falls between the Category IIB and Category III classifications is:

> They [the censors] will only say 'you need to remove this, if not it will be Category III'. It is up to you whether you want to cut it or not. They never impose that you must… You make your own decision because they never force you to do anything. So, this is a kind of advice and normally, the film investors will ask the director to trim it to avoid the film from being categorized as Category III so that they wouldn't lose that much at the box office.

However, Tam did caution that 'unjustified censorship or excisions will definitely affect the creative completeness or totality of vision that the filmmaker chooses to present to his or her audiences'.

In Australia, the Classification Board and the Classification Review Board are not empowered to require alteration to be made to films submitted to them for classification purposes. The classifiers only determine the classification category and the consumer advice to be given to a submitted film. However, if the classifiers find that the film contains content or portrayals that are prohibited by the classification law[106] or guidelines,[107] they may refuse classification (the RC category), which means that the film is banned in Australia. Greg Denning summarized the issue of alteration to films in the country as follows:

> Classifiers do not have the power to require alteration to be made to submitted films. They can only recommend the classification category…. They will also give you the specifics of what scenes or what contents pushed the film into the next level of classification. So, if you are looking to edit the film down, they may give you guidance on that.

Discussion with censors regarding classification category

Related closely to the issue of alteration to films is the issue of determination of classification category. There is no provision in the Film Censorship Act 2002 enabling film practitioners in Malaysia to discuss with censors the classification category to be given to their film. All of the Malaysian interviewees thought the opportunity to discuss classification issues with censors is important. The lack of a formal channel to do so could encourage abuse of power and the fieldwork carried out in Malaysia suggests that certain prominent producers receive 'better deals' compared to independent practitioners.[108] The former often have opportunities to negotiate with censors for a 'better censorship decision' whereas the opportunity to do so is not available to the less established practitioners.[109]

Every Malaysian interviewee, in particular the producers and distributors, agreed that the classification category a film receives affected its commercial viability. They were of the opinion that a restricted category will affect box office receipts as audiences under the age of 18 – which constitutes a huge pool of cinema-goers – would be barred from having access to the film. Since the classification category a film receives affects its commercial viability, film practitioners should be given equal opportunities to negotiate with the censors regarding the classification they desire for their films. In relation to the issue of alteration, some of the Malaysian interviewees, especially the producers, were willing to make excision to their films in order to secure a particular classification – the always targeted 'U' classification – which would allow the film to be viewed by all levels of society. For example, Ruhani Abdul Rahman noted that 'it is important to get a 'U' [classification] here as you will then get more audiences', while Ahmad Puah Onah disclosed that his priority when producing a film was to make it 'suitable for the general audience' because 'I want the widest audience to watch it.'[110]

In Hong Kong, when a film is submitted to the censorship authority, it is to be accompanied by a statement as to the classification category which is sought for the film. The censorship guidelines provide that censors should accommodate, as far as possible, the classification sought and if that is not possible, advice may be given as to the excision that can be made to the film to secure the desired classification category.[111] All of the Hong Kong interviewees agreed that the classification category a film received affected its commercial viability. Wellington Fung, for example, noted that 'when I produce a film, I don't go for Category III because I prefer to have more audience'. Fung added that when he was an executive producer at Cinema City, 'we always went for Category I so that the whole family could get into the cinema'. Nansun Shi, a fellow film producer and co-founder of Film Workshop, noted that 'it is unavoidable that a film with restricted classification will have much smaller audiences in Hong Kong', while Bill Kong noted that Category I and Category IIA are the best as they are 'for all ages, watchable by all people'. The interviewees also agreed that the opportunity to discuss classification categories with the censors is very important.

The importance of securing the right classification category was also evident when most of the interviewees disclosed that they would agree to excision being made to their films in order to secure a particular classification. Benny Chan said:

> If my film is classified Category III, it will affect its commercial viability and therefore, I will re-edit the film so that it will get a Category II classification. Categories IIA and IIB are the most favoured categories in Hong Kong in terms of the marketability of a film.

Wellington Fung described the compromise made in removing certain content from a film in order to get a lower classification as 'a sensible commercial decision' while Bill Kong, arguably the most successful film producer working in Hong Kong today, said that his company, Edko Films, did make alterations to their films 'to avoid getting Category III'. Another example is Lo Chi Leung who removed a shot from his film *Double Tap* (2000) in order for the film to be classified Category IIB:

> The excised shot is just a few seconds long, not the entire scene. I excised it because otherwise it will be classified Category III and therefore, those under 18 will not be allowed to watch it and this will greatly affect the box office of the film.

On the contrary, Mabel Cheung noted that she would not alter her film in order to secure a lower classification if she thought that the content (that pushed the film into a higher classification) was necessary to the film. Cheung said:

> The censorship guidelines are clear, so I will know before I make my film whether it will fall under Category III or not.... I know that and if I still shoot it, that means I must have done it for a reason. For example, I think that the love scene is necessary for the story or maybe the foul language is necessary in my film about triad society. If I cut out the love scenes or foul language, it will not be the same film anymore.... But if it is just one line or a shot that gets the film into trouble, maybe I will consider [excising it].

As in Malaysia, the relevant legislation in Australia does not make provision for film practitioners to indicate, or discuss with classifiers, the classification category to be given to their film. This omission, on paper, would appear to be able to affect a film's potential in the market as all of the Australian interviewees agreed that the classification category received for a film would affect its box office performance. For example, Greg Denning pointed out that:

> Obviously if you have a family film, you would want a G or a PG, if you have a film that is targeted at people under 15 years old, you wouldn't want anything more than an M classification... sometimes for certain films, like horror films, you would want an MA15+ because the truth is, people might not want to see an M rated horror movie... so it very much depends on the genre of the film.

The admissions by most of the interviewees that they are willing to make alterations to their films in order to secure a particular classification also underlined the importance of having the 'right classification'.[112] Most of the Australian interviewees were also of the opinion that the opportunity to discuss with classifiers is important because they would be adversely affected if their films were classified in a restricted category. The importance of the opportunity to discuss with classifiers was stressed by many interviewees including Ray Lawrence who stated that 'the opportunity to do so is so important that it should be [provided] in the guidelines.'

The provision of reasons for decisions

In Malaysia, the provision of reasons for censorship decision to film practitioners is very much dependent on the panel of censors assigned to examine the film concerned. This is so, even though it is expressly provided under the Film

Censorship Act 2002 that when censors approve a film for exhibition subject to alteration, or when approval for exhibition is refused, they must furnish in writing their reasons for requiring such alteration or for the refusal.[113] The Malaysian interviews confirmed the fact that the Board of Censors and Appeal Committee rarely furnish film practitioners with written reasons for the decisions they make. What is normally provided to film practitioners is the time code of the scenes (the running time) to be excised and little else. U-Wei Haji Saari, for example, noted that the censors 'don't provide the reasons, they just give the points where it [a scene or shot] has to be taken out'. Most of the Malaysian interviewees also revealed that they did encounter difficulties in their attempts to obtain censorship reasons from the Board of Censors. For example, when asked whether difficulties had been encountered in obtaining reasons, Yasmin Ahmad replied: 'Yes, for *Sepet.* They don't feel as if they owe you an explanation … they are just too lazy to provide you with an explanation or reasons!' Shuhaimi Baba also encountered problems in obtaining reasons for decisions from the censors. In reference to *Ringgit Kasyorga*, the director-producer stated that the censors just asked her to 'take this out, take that out from this minute to that minute'. No reasons were given to her, only the running time of the scenes that had to be removed from the film. Lorna Tee noted that:

> In Malaysia, you will never get feedback as to why it is censored and their decisions are final… you don't get a letter stating why certain contents are censored, they just let you know what to take out by describing the scenes that must be removed... it is never the reasons.

On the rare occasions where reasons were provided, film practitioners found these reasons to be 'brief and inadequate' (for example, 'this film is not suitable for Malaysian audiences'),[114] 'juvenile',[115] 'shallow'[116] and 'laughable and bizarre'.[117] The quality (or the lack of it) of the reasons given by the Malaysian censors can be illustrated by the experience that the director-producer and the distributor of the film *I Don't Want to Sleep Alone* had with the Board of Censors. This film was initially banned by the Board (later approved for exhibition by the Appeal Committee subject to five scenes being excised from the film) and the reasons given included:[118]

1 the film portrayed an image of Malaysia which is different from the one projected by the government's tourism campaign to promote the *Visit Malaysia Year 2007* program;
2 the film dealt with the haze issue;[119]
3 the film portrayed Malaysia as being populated by many migrant workers; and
4 the film contained scenes where there is a lot of rubbish on the streets, giving the impression that the country is dirty.[120]

No further comment is needed here to make the case that it is a very poorly reasoned censorship decision.

In Hong Kong, censors are required under the Film Censorship Ordinance to provide reasons for the censorship decisions they make.[121] All of the Hong Kong interviewees responded positively that they never encountered any difficulty in obtaining reasons for censorship decisions.[122] Additionally, there were also no complaints or dissatisfaction expressed over the quality or rationality of the reasons provided.

In Australia, although there is no express provision in the Classification (Publications, Films and Computer Games) Act 1995 requiring the classifiers to provide reasons for their decisions, all of the Australian interviewees reported that they had not encountered any difficulty in obtaining reasons for the classification decisions made on their films. There was no problem at all in obtaining the reasoning behind why a determination was made.[123] When queried further on the quality of the reasons provided, some of the interviewees commented that 'they gave us descriptions of why they came to their decisions but we do not necessarily agree with them'.[124]

It is likely that the practice of providing reasons to film practitioners is partly due to good administrative practice on the part of the decision-making entities and partly due to the influence of section 13 of the Administrative Decisions (Judicial Review) Act 1977 which provides that any person who is entitled to apply for judicial review of any decisions reviewable under section 5 of the same Act may request the decision-maker for a statement of reasons for the decision.

Appeal against censorship decisions

There are two concerns in regard to appeal against film censorship decisions: first, the potential adverse effect of members of the public having the right to appeal against censorship decisions and second, not having the right to make oral representations during the appeal process.

Appeal by members of the public

In Malaysia, members of the public are not afforded an express right under the Film Censorship Act 2002 to appeal against decisions made by the Board of Censors. There was a split in opinion amongst the Malaysian interviewees as to whether members of the public should be given the right to appeal. Those in favour of the public having such a right were of the view that they would not experience any problems if that right were exercised.[125] Interviewees who were not in favour of granting members of the public the right to appeal thought that it could be abused to sabotage films.[126] Yasmin Ahmad, who experienced unwarranted criticism of her films from the Malay media, was sure that there were people who would attempt to undermine certain filmmakers by stopping their films from being released. Ruhani Abdul Rahman, who was of the same opinion, added that such a right would create more problems for film practitioners because there would always be people with ulterior motives who wanted films produced by certain individuals or companies to be banned or, at least, encounter censorship issues.

In Hong Kong, a person who is aggrieved by the exhibition or distribution of a film can appeal against the censorship decision.[127] All of the Hong Kong interviewees were of the opinion that in an open and democratic society, members of the public should have the right to appeal against censorship decisions. The interviewees did not foresee any adverse effects from the exercise of such a right, having faith in the wisdom of the Board of Review to deal with such appeals appropriately. For example, Mabel Cheung noted that 'I do not know of any film that, because of the complaint or appeal made [by a member of the public], its classification category was changed. In Hong Kong, I have never heard of that'.

In Australia, there are four categories of person who can appeal against a classification decision, one of which is 'a person aggrieved by the decision'. The term 'person aggrieved' is defined as someone who can demonstrate an interest in the subject matter of the film in question that extends beyond that of an ordinary member of the public. Opinions were evenly split amongst the Australian interviewees as to whether this category of person should be afforded the right to appeal. Peter Campbell, who thought that members of the public should not have the right to appeal, said that 'they have the choice to go see it or not'. Campbell had to undergo two 'battles' with the Review Board because the initial classification decisions on two films – *Irreversible* (Gaspar Noe, 2002) and *9 Songs* (Michael Winterbottom, 2004), both containing strong sex scenes, which his company distributed – were appealed against by individuals who purported to represent community interest groups or organizations.[128] Campbell disclosed that these individuals were given credence by the Review Board although they had objected to those films without even having seen them. Because of the appeals, Campbell had to go through a lot of trouble to get the films released. The distributor also pointed out that subsequent to the appeal, the same individuals lobbied the South Australian Attorney General to call for the banning of the film *9 Songs* and 'that was pushed through with great pressure' in South Australia.[129] The banning of the film in that state 'cost us a fortune and it nearly wiped us out [of business]'.[130] Greg Denning, a fellow practitioner in the distribution sector, was also of the opinion that allowing the public to appeal would 'become very burdensome and, in practice, it can potentially be a nightmare'. This view was also shared by Joel Pearlman, noting that the ability of members of the public to appeal against classification decisions could 'create a lot of chaos' that could 'lead to practical challenges'.

The right to make oral representations

Film practitioners in Malaysia have no statutory right to make oral representations to members of the Appeal Committee when they appeal against censorship decisions made by the Board of Censors. All of the Malaysian interviewees agreed that it is very important that such a right be guaranteed in the law because without an express provision, the discretion lies with the Committee and this has caused favouritism practices where only certain film practitioners are given the opportunity to make oral representations. The interviewees considered the opportunity to have access to the Committee to argue their case vital as it would affect the outcome of the appeal positively. For example, Yasmin Ahmad noted that she managed to convince the Committee (during the appeal process) to revoke some of the excisions required by the Board on her film *Sepet.* Most of the Malaysian interviewees also expressed the wish that the right to make oral representations is provided under the Film Censorship Act 2002.

In stark contrast, Hong Kong film practitioners are entitled to make both oral and written representations to the Board of Review when the censorship decision made on their film has been appealed against by themselves, by the Film Censorship Authority or by a member of the public. Although they had not personally needed to appeal,[131] all of the Hong Kong interviewees thought that the right to make oral representations is very important (and some said necessary) as it would have a positive effect on the outcome of the appeal.[132]

In Australia, the classification law does not provide film practitioners with an express right to make oral representations before the Classification Review Board when they appeal against a decision made by the Classification Board.[133] Like their Malaysian and Hong Kong counterparts, the Australian interviewees were also of the opinion that the opportunity to make oral representations at the appeal stage is very important.[134] Although such a right is not expressly provided by statute, several interviewees who had gone through the appeal process reported that they were given ample opportunity to do so before the Review Board.[135]

Although film practitioners are afforded the opportunity to make oral representations, not every interviewee was entirely satisfied with what they were allowed to submit before the Review Board. The frustration highlighted was that film practitioners are not allowed to reference previous classification decisions during their submission:[136]

> We are not allowed to reference any previous decisions or any films that have been classified in the past. To give you an example, if I got a horror film that got up to appeal that I think it should be classified MA15+ but is given an R18+, I would love to be able to go in with a list of previous horror films that contain similar content that were classified MA15+. You are essentially asked to consider every previous decision irrelevant.... We are not allowed to specifically reference any of those films. It doesn't really enable you to bring a concise case before the appeal board. I guess what that means to a distributor is that there is a high degree of uncertainty when you go to appeal as well as a very high cost.

Availability of judicial review

The Malaysian interviewees were of the opinion that they should have the right to apply for judicial review to challenge film censorship decisions. All of the interviewees agreed that judicial review is vital in view of the existing censorship system. Tsai Ming-liang, for example, noted that the availability and awareness of judicial review would make censors 'more cautious when they are making censorship decisions', while Amir Muhammad said that judicial review is needed to counter the wide discretionary powers wielded by censors and the Home Minister. However, due to factors such as the cost and time involved in an application; the lack of confidence in the judiciary and the administration of justice; and the foreseeable repercussions of an application on the applicant-film practitioner should the censors harbour a grudge, most of the Malaysian interviewees would not be prepared to mount a challenge in court even if they were dissatisfied with the censorship decision made on their film.[137]

The issue of availability of judicial review and whether it is the best option to solve censorship problems is further examined in Chapter 6 where the book focuses on the principles, the remedies and the viability of judicial review applications under common law in general and under Malaysian jurisprudence in particular.

It is notable that all of the Hong Kong interviewees believed that the availability of judicial review is important in a jurisdiction with a state-based censorship system. However, some of these interviewees, for example Benny Chan and Gordon Chan, went on to emphasize that it is very unlikely that they would need to have recourse to it because the Hong Kong film censorship system works very well.

All of the Australian interviewees also stated that the availability of judicial review is important (and some said necessary), in a film censorship system. Judicial review applications challenging classification decisions have been filed in Australia under the Administrative Decisions (Judicial Review) Act 1977 before and after the introduction of the Classification (Publications, Films and Computer Games) Act 1995. These are discussed in Chapter 6.

At the end of every interview, the interviewees were asked whether there is any reform to the film censorship law, guidelines and process that they hoped to see take place. The Malaysian interviewees, in general, expressed the hope that they would have more freedom for creative expression. This commonly held aspiration was encapsulated by Tsai Ming-liang, who noted that 'with all these censorship restrictions, there is no freedom to be creative. There is no space for artists in Malaysia to pursue their creative works and to develop!', and Aziz M. Osman, who hoped that 'changes will be made to the censorship system so that filmmakers will have more freedom… so that when we work, we will only give priority to the material itself rather than [the consideration of] "will it be approved by the censors"'.

More specifically, the Malaysian interviewees wanted members of the Board of Censors and the Appeal Committee to be carefully selected so that only suitable and competent individuals are appointed as censors.[138] U-Wei Haji Saari, forthrightly commented that 'only intelligent people should be in the censorship board!' while Ahmad Puad Onah and Ruhani Abdul Rahman proposed the composition of the Board and the Committee should include people with film knowledge or filmmaking experience and that the Home Minister should not just 'give out the jobs to retirees'.[139] Some of the interviewees also hoped changes would be made to the mode of appointment (to be more transparent and inclusive) and the security of tenure of censors so that they would be able to make decisions independently from political influence or pressure.[140] The interviewees, particularly the directors, also suggested that classification of film is the way forward for the

Malaysian system. They wanted films to be classified, not censored, so that films could be distributed and exhibited in their intended version without any alteration if they were classified in a restricted category.[141] Tsai Ming-liang, for example, stressed that 'there should be classification categories based on age, not morals. A good classification system is justifiable and at the same time will provide film practitioners with more creative space'. In regard to the censorship guidelines, the interviewees hoped that an overhaul would be made – which would include clearer and more precise provisions – with their participation sought in the process. The interviewees would like the right to make oral representations at the appeal stage provided in the law and judicial review made available to them, to be resorted to when the need arises.

As noted above, the Hong Kong interviewees were satisfied with the film censorship system and were of the opinion that it worked very well. When asked what reforms to the system they hoped to see take place, most of the interviewees were of the opinion that change was not necessary. Only two suggestions were made in the 12 interviews conducted with Hong Kong film practitioners. First, Mabel Cheung suggested that the application of the censorship guidelines could be more lenient in relation to language. Second, Cheung, Patrick Tam and Lo Chi Leung proposed that it would be better if the number of censors assigned to examine a film could be increased, so that it would not be a single censor examining a film and making the decision. These issues are further discussed in Chapter 7.

The Australian interviewees were also satisfied with their country's film classification system and most could not suggest any changes to it. Rolf de Heer, for example, answered 'there are none that I can think of' when queried whether there are any reforms to the classification law, guidelines and process that he would like to see. However, two of the interviewees raised concerns regarding the reclassification of films.[142] They considered that once a film was classified, it should remain so and there should not be any reclassification exercises. A film distributor and an exhibitor hoped that 'advertising approval to trailers [could be given] based on the content of the trailer and not based on what the film's classification is'.[143] Lastly, it was suggested by an interviewee-distributor that film practitioners should be allowed to make reference to past classification decisions when they appealed against a classification decision so that they could present a concise argument before the Classification Review Board. These issues are further discussed in Chapter 7.

Summary

The fieldwork conducted in Malaysia confirmed the problems and concerns raised by the key issues of the censorship system identified in Chapter 4, while the comparative fieldwork conducted in Hong Kong and Australia strongly suggested that the Malaysian film censorship system should be reformed to promote the artistic vibrancy and commercial viability of the country's film industry. To summarize the foregoing discussions in this chapter, there are eight areas of concern that should be addressed in the Malaysian film censorship system:

1. the suitability, competence and independence of film censors in carrying out their duties as well as the Home Minister's discretionary power to ban films;
2. the Home Minister's power to exempt a film from censorship at his absolute discretion;
3. the omission of provisions in the law and guidelines requiring the artistic merit of a film, as well as the prevailing community standards, to be taken into account in the process of making censorship decisions;
4. the defective Film Censorship Guidelines 1993, application of which has resulted in inconsistent censorship decisions and has impeded film practitioners' freedom of expression;
5. the power of censors to require alteration to be made to films and the non-availability of a formal channel where every film practitioner may discuss classification categories with the censors;
6. the non-provision of, or the lack of rational, reasons for censorship decisions;
7. the possible abuse of the opportunity to appeal against censorship decisions by members of the public and the lack of an express right to make oral representations at the appeal stage of a censorship process; and
8. the availability and viability of judicial review applications in challenging film censorship decisions.

Over the course of the research, a small number of concerns were also identified in the Hong Kong and Australian systems. These concerns are discussed in Chapter 7.

6 Judicial review of film censorship decisions

Introduction

Earlier chapters of this book have compared the film censorship system in Malaysia with the systems in Hong Kong and Australia as set out in the laws, guidelines and processes (Chapter 3); examined the key issues that arise from these systems (Chapter 4); and analysed the opinions of film practitioners on those issues (Chapter 5).[1] This has shown that the Malaysian film censorship system constitutes one of the factors that affects the artistic vibrancy and commercial viability of the country's film industry. As explained in Chapter 1, the final part of the book comprises this and the following chapter, each considering an alternative to deal with the adverse effects of the Malaysian film censorship system. This chapter will explore the possibilities of judicial review of film censorship decisions while the next chapter proposes reforms to the system itself. The book is primarily concerned with the Malaysian film censorship system and, hence, the focus of discussion and analyses in this chapter is mainly on judicial review in the Malaysian context. References to the jurisprudence of other common law jurisdictions are made when relevant and necessary.

Judicial review is a process by which the court exercises its supervisory jurisdiction over the proceedings and decisions of public bodies or authorities. Since film censorship is a matter under the purview of the government (and thus within the public domain), judicial review appears to be the only legal channel that film practitioners can have resort to, as they are not able to commence a court action against censorship authorities under the law of tort or law of contract in the event that they are aggrieved by the censorship decisions made about their films. Therefore, it is important to investigate the potential of this branch of public law as a possible alternative to law reforms.

There has not been any application for judicial review challenging film censorship decisions in Malaysia and Hong Kong but there have been numerous such applications in Australia. The fact that judicial review is not utilized in Malaysia and Hong Kong does not mean that it cannot be an important or effective measure. The awareness of its availability as well as effectiveness may 'cast a shadow' on censorship authorities to perform their duties with more care as their decisions may be liable to be challenged and quashed in court. In principle, this awareness will encourage a more careful and thorough decision-making process, resulting in sounder film censorship decisions. Matthew Groves, an administrative law scholar, is of the view that judicial review 'clearly has the potential to affect the ultimate or substantive outcome of administrative decision-making',[2] but since the empirical research on the relationship and impact of judicial review upon public authority decision-making has yet to produce a definite picture of the effects of the law, it may only be stated up until this point that judicial review does have an impact and it is heavily dependent on the context of the jurisdiction concerned and the matter under review.[3] Additionally, film practitioners interviewed for this book generally agreed that judicial review is vital in a state-based film censorship system and many of them would be prepared to use it in particular circumstances.[4] Therefore, the following discussion and analyses are not only of academic interest but also serve practical purposes.

This chapter will first lay out the basic common law principles of judicial review, including its basis, objectives and scope. The development of the law that has taken place in Malaysia will then be discussed. This section of the chapter will establish that film censorship decisions in Malaysia (as well as in Hong Kong and Australia) are susceptible to judicial review and it will be followed by a discussion of the grounds on which film practitioners can rely to challenge censorship decisions. It will be demonstrated by actual and hypothetical examples that the conventional grounds of judicial review are sufficient to deal with censorship issues. Subsequently, the chapter will discuss the issue of availability of judicial review to film practitioners. Despite the many obstacles such as ouster clauses, *locus standi* and other rules and practices, this section of the chapter will establish that judicial review is available to film practitioners. There is no absolute legal impediment for a film practitioner seeking public law remedies from the courts. The possible outcome of a successful judicial review application will be examined by exploring the various remedies at the courts' disposal. This section will establish that given the right judicial approach, film practitioners would be able to obtain adequate and effective remedies against censorship authorities in response to their grievances. The final section of the chapter will seek to answer the pertinent question of whether judicial review application is the best option available to film practitioners. Despite the desirability of judicial review in theory, in the current climate, it is not the best option in Malaysia because of three factors: the cost and time it involves, the current state of the judiciary and the possible repercussions on the film practitioner concerned if a judicial review application were to be made. Although not the best option, all of the interviewees were of the opinion that the availability of judicial review is still very important.

The definition and basis of judicial review

Judicial review, which is an essential component of the rule of law,[5] is the process by which the High Court exercises its supervisory jurisdiction over the proceedings and decisions of inferior courts, tribunals and other bodies or persons who carry out quasi-judicial functions or the performance of public acts or duties. This jurisdiction was originally derived from the common law and exercised by the prerogative writs of *mandamus*, *certiorari* and prohibition but it is now conferred and regulated by the statutes and rules of court.[6]

Judicial review provides the means by which judicial control of administrative action is exercised and the subject matter of every judicial review is either a decision made by some person or body of persons or a refusal by him or her to make a decision.[7] In the case of *Council of Civil Service Unions v Minister for the Civil Service* (hereinafter referred to as 'the *GCHQ* case'),[8] Lord Diplock noted that:[9]

> For a decision to be susceptible to judicial review, the decision-maker must be empowered by public law (and not merely, as in arbitration, by agreement between private parties) to make decisions that, if validly made, will lead to administrative action or abstention from action by an authority endowed by law with executive powers.

Lord Diplock also noted that the ultimate source of the decision-making power is 'nearly always nowadays a statute or subordinate legislation'.[10]

The basis of judicial review is the doctrine of *ultra vires* or excess of jurisdiction.[11] This doctrine allows courts to strike down decisions made by authorities exercising public functions which they have no power or jurisdiction to make.[12] No authority whether administrative, legislative or quasi-judicial can exceed the power given to it and any decision taken in excess of its powers is invalid.[13]

Application for judicial review may also heighten awareness of its potential impact and this awareness may in turn promote higher standards of public administration, especially in decision-making processes.

The scope and principles of judicial review

Generally, a body of persons or authority is subjected to judicial review if the duty that is being carried out is a public duty or a duty with 'public element'.[14] The scope of judicial review therefore includes decisions made by inferior courts or tribunals and decisions made by administrative bodies or their officers that involve public law. The traditional test for determining whether a body of persons or authority is subject to judicial review is the source of its power – whether the power is derived from statute or prerogative.[15] If the source of power is a statute or subordinate legislation, then it will most likely be amenable to judicial review. However, this is not the sole test, as pointed out by Lloyd LJ in the case of *R v Panel on Take-Over and Mergers, Ex parte Datafin plc* where Lloyd LJ noted that it is equally important to look at 'the nature of the power' because:[16] 'If the body in question is exercising public law functions, or if the exercise of its functions have public law consequences, then that may… be sufficient to bring the body within the reach of judicial review.'

If a body of persons or authority is established under legislation and the decision made by that body or authority under its statutory power has a public element, it will be susceptible to judicial review. The film censorship decision-making entities in Malaysia, Hong Kong and Australia are established under legislative instruments (the Film Censorship Act 2002, the Film Censorship Ordinance and the Classification (Publications, Films and Computer Games) Act 1995 respectively) and the decisions they make under their respective statutory powers have public elements and consequences. Thus, they are well within the scope of judicial review.

The conventional principles of judicial review were stated in the case of *Chief Constable of the North Wales Police v Evans*[17] where the House of Lords held that judicial review is supervisory in nature where the court neither probes into the merits of the decision nor substitutes its own decision for that of the body or authority concerned. Thus, judicial review is concerned not with the merits of the decision in respect of which the application is made, but with the decision-making *process* itself.[18]

The duty of the court is therefore to confine itself to the issue of legality and its concern is whether the decision-making entity has exceeded its powers, committed an error of law, committed a breach of the rules of natural justice, made a decision which no reasonable decision-maker could have reached or abused its powers.[19] The approach adopted by the court is to quash the challenged decision (if there is a ground to do so) and remit the matter back to the original decision-maker to be reconsidered.

The courts in Malaysia have adhered to these conventional principles as practiced by the English courts.[20] They have, in numerous cases, referred to and cited with approval the common law principles and scope of judicial review.[21] However, with judicial activism, the conventional principles that judicial review is concerned with the decision-making process and not the merits of the decision itself and that the court, acting in its supervisory jurisdiction, does not substitute its own decision for that of the original decision-maker have been departed from in appropriate circumstances. Since the mid-1990s, judicial review in Malaysia has developed beyond its 'supervisory functions'; in suitable cases, review on the merits of the decision has been carried out. The courts also do not limit themselves to quashing the challenged decisions and remitting them back to the original decision-makers but have advanced further to substitute their own decisions for those of the decision-makers. This approach is to be preferred in cases where fundamental liberties are breached because if judicial review is confined to only scrutinising the decision-making process (and not the merits of the decision itself), 'the result of a successful judicial review application is often that the decision-maker has merely to find a more acceptable process for reaching the same result'.[22]

Two Malaysian cases illustrate the point. In the case of *Tan Tek Seng v Suruhanjaya Perkhidmatan Pendidikan*,[23] the appellant, who was a school headmaster, was found guilty of the offence of criminal breach of trust. Following the finding of guilt, the state education department recommended to the first respondent (the Education Service Commission) that the appellant should continue in service but suffer a reduction in rank as a punishment. The first respondent did not accept the recommendation and without being afforded an opportunity to be heard, the appellant was dismissed. The appellant sought numerous declarations from the court, one of which was to declare that his dismissal was null and void. The Court of Appeal held, amongst other things, that 'the requirement of fairness which is the essence of article 8(1) when read with article 5(1) [of the Malaysian Federal Constitution] ensures not only that a fair procedure is adopted but also that a fair and just punishment is imposed according to the facts of a particular case'.[24] The Court of Appeal was of the view that dismissal was too severe a punishment to impose upon the appellant, it was disproportionate in the circumstances of the case and that some lesser punishment ought to have been imposed. The court then made an order substituting the punishment of dismissal with that of the punishment of reduction in rank of the appellant.[25]

In the case of *Rama Chandran R v The Industrial Court of Malaysia*,[26] the appellant's service was terminated by his employer and the dispute was subsequently heard in the Industrial Court. The appellant contended that his dismissal was without just cause and excuse, and that it was an act of victimization. The Industrial Court however ruled that the appellant had been dismissed with just cause and excuse. On appeal to the Federal Court, it was held that the Industrial Court Chairman had not addressed his mind to the issue of bias raised by the appellant, which was the crux of his complaint. The Industrial Court had therefore committed an error which went to its jurisdiction and the decision was quashed. The central issue that arose in the Federal Court was whether the extent of the court's powers in review jurisdiction includes the power to make consequential orders for fair compensation in favour of the appellant instead of remitting the matter back to the Industrial Court. The Federal Court stated that sending the case back to the Industrial Court would be time-consuming and would involve the appellant in continued and prolonged litigation which would cause him harm and injustice. The Federal Court held that, in appropriate circumstances, it had the power not merely to quash the Industrial Court's decision but to go on to make a finding that an employee has been dismissed from service without just cause or excuse and, where necessary, proceed to award fair compensation. The Federal Court then assessed the amount of compensation and awarded the sum to the appellant.

The above cases show that, under appropriate circumstances, the courts substitute their own decisions for those of the original decision-makers. It must be pointed out that these cases are industrial relations matters and, since there has never been any judicial review application challenging a film censorship decision in Malaysia, it is difficult to conclude with certainty that the courts would adopt a similar approach to film censorship decisions. However, it appears that there is no compelling reason as to why the courts would not adopt the same approach in film censorship matters to quash censorship decisions made by the Board of Censors, the Appeal Committee or the Home Minister and proceed to decide on the matter without reverting it back to the original decision-maker. The court may also make consequential orders and the remedies that could be granted are discussed further on in this chapter.

The grounds of judicial review

In 1985, the various conventional grounds upon which judicial review may be made were conveniently reformulated by the House of Lords in the landmark *GCHQ* case[27] where Lord Diplock simplified and narrowed down the grounds into three headings in the following classic dictum:[28]

> Judicial review has I think developed to a stage today when without reiterating any analysis of the steps by which the development has come about, one can conveniently classify under three heads the grounds upon which administrative action is subject to control by judicial review. The first ground I would call 'illegality', the second 'irrationality' and the third 'procedural impropriety'. That is not to say that further development on a case by case basis may not in course of time add further grounds. I have in mind particularly the possible adoption in the future of the principle of 'proportionality'[29]
>
> By 'illegality' as a ground for judicial review I mean that the decision-maker must understand correctly the law that regulates his decision-making power and must give effect to it… By 'irrationality' I mean what can by now be succinctly referred to as '*Wednesbury* unreasonableness' (*Associated Provincial Picture Houses Ltd v Wednesbury Corporation* [1948] 1 KB 223). It applies to a decision which is so outrageous in its defiance of logic or of accepted moral standards that no sensible person who had applied his mind to the question to be decided could have arrived at it… I have described the third head as 'procedural impropriety' rather than failure to observe basic rules of natural justice or failure to act with procedural fairness towards the person who will be affected by the decision. This is because susceptibility to judicial review under this head covers also failure by an administrative tribunal to observe procedural rules that are expressly laid down in the legislative instrument by which its jurisdiction is conferred, even where such failure does not involve any denial of natural justice.[30]

Under 'illegality', the question that the court will ask is whether the decision-maker strayed outside the power or purposes defined by the governing legislation. Under 'irrationality', the question is whether the power under which the decision-maker acts has been improperly exercised, while under 'procedural impropriety', the question is whether the decision made was procedurally unfair.[31] These grounds of review are not exhaustive,[32] they may overlap[33] and they are convenient groupings or headings.

The grounds mentioned above are for judicial review of administrative actions in exercising discretionary powers and they will be discussed separately below in relation to film censorship.[34]

Illegality

Illegality arises where the decision-making entity acts without or in excess of its jurisdiction or power. A decision is illegal if it contravenes or exceeds the terms of the power which authorizes the making of the decision or if it pursues an objective other than that for which the power to make the decision was conferred.[35] In deciding whether a decision is illegal, the court will construe the content and scope of the legislation empowering the making of the decision to determine whether the decision falls within its 'four corners'.[36]

In regard to film censorship, four common errors may be committed by censors that would render the censorship decision illegal. The first is where censors make a decision which they are not empowered to make under the film censorship legislation. An actual decision may be highlighted here as an illustration. In 2008, a film entitled *Malaysian Gods* (Amir Muhammad) was approved by the Board of Censors under section 10(1) of the Film Censorship Act 2002 but in addition to the approval granted, a prohibition was imposed on the said film from being exhibited or distributed to the public.[37] This is 'illegal' as the Board is not empowered under the governing law to make such decision. The Act only empowers the Board to make three types of censorship decision: approve the film for exhibition without any alteration (section 10(1)(a)), approve the film for exhibition with such alteration as it may require (section 10(1)(b)) or refuse to approve the film for exhibition (section 10(1)(c)). The Board is not empowered to approve a film but at the same time bar its exhibition and distribution in the country.

The second error is where censors exercise the discretionary powers conferred on them for an 'extraneous', 'improper' or 'ulterior' purpose. If a power is granted for one purpose but is exercised for a different purpose, that power has not been validly exercised.[38] It is apparent from the fieldwork conducted in Malaysia that this error is at times committed by censors. U-Wei Haji Saari noted that the censors will ban a film or require scenes to be excised when they feel the content is offensive to them (or made them feel uncomfortable) regardless of whether such content is in fact prohibited or not and without regard to whether the content is acceptable to society.[39] Fellow film director James Lee discovered that the censors 'will just ban' a film if they feel its release will be a subject of complaints by certain quarters of society[40] while film distributor Leonard Tee remarked that 'if the censors don't understand the film, they will think that it is "dangerous" and they will just ban it'.[41] These are examples where censors exercise the discretionary power conferred on them for an 'extraneous' or 'improper' purpose. A hypothetical example may also be included here. It is plausible that a film could be refused approval for exhibition by censors or the Home Minister under the pretext that its exhibition would be 'contrary to public interest'[42] where in fact the film is banned because it contains content that is critical of the government.

The third error is where the exercise of the discretionary power is based on irrelevant considerations or where the decision is made without due regard to relevant considerations. In a decision-making process involving the exercise of discretionary power, the decision-maker must take into account considerations which are relevant to the objectives of the legislation in question while ignoring considerations that are irrelevant.[43] If the exercise of a discretionary power was influenced by considerations that cannot lawfully be taken into account, that power has not been validly exercised.[44] The influence of irrelevant considerations or immaterial factors will be apparent if the decision-maker has set them out as reasons for the decision. In cases where the reasons for decision are not provided and there is no material to show what considerations influenced the decision-maker, the court may determine whether such influence is to be inferred from the surrounding circumstances.[45] If the influence of irrelevant consideration is established, it is not necessary to prove that such consideration was the sole or dominant influence. It is sufficient to prove that the influence was material or substantial.[46] If it is alleged that relevant considerations have not been taken into account, the court will assess the actual or potential importance of the relevant considerations that were overlooked.[47] A case in point is the banning of *Lelaki Komunis Terakhir* (*The Last Communist*) in 2006 by the Home Minister where, subsequent to making his decision, the Minister disclosed to the press that he had considered the fact that it was insensitive to release the film at a time when the United Malays National Organization (which has long been the governing political party in Malaysia and in which the Minister served as its Secretary General at the material time) was celebrating its sixtieth anniversary and that the film did not show enough violence or portrayals of violent acts to reinforce the perception that communists are violent people.[48] These two irrelevant considerations were taken into account in making the decision to ban the film while not having regard to relevant considerations, such as the fact that the film had been approved without any cut and classified ‘U’ (suitable for viewing by all levels of society) by the Board of Censors, and the consideration of whether excision of certain content of the film would suffice instead of an outright banning of the entire film.

The fourth error is where there is non-exercise of discretion on the part of the censors in making a decision. A decision-making entity exercising discretionary powers is obligated to apply its mind to the facts, merits and circumstances of each case that comes before it for decision and it must not allow another unauthorized person or entity to decide the matter on its behalf. Film censors must also not fetter their own discretion and must not act under dictation or act mechanically by relying on instructions or ‘opinions’ of another entity without exercising independent judgment.[49] If this principle is not observed, the ensuing decision may be liable to be quashed under the ground of illegality. An example of this situation may be the withdrawal of the release of *Bruce Almighty* (Tom Shadyac, 2003) from Malaysian cinemas. The film is a comedy about a television reporter who complains about life and ends up being given the power by God to control the universe. It was initially approved for exhibition (and promotional activities were ongoing to promote the upcoming release of the film) but was subsequently withdrawn in an abrupt manner. There was circumstantial evidence that the decision of the Board of Censors to withdraw its approval was ‘influenced’ by statements and ‘opinions’ issued by other government departments on the suitability of releasing the film in Malaysia.[50]

Irrationality

‘Irrationality’ is also sometimes referred to as ‘unreasonableness’ and these terms are used interchangeably. The famous formulation of this ground can be found in the case of *Associated Provincial Picture Houses Ltd v Wednesbury Corporation*[51] where Lord Greene held that the court can interfere if a decision is 'so unreasonable that no reasonable authority could ever come to it'[52] In the case of *R v Secretary of State for the Environment, Ex parte Nottinghamshire County Council,*[53] the House of Lords held that the threshold of unreasonableness was to be 'extreme' and it was formulated to include decisions which are so absurd or outrageous in their defiance of logic or of accepted moral standards that the decision-maker must have taken leave of his senses.

Irrationality or unreasonableness is also used to denote extreme behaviour, for example acting in bad faith (*mala fide*) or a decision which is 'perverse' or 'absurd'.[54] A decision may also be held to be unreasonable if it is unduly oppressive as it subjects the affected parties to excessive hardship or to unnecessary infringement of their rights.[55] A decision is also irrational if it lacks ostensible logic or comprehensible justification. Other instances of irrational or unreasonable decisions include decisions that are made in an arbitrary fashion, decisions made in the absence of logical connection between the evidence and the ostensible reasons for the decision as well as decisions made without evidence to support them.[56] The Home Minister's arbitrary banning of *Lelaki Komunis Terakhir* again serves as an example for this ground of judicial review. Besides the outright banning of a film, censorship by way of excision without intelligible justification may also render such decision liable to be quashed under this ground.

Procedural impropriety

'Procedural impropriety' arises where the decision-maker has acted without complying with mandatory procedural rules laid down in the legislation empowering the making of the decision or has failed to observe the rules of natural justice. The term 'natural justice'[57] is being increasingly replaced by a general duty to act fairly,[58] which is a key element of procedural propriety.[59] Whether fairness is required and what is involved in order to achieve it in a decision-making process is for the court to decide as a matter of law, not for the decision-making entity to decide as a matter of discretion.[60] There is a presumption that procedural fairness is required whenever the exercise of a power adversely affects an individual's rights protected by common law or by legislation.[61] When a mandatory procedure is laid down in the legislation, it must be followed by the decision-maker in the process of making a decision[62] and the court may, on an application for judicial review, decide on the extent to which the legislative procedure has been fulfilled. If the procedure is not followed, the ensuing decision may be quashed under the ground of 'procedural impropriety'.

The two most important principles under the ground of 'procedural impropriety' (or rather 'procedural fairness') in regard to film censorship are the right to an oral hearing and the right to a reasoned decision. A person who is entitled to be heard orally[63] or who is given an oral hearing as a matter of discretion must be allowed an adequate opportunity to present his or her case.[64] It is of course important for film practitioners to be able to make oral representations to censors as well as to members of the Appeal Committee before their films are banned or subject to excision. The importance of making oral representations was highlighted and stressed by film practitioners interviewed for this book[65] but unfortunately, the right is not guaranteed under the Film Censorship Act 2002.

As regards the right to reasoned decision, in common law there is no general duty on the part of the decision-maker to provide reasons for the decisions they make. However, under certain circumstances such a duty may exist and failure on the part of the decision-maker to provide reasons may give grounds for challenging the decision made on the ground of procedural impropriety.[66] These circumstances would include situations when reasons for a decision are expressly or impliedly required by legislation, where the relevant legislation provides a right to appeal and reasons are needed so as to enable the affected person to exercise effectively that right of appeal or where natural justice or fairness itself requires that reasons be given.[67]

If the film censorship legislation provides that film practitioners are entitled to an oral hearing or to make oral representations in an appeal against censorship decisions or they are entitled to reasoned censorship decisions, failure on the part of the censors to so provide will give rise to this ground of challenge and the decision in question may be liable to be quashed by the court. As discussed in Chapter 4, section 10(3) of the Film Censorship Act 2002 provides that if the Board of Censors approves a film subject to alteration being made or refuses to approve a film for exhibition, written reasons must be given to the owner of the film concerned. A Malaysian film practitioner whose film was banned or approved subject to alteration but was not furnished with written reasons for the censorship decision may use this ground to challenge the decision-making process in which the decision was made.[68]

Proportionality

In view of the development of the law in Malaysia, this ground of judicial review may be discussed under two separate sub-headings: common law proportionality, which originated from the English courts, and constitutional review proportionality, which is a part of the Malaysian administrative law jurisprudence based on the Federal Constitution and inspired by Indian jurisprudence – both of which could be open to film practitioners to challenge censorship decisions that are 'disproportionate'.[69]

Common law proportionality

'Proportionality' was suggested by Lord Diplock in the *GCHQ* case[70] as the possible fourth ground of judicial review in English law. The principle of proportionality requires that administrative measures must not be more drastic than is necessary for attaining the desired result and it requires the court to determine whether the decision made or action taken was really needed.[71] The reluctance of the English courts to accept proportionality as a ground of judicial review is based on the view that it lowers the threshold of judicial intervention and involves the courts in considering the merits of the decision challenged.[72]

Nevertheless, proportionality has in fact been applied, albeit under limited circumstances, since the 1950s by the English courts in numerous cases including *R v Northumberland Compensation Appeal Tribunal, Ex parte Shaw*[73] and *R v Barnsley Metropolitan Borough Council, Ex parte Hook.*[74]

Constitutional review proportionality

Constitutional review proportionality as a ground of judicial review was first introduced in Malaysia in the case of *Tan Tek Seng v Suruhanjaya Perkhidmatan Pendidikan*[75] where the Court of Appeal utilized provisions of the Federal Constitution[76] to rule that fair procedure must be adopted in a decision-making process and that actions taken or decisions made by authorities must be proportionate in the circumstances of the case. The main constitutional provision that the Malaysian courts rely on for this unique ground is article 8(1) which reads: 'All persons are equal before the law and entitled to the equal protection of the law'.[77] In the case of *Dr Mohd Nasir bin Hashim v Menteri Dalam Negeri Malaysia,*[78] the Court of Appeal took the opportunity to elucidate the principle as it has been used by the Malaysian courts:[79]

> [Article 8] guarantees fairness of all forms of State action... [The court] must also bear in mind the principle of substantive proportionality that art 8(1) imports... In other words, not only must the legislative or executive response to a state of affairs be objectively fair, it must also be proportionate to the object sought to be achieved. This is sometimes referred to as 'the doctrine of rational nexus'. A court is therefore entitled to strike down State action on the ground that it is disproportionate to the object sought to be achieved.[80]

In film censorship matters, proportionality could be relied upon as a ground to challenge refusals of approval for exhibition and distribution of films. A decision to refuse approval (that is, to ban) a film due to specific and identifiable content in the film may be found to be disproportionate to the objective sought to be achieved by the censors if a less drastic decision could be made, such as requiring the objectionable content to be excised from the film before approval is granted. This is because it may not always be necessary to ban a film simply because it contains content that is prohibited under the censorship guidelines. For example, the Hong Kong Board of Review could be understood to have acted 'proportionately' by not banning the French film *Irreversible* (Gaspar Noe, 2002) but approving it for exhibition subject to age restriction and minor excisions to be made to the film. In Hong Kong and Australia, there are many such examples.

The availability of judicial review to film practitioners: the filter mechanisms

The availability of judicial review to an applicant in Malaysia is generally subject to five considerations. They are:

1 whether the application is time-barred;[81]
2 whether the decision sought to be challenged by the application is reviewable and therefore justiciable;
3 whether the judicial review jurisdiction of the court is ousted by an effective ouster clause;
4 whether the applicant has the required standing to make the application; and
5 whether the rule of exhaustion of alternative remedies operates (in the circumstances of the case) to bar the application.

On the first consideration, Order 53 rule 3(6) of the Rules of the High Court 1980 prescribes that an application for judicial review should be made promptly and in any case within 40 days after the date when the grounds for the application first arose or when the decision is first communicated to the applicant. The time period of 40 days may be extended by the court if there is an application for extension of time supported by good and valid reasons.

On the second consideration, film censorship is neither an unreviewable discretion nor a non-justiciable issue in Malaysia.[82] 'Justiciability', as explained in the *Judicial Review of Administrative Action*, means:[83]

> In the judicial review context, it should refer to the government decisions which should be immune from judicial review, either totally or partially, for political reasons or because the courts are ill-equipped to engage in the review, even though the review is not on the merits. Some areas of government decision-making are best left to other branches of government for political reasons. These include treaty making, proroguing and dissolving of parliament, making peace, and conduct of international relations. There might well be aspects of activities in these areas which are properly susceptible to judicial review, but there will be a natural judicial reluctance to get involved, even at the margins of judicial review.

Having examined the first two considerations, the discussion will now turn to the remaining three – the effect of ouster clause, the standing requirement and the rule of exhaustion of alternative remedies.

The effect of ouster clauses

Ouster clauses, otherwise known as privative or finality clauses, are widely used in Malaysian legislation. It is a legislative trend to insert such a clause into statutes to make administrative decisions or actions 'court-proof'. There are a variety of ouster clauses, some declare the administrative decisions to be 'final' or 'conclusive', like section 23(2) of the Film Censorship Act 2002;[84] some declare that the decision is not subject to an 'appeal' or 'review' in any court as in section 48 of the Act.[85] There are also ouster clauses which go further and seek to bar the courts from 'reviewing, calling into question, and quashing' an administrative decision.

The leading common law case in this area is *Anisminic Ltd v Foreign Compensation Commission*,[86] (hereinafter referred to as 'the *Anisminic* case') where the House of Lords restricted the scope of an ouster clause by giving a wide and liberal interpretation to the concept of 'excess of jurisdiction'. This case is important in two aspects. First, it diluted the efficacy of ouster clauses by confining their protection to non-jurisdictional errors. Second, it extended the scope of jurisdictional errors. The House of Lords construed 'jurisdictional errors' broadly as to include errors of law therein[87] and it practically rendered obsolete the technical distinction between 'error of law going to jurisdiction' and 'error of law within jurisdiction'.[88]

In Malaysia, until the case of *South East Asia Fire Bricks Sdn Bhd v Non-Metallic Mineral Products Mfg Employees Union*[89] (hereinafter referred to as 'the *Fire Bricks* case') in 1980, judicial interpretations on the effect of ouster clauses did not show a uniform approach.[90] Some judges interpreted such clauses restrictively, while others did so liberally. However, no ouster clause was taken to exclude completely judicial review of administrative action.[91] The general approach taken was that an ouster clause would not oust the supervisory jurisdiction of the court to review a decision on the grounds of jurisdictional error as well as error on the face of the record.[92] However, in 1980, the Privy Council's decision in the *Fire Bricks* case changed the Malaysian courts' earlier approach and perpetuated the error of law and error of jurisdiction dichotomy. It was, in effect, a step back from the *Anisminic* case for Malaysia. The Privy Council's ruling in the *Fire Bricks* case was accepted and applied by the Malaysian courts in a series of cases where, in most of them, the courts have refused to review administrative decisions on the ground of error of law.

Fortunately, in 1995 the Court of Appeal in the case of *Syarikat Kenderaan Melayu Kelantan Bhd v Transport Workers' Union*[93] took the step of departing from the rule of *stare decisis*. The court refused to be bound by the decision of the Privy Council in the *Fire Bricks* case on the issue of the scope of judicial review in the face of an ouster clause. The Court of Appeal held that an inferior tribunal or other public decision-making authority, whether exercising a quasi-judicial or administrative function, has no jurisdiction to commit an error of law, whether the error is jurisdictional or not. Since the body under review has no jurisdiction to commit an error of law, its decision will not be immune from judicial review even in the face of an ouster clause, howsoever widely drafted the clause may be.[94] The Court ruled to 'abolish' the distinction between an error of law and an error of jurisdiction set out in the *Fire Bricks* case. Consequently, all errors of law are now reviewable by the High Court, substantially enlarging the scope of judicial review.

The proposition in the *Syarikat Kenderaan Melayu Kelantan Bhd* case in regard to the error of law concept – which draws from a broad understanding of *Anisminic* – has been accepted by the apex court in Malaysia in the cases of *Kumpulan Perangsang Selangor Bhd v Zaid bin Hj Mohd Noh*[95] and *Hoh Kiang Ngan v Mahkamah Perusahaan Malaysia.*[96] The current judicial position on the effect of ouster clauses is that the High Court need not ascertain whether an error of law committed by the decision-making entity goes to jurisdiction or not. An error of law, whether jurisdictional or otherwise, becomes reviewable even in the presence of an ouster clause. Therefore, sections 23(2) and 48 of the Film Censorship Act 2002 would not effectively oust the courts' jurisdiction to review film censorship decisions if the decision challenged is tainted with error or errors of law. Whenever an error of law is committed by the decision-making entities, no ouster clause, however widely drafted, may exclude judicial review of the decision made and the cases make clear that errors of law include such matters as the decision-maker taking into account irrelevant considerations; or omitting to take into account relevant considerations; or when the decision-maker misconstrues the relevant statutory provision; or misapplies the principle of the law.

The locus standi *requirement*

The purpose of the *locus standi* rule is to resolve the conflict between two competing aspects of public interest: the desirability of encouraging individuals to participate in the enforcement of law and the undesirability of encouraging 'professional' litigants or meddlesome interlopers invoking the jurisdiction of the courts in matters in which they are not concerned.[97] Before the year 2000, there was no express provision governing the *locus standi* requirement of judicial review application in Malaysia. The Rules of the High Court 1980 and the Courts of Judicature Act 1964 were silent as regards the issue of standing of a judicial review applicant. The rule as to *locus standi* has therefore evolved over time through the courts.[98] A case which is relevant to both film censorship and *locus standi* is *George John v Goh Eng Wah Bros Filem Sdn Bhd,*[99] where the applicant sought leave to apply for a *certiorari* to quash the censors' decision in approving the publicity materials of a film entitled *Happy Bigamist* (Anthony Chan, 1987) which depicted a person living happily with two wives in one house.[100] The High Court took a liberal stand on the *locus standi* requirement and in holding that the applicant had the required standing to file the application, stated that: 'In order to have *locus standi* to invoke the jurisdiction of judicial review, the applicant should claim, if not a legal or equitable right, at least *sufficient interest* in respect of the matter to be litigated'.[101]

When the Rules of the High Court 1980 were amended in 2000, the existing Order 53 (which provides for the rules of application for judicial review) was replaced with a completely new Order 53. The *locus standi* requirement is now provided under rule 2(4) and it reads: 'Any person who is adversely affected by the decision of any public authority shall be entitled to make the application'. The Court of Appeal in the case of *QSR Brands v Suruhanjaya Sekuriti*[102] pointed out that the phrase 'adversely affected' in Order 53 rule 2(4) should be construed in a flexible manner and held that:[103]

> If the court is satisfied that the applicant has neither a sufficient personal interest in the legality of the impugned action… nor is the application a public interest litigation, then leave may safely be refused on the ground that the applicant is not a person 'adversely affected'.

In film censorship matters, *locus standi* or standing will not be an issue if the application for judicial review is made by the affected film practitioner – the film's director, producer, distributor or exhibitor – because they have personal interest in the decision. Furthermore, when a decision to ban a film is taken or when a censorship decision is made in an *ultra vires* manner, the fundamental liberties of the film practitioner concerned as guaranteed under articles 5 and 10 of the Malaysian Federal Constitution are infringed[104] and their interests in the film are affected. The film practitioner concerned will be 'adversely affected' and thus have the required *locus standi* to move the court by way of an application for judicial review.

The rule of exhaustion of alternative remedies

Must alternative remedies be exhausted before recourse may be had to judicial review? The courts in exercising their discretion will not normally make judicial review available to an applicant where there is an alternative remedy by way of appeal.[105] However, in deciding whether or not to disallow judicial review on the ground of non-exhaustion of existing alternative remedies, the court will consider the efficacy, benefit, convenience and adequacy of the alternative remedies available to the applicant. The existence of an appeal provision in the relevant legislation is therefore not a conclusive ground to refuse judicial review.[106]

There is no law requiring an applicant to exhaust all alternative remedies before an application for judicial review can be commenced.[107] The Court of Appeal in the case of *QSR Brands v Suruhanjaya Sekuriti,*[108] held that the existence of an alternative remedy available to the litigant would not on its own bar the court from hearing a judicial review. The approach is that the court will take into account the availability of the alternative remedy when deciding whether to grant the relief sought. The decided cases show that the rule of exhaustion of alternative remedies is not an absolute rule in Malaysia. It is not always the case that the court will not grant judicial review where an alternative remedy exists. Judicial review will be granted if the alternative remedy is not as effective, efficacious or convenient as judicial review.[109] It will also be granted if the application will resolve the issue directly and expeditiously,[110] if the case raises important public law issues[111] or if the applicant can demonstrate that the decision challenged is *ultra vires*, if there is blatant failure to perform a statutory duty or if there is an abuse of power or a breach of the principles of natural justice.[112]

In regard to film censorship, the rule will come into play when a film practitioner applies for judicial review to challenge the Board of Censors' decision without first appealing to the Appeal Committee. It is very likely that the court will dismiss the application unless the applicant-film practitioner can demonstrate illegality, abuse of power or a breach of the rules of natural justice; or that the application will resolve the issue directly, expeditiously, or effectively; or that the case raises important public law issues. Therefore, in such a situation, the film practitioner concerned would do better by first exhausting the appeal procedure provided under the Film Censorship Act 2002 before filing an application for judicial review.

Remedies available under judicial review application: what can the applicant-film practitioner achieve?

The superior courts in Malaysia have two types of power in judicial review matters. The first is the inherent powers of the High Court based on common law and the second is the additional powers of the High Court granted under paragraph 1 of the Schedule to the Courts of Judicature Act 1964 read together with section 25(2).[113]

From these powers, the courts have at their disposal a wide variety of remedies, which may be grouped into two categories: the common law remedies and the additional powers remedies. The Courts of Judicature Act 1964,[114] the Rules of the High Court 1980[115] and the Specific Relief Act 1950[116] are applicable to the grant of judicial review remedies to successful applicant-film practitioners.

Common law remedies

The common law remedies are comprised of orders or writs of *habeas corpus*, *mandamus*, *certiorari*, *quo warranto*, and prohibition (the prerogative writ remedies), as well as declaration, injunction, monetary compensation and damages (the non-writ remedies). In an application for judicial review challenging a film censorship decision, the court may grant the following common law remedies:

1 *Certiorari*, to quash the decision if it is made in excess of jurisdiction, in breach of the rules of natural justice, or where there is an error of law or abuse of power. When this remedy is granted, the court may direct the censorship authority concerned to reconsider the matter afresh. *Certiorari* is the most commonly sought writ and is the principal means of invoking judicial review over any authority determining the rights of the people.[117] It appears to be the most effective common law remedy for film practitioners challenging a censorship decision that is illegal, irrational, unfair or disproportionate.

2 *Mandamus*, to compel the decision-making entities to perform their duty, or to keep the entities within the limits of their jurisdiction. When discretion is vested in an authority by law, and that authority does not exercise, or abuses, the discretion, *mandamus* can be issued to compel the authority concerned to exercise its discretion properly and in accordance to law.[118] A film practitioner may apply for an order of *mandamus* to compel censors to perform their duty expeditiously if there is unnecessary delay in the making of a censorship decision. This is to avoid films from being held-up over a long period of time by the censors concerned.[119]

3 Declaration, to declare that a censorship decision is null, void and of no effect. However, a declaration merely declares the position of the law under a set of facts and does not quash the decision in question. A declaration has no coercive force, but it may effectively undermine the enforceability of a challenged decision.[120] This remedy may also be sought to declare certain censorship guidelines or practices to be invalid.

Additional powers of the High Court: the moulding of relief

The additional powers of the High Court are much wider and more dynamic than its inherent powers. Paragraph 1 of the Schedule to the Courts of Judicature Act 1964 read in conjunction with section 25(2) of the same Act[121] provides that the High Court shall have the following additional powers:

> Power to issue to any person or authority directions, orders or writs, including writs of the nature of *habeas corpus*, *mandamus*, prohibition, *quo warranto*, and *certiorari*, or any others, for the enforcement of the rights conferred by Part II of the Constitution, or for any of them, or for any other purpose.[122]

The Federal Court in the case of *Rama Chandran R v The Industrial Court of Malaysia*[123] held that since paragraph 1 carries the caption 'Additional Powers of High Court', the powers granted therein are therefore over and above those inherent powers already enjoyed by the High Court.[124]

Paragraph 1 of the Schedule to the Courts of Judicature Act 1964 is couched in comprehensive phraseology and therefore confers wide powers on the High Court.[125] The language used to describe the nature of the power, the purpose for which, and the person or authority against whom, it can be exercised, encompasses many areas and prescribes a lot of power to the court. Although the provision carries the caption 'Additional Powers of the High Court', the Court of Appeal and the Federal Court also enjoy the powers stipulated therein.[126] Under paragraph 1, the courts can issue writs in the nature of prerogative writs as understood under the common law, but the scope is much wider than that as the use of the phrase '*writs, including writs of the nature of*' does not equate the writs that can be issued in Malaysia with those in England (or other common law jurisdictions without a similar provision). The High Court can also issue directions, orders or writs other than the prerogative writs. The phrase '*or any others*' empowers the court to grant other remedies besides writs and this would include declaratory and injunctive relief. The phrase '*directions, orders*' then allows the High Court to mould consequential relief after having disposed of the main remedy or remedies sought.[127] It enables the court to mould the relief (remedy) to suit the factual matrix of each case, and such powers can be utilized for the enforcement of rights, may it be fundamental rights or any other rights. Therefore, instead of only quashing a film censorship decision (with an order of *certiorari*) and remitting it back to the censorship decision-making entities to reconsider the matter afresh, the court can go a step further to mould the relief according to the needs of the situation or the applicant. It needs to be stressed that the moulding of judicial relief is a salient feature of the additional powers of the High Court and orders as well as directions may be made against '*any person or authority*' and not limited to public authorities only.

The concept of moulding of relief was introduced in Malaysia in the case of *Hong Leong Equipment Sdn Bhd v Liew Fook Chuan*[128] where the Court of Appeal, after basing itself on the similarity between article 226(1) of the Indian Constitution and paragraph 1 of the Schedule to the Courts of Judicature Act 1964, held that in the field of public law remedies, the High Court is not confined to the grant of usual prerogative orders known to the English common law, but is at liberty to fashion appropriate remedy to suit the circumstances of the case. Sri Ram JCA stated:[129]

> It is plain that Parliament intended that the High Court should be empowered to grant relief which is ordinarily beyond the scope of the usual public law remedies. That intention finds expression in the word 'including' which has been interposed between the phrase 'directions, orders or writs' and the phrase 'writs of the nature of *habeas corpus*, *mandamus*, prohibition, *quo warranto* and *certiorari*, or any others'. So too, the phrase 'or for any other purpose', with which the paragraph concludes, makes clear the wide area in which the remedies are to operate. These matters, in my judgment, reflect the conferment of a wide power upon the High Court in the matter of public law remedies.

The additional powers may be utilized by the superior courts over and above their inherent powers in an application for judicial review challenging film censorship decision. It is argued here that the courts, sourcing their additional powers from paragraph 1, may:

1 order the Board of Censors, the Appeal Committee or the Home Minister to reconsider their decision based upon directions issued by the court;
2 direct the Board, the Committee or the Minister to review or to make a fresh decision within a prescribe timeframe;
3 order the Film Control Division of the Home Ministry to pay the applicant-film practitioner compensation or damages if an approval for exhibition and distribution of a film is subsequently revoked without justification and such revocation has caused financial losses to the film practitioner concerned;
4 order the Board, the Committee or the Minister to restore (or return) excised parts of the film submitted to the film practitioner concerned;
5 overturn the censorship decision made by the Board, the Committee or the Minister if the court finds the decision is tainted with illegality or irrationality, or is made under an unfair procedure or is disproportionate with the object sought to be achieved;
6 make its own censorship decision about the film concerned.

The combination of the two categories of powers, inherent and additional powers, ensures that the applicant-film practitioner will obtain from the court remedy or remedies that are adequate and appropriate to the circumstances of the case.

Judicial review of film censorship decisions: the best option?

It appears that there have been no judicial review applications challenging film censorship decisions in Malaysia and Hong Kong. In Australia, there have been a number of such applications but only two of them are directly relevant to the scope of this book[130] – *Village Roadshow Corporation Ltd v Sheehan*[131] and *Family Voice Australia v Members of the Classification Review Board.*[132] In the former case, the applicant sought judicial review to challenge the Board of Review's decision in confirming the Censorship Board's decision to classify the film *Full Metal Jacket* (Stanley Kubrick, 1987) for restricted exhibition (that is, an 'R' category)[133] under the Film and Video Tape Classification Act 1984 (NSW), and the respondent's personal decision not to reconvene the Board of Review to consider its decision further following a written request by the applicant. The applicant was the distributor of the film and the respondent chaired the Board of Review. The applicant argued that the Board of Review had failed to take into account relevant considerations (that is, the suitability of the film for viewing by persons between the ages of 15 and 17 years) and that the members of the Board of Review had 'slavishly followed' the classification guidelines and had not applied themselves to the merits of the case. Both grounds failed as the Federal Court found that there was no evidence that the Board of Review had failed to take into account whether the film was suitable for viewing by persons between the ages of 15 and 17 years and there was also no evidence to suggest that the Board of Review had abdicated its responsibility to make an independent decision in the matter. However, the court was of the opinion that the respondent's personal decision not to submit to the Board of Review the applicant's request to reconsider the matter (with new evidence said to support it, like the censorship decisions on the film in New Zealand and the United Kingdom which gave the film lower classification categories) had deprived the applicant of an opportunity for a full and fair determination of its request for an 'M' classification of the film. The court proceeded to quash the decision of the respondent not to permit the Board of Review to reconsider its decision. The court then ordered the Board of Review to reconsider the matter. However, the subsequent reconsideration did not result in a change of the film's earlier 'R' classification.

In the latter case, the applicant – Family Voice Australia – sought judicial review (under section 5 of the Administrative Decision (Judicial Review) Act 1977) of the Classification Review Board's decision to classify a modified version of the film *Salo o le 120 Giornate di Sodoma* (*Salo, Or the 120 Days of Sodom*, Pier Paolo Pasolini, 1975)[134] in DVD format along with additional materials (including documentary features and behind-the-scenes footage of the film in production) R18+ with the consumer advice: 'Scenes of torture and degradation, sexual violence and nudity'.[135] In arriving at its decision, the five-member panel of the Review Board found that the impact of the film was high (with portrayals of mental and physical violence, nudity and sexual violence) but justified by the historical, political and cultural context of the film as provided by the additional documentary material included in the DVD format that would 'mitigate the level of potential community offence and the impact of the classifiable elements to the extent that the film can be accommodated within the R18+ classification'.[136] Family Voice Australia, in its application, contended that the Review Board's decision was affected by an error of law and that the Review Board erred by failing to comply with the Guidelines for the Classification of Films and Computer Games as required under the Classification (Publications, Films and Computer Games) Act 1995 and the National Classification Code. The applicant's allegations included:

1 The Review Board did not consider the cumulative effect of the individual classifiable elements in the film.
2 The Review Board failed to consider whether the depictions of cruelty and violence were detailed and of high impact.
3 The Review Board erred in finding that the sexual activity depicted in the film was permissible because of context.
4 The Review Board failed to consider whether depictions of sexual violence in the film were gratuitous, exploitative or offensive.

The Federal Court held that the Review Board had appropriately directed its attention to, and considered each of the classifiable elements in the film and subsequently made their decision to classify the film R18+. The judicial review application was dismissed as the Court was satisfied that the Review Board had considered all relevant issues, directed itself correctly as to the statutory criteria and applied the Act, the Code and the Guidelines without committing any error of law in the course of making the decision.

Although every Malaysian film practitioner interviewed for this research agreed that it is important to have the option of challenging film censorship decisions by way of judicial review, less than 50 per cent of them stated that they would be prepared to do so if dissatisfied with a decision. The Malaysian interviewees were reluctant to pursue judicial review as the solution to their censorship woes for three reasons:

1 the cost and time involved in an application for judicial review;
2 the lack of confidence in the judicial system; and
3 the subsequent negative effects or repercussions of an application on the applicant-film practitioner.

Ruhani Abdul Rahman thought it would be burdensome to incur extra expenses in addition to the large amount of money already spent on producing a film. Additionally, a judicial review application would take a long period of time to be disposed of by the court and the delay would cause the film to 'be stuck there for years!'[137] The producer also acknowledged that she could not afford to have her film 'held up' for a long period of time as it was imperative that the film be released for exhibition and distribution in order for her to recoup the investment, which was often made up of a combination of her production company's capital and loans from financial institutions. U-Wei Haji Saari also agreed that the cost which would be incurred and the foreseeable delay caused by a judicial review application were prohibitive factors that would drive film practitioners away from this course of action.[138] Khoo Eng Yow was of the opinion that it was an exercise in futility to challenge a censorship decision in court due to the current judicial climate in Malaysia. The lack of confidence in the impartiality of the courts, which the interviewee perceived to be biased in favour of the authorities and the government, is the main reason why he would not bother to pursue judicial review in the event he was aggrieved by a censorship decision.[139] Leonard Tee, an independent film distributor, also shares the same opinion.[140]

The other factor that contributes to the reluctance of Malaysian film practitioners to pursue judicial review application is the subsequent effect that such application might have on them. The author's impression, from the interviews conducted and from informal conversations with other film practitioners, is that most of the film practitioners in the Malaysian film industry have reservations about resorting to judicial review because they want to maintain a cordial relationship with the censors. They would not want that relationship to become confrontational because the hostility would cause more 'problems' for them in the future. Aziz M. Osman for example, admitted that he 'would not dare' to make an application for judicial review to challenge a censorship decision on his film even if he was dissatisfied with it.[141] When probed further for the reasons behind his reluctance, Aziz stated that it was for his 'survival' in the film industry and further noted that he had learned his lesson in that there was no point in going against the censorship authorities.[142] Even so, it was striking that the Malaysian interviewees believed it was important for the option of judicial review to be available.

Like their Malaysian counterparts, all of the Hong Kong interviewees were also of the opinion that the availability of judicial review is important. It is pertinent to note that the Hong Kong interviewees also expressed their satisfaction with censorship decisions and were of the view that the film censorship system in Hong Kong functions very well. Therefore, there would be hardly any occasions where it would be necessary for them to resort to judicial review.[143] However, the interviewees appeared to be willing to do so in the unlikely event they were aggrieved by a censorship decision. Mabel Cheung, for example, stated that she would 'do anything to fight for my films if I think the [censorship] decision is not fair'[144] while Patrick Tam said that the decision as to whether to apply for judicial review would depend on the situation:[145]

> If it [the censorship] is very minor, I won't take the trouble to go against it... But if it is unreasonable or damaging to the film, I will challenge it. The right to file an application for judicial review is important especially if you think your film was unfairly treated or mistreated.

Tam's position was shared by Kenneth Bi who noted that 'it would depend on the film. If the film is about politics, yes! If it is just sex, like showing one breast as opposed to two, then I probably wouldn't.[146] Wellington Fung pointed out that when the consideration of whether to challenge a film censorship decision in court arises, 'commercial judgment' will inevitably favour options other than having resort to judicial review simply because it would 'hold up the whole thing [the distribution and exhibition of the film concerned] where commercially, we will lose more'.[147] Besides commercial considerations, no other reasons or factors were highlighted by the Hong Kong interviewees.

Similar to the Malaysian and Hong Kong interviewees, all of the Australian interviewees agree that the availability of judicial review is important. For example, Rolf de Heer noted that 'it is extremely important that judicial review is available' and that he would have recourse to it if he was dissatisfied with the classification decision passed on his film. However, the filmmaker also said that it was unlikely that he would need to challenge classification decisions in court because the Australian system is not restrictive and that his interests in filmmaking do not clash with it.[148]

The majority of the Australian interviewees were certain that they would have recourse to judicial review in the event they were dissatisfied with classification decisions about their films. For example, when asked whether he would file a judicial review application if dissatisfied with the Classification Review Board's decision, Ray Lawrence answered 'of course, I would' without any hesitation.[149] Tony Ayres was of the opinion that 'it will be an issue when a film goes from an MA to R [classification] because it affects the box office… If I was in that situation, I would have recourse to judicial review'.[150] An interviewee who requested anonymity noted that 'judicial review is of course important. If you take that away, you are giving total autocracy to the censors!' In contrast, only three interviewees were unsure as to whether they would seek judicial remedies from the court. Richard J. Frankland, who was dissatisfied with the classification his film *Stone Bros* received, noted that he was not sure whether he would pursue judicial review because his production company had already lost a lot of money on the film and it was not certain whether it was feasible to incur further expenses to mount a court action. Greg Denning of Icon Film Distribution Australia noted that the time factor would be 'very prohibitive' because 'normally we have release date, so we are up against time… the issue is whether we can get the judicial review application heard in time'.[151] Peter Campbell noted that 'it would depend on how much you had invested in the film. If you were involved in the financing, then you should… but now, as a distributor, there are so many films out there and so there is more choice. If it is going to be problematic, you should be more selective with the films that you are going to distribute'.[152]

In summary, although a successful applicant-film practitioner could obtain appropriate and adequate remedies from the court, judicial review is still not the best option. It is likely to be slow and expensive and risks harming relations with the censors. Therefore, it would be more beneficial to the Malaysian film practitioners and industry if the film censorship system itself is reformed while judicial review is kept available as the final resort, as well as to influence censors to carry out their duties legally, rationally, fairly and proportionately. Equally, this makes it valuable to understand the ways in which judicial review *is* available under the current Malaysian film censorship system, and the sorts of remedies that it could provide. Even if judicial review is not put into action in court, 'the shadow of the law' could affect film censors, potentially encouraging the making of better censorship decisions – both procedurally and substantively. At least, that is the clear understanding of the film practitioners interviewed as part of the research. Proposals for the reform of the Malaysian film censorship system will be the focus of the following chapter.

7 Conclusion

Proposals for the reform of the Malaysian film censorship system and further research

Introduction

Having identified, discussed and established the areas of concern in the Malaysian film censorship system in Chapters 3 to 5 and considered, in Chapter 6, judicial review as an alternative to deal with challenges occasioned by film censorship, this chapter will propose changes to the system that are likely to promote the artistic vibrancy and commercial viability of the country's film industry. The proposals made are primarily aimed at providing greater transparency and accountability to the film censorship system, to reconcile the system with the free speech principle, as well as to improve the system to make it more responsive to the needs of film practitioners and conducive to the growth of the film industry.

In general, the proposals for reform involve amendments to the film censorship law, revision to the censorship guidelines and changes to the censorship process. The amendments to the Film Censorship Act 2002 will ensure transparency in the process of appointing decision-makers; structure and confine the presently unconstrained discretionary powers of the decision-making entities; ensure film practitioners are furnished with written reasons for censorship decisions; and guarantee film practitioners the right to make oral representations at the appeal stage of a censorship process and the right to make judicial review applications. The Film Censorship Guidelines 1993 were revised in March 2010, after fieldwork for this book was completed. However, the 2010 version of the guidelines did not significantly improve (or remove the 'defects' of) the earlier guidelines but appear to be even more vague and convoluted. Therefore, this chapter considers both versions of the guidelines in relation to possible future reform. The proposed revision to the guidelines entails clearer descriptions of the content that is prohibited in films; the requirement to take into account the context of a film as well as the degree, intensity and realism of presentation of censorship elements in the decision-making process; and a clear schedule setting out the limits of each censorship element under every classification category. And finally, the proposed changes to the censorship process would do two further things: first, provide a formal channel for film practitioners to discuss with censors the issue of classification category and second, avoid unnecessary re-examination of films brought about by public complaints.

The eight areas of concern in the Malaysian film censorship system will be discussed separately, for each the discussion will begin with a statement about the issue or problem in that particular area as revealed in earlier chapters followed by the proposal for reform. All of the proposals are made based on analysis of the laws, guidelines, and processes as they are expressed on paper, the censorship practices in all three jurisdictions, the interviewees' opinions of the issues and, where relevant, the literature about free speech as well as constitutional and administrative law principles. The chapter concludes by noting the areas of concern that arise in the two comparative jurisdictions, Hong Kong and Australia, for further research.

The areas of concern in the Malaysian film censorship system and proposals for reform

Decision-making entities

There are three concerns about the decision-making entities in Malaysia: first, the suitability and competence of the appointed film censors; second, the independence of film censors in making their decisions; and third, the Home Minister's absolute discretionary power to ban films.

Suitability and competence of film censors

The suitability and competence of film censors is an issue of concern raised strongly by the Malaysian interviewees.[1] They stated that they doubted the ability of the members of the Board of Censors and the Appeal Committee[2] to make sensible, appropriate and credible censorship decisions because the members had little, if any, knowledge of film or experience in filmmaking. The appointed film censors were also seen as not the best people to sit on the Board (or the Committee) because they could not understand and appreciate the artistic merits of films they examine;[3] they were out of touch with contemporary audience standards;[4] and did not care about the potential adverse effects of their decisions on the integrity of the films they examined.[5] Additionally, the method, criteria and process of selection and appointment of film censors not being made public was a source of concern to the interviewees. Most film practitioners do not know the identity of the censors who will eventually be examining their films.

It is proposed that sections 4 and 22 of the Film Censorship Act 2002, which provide for the appointment of members of the Board and the Committee respectively, be amended to guarantee transparency in the selection and appointment processes. Suitable and competent members of the public should be given the opportunity to apply and be appointed as film censors, as in Hong Kong and Australia.[6] Film practitioners should also be allowed to nominate individuals to be appointed to the Committee as, ideally, the film fraternity should have some representation in the decision-making entities. It is envisioned that a balanced composition of professionals and experts from various disciplines as well as people of diverse background, age and profession would be appointed as censors instead of only conservative former bureaucrats, which appears to be the current situation. Additionally, the appointments of film censors should be gazetted as occurs in the Hong Kong model[7] to avoid anonymity.[8] For Amir Muhammad, a censorship board should consist of a balanced mix of people: 'the composition [of the Board] is odd in that everybody is old… and you find the oddest things being cut out… I think it should consist of a variety of people'. U-Wei Haji Saari was of the opinion that only individuals who are 'open minded, sensitive and understand film as an art form should be appointed as censors',[9] Ruhani Abdul Rahman expressed hope that the Board would consist of more young censors ('not only retirees!') because the predominant film-goers in Malaysia are those between the ages of 16 to 40, a view shared by Shuhaimi Baba, while Saw Teong Hin hoped that the appointment of censors would be transparent so that film practitioners would know who was accountable for the decisions made.[10] The director described the present situation as 'cloak and dagger' as most film practitioners do not know who is in charge and 'the goal post keeps shifting'.[11]

It is very important that only suitable and competent individuals are appointed as censors because they will be making determinative judgments on the availability or otherwise of films to the public. The fieldwork suggests that their decisions have serious repercussions on both the artistic and commercial viability of the film industry. For example, a decision to approve a film subject to alteration could 'destroy' its narrative and aesthetic aspects as well as cause the film to lose its appeal to audiences. Therefore, it is crucial to have the right individuals involved in the decision-making entities. As discussed in Chapter 1, leading free speech theorists and writers, including Schauer and Barendt, emphasized the importance of *who* the person was making censorship decisions.[12] Interviewees emphasized that there should be some members – at least on the Appeal Committee – with an understanding of cinema and an ability to consider film from artistic viewpoints in exercising judgment. It is worth noting again that the Hong Kong Board of Review always has at least one member who is a well-respected figure from the film fraternity.[13] However, despite there being no film practitioner sitting on the Classification Review Board in Australia, the Australian interviewees did not raise any concerns regarding this matter. It appears that other elements of the Australian system and the general competence of the censors underlie this. At the very least, film practitioners should be allowed to nominate candidates for the decision-making bodies in a more transparent selection process, but the most important issue is obtaining a good range of competent people in the role.

By having the decision-making entities staffed with competent members, the censorship decisions made would be more credible and appropriate, and that would be beneficial to film practitioners and their Malaysian viewers. It would also remove one of the 'disturbing features of administrative censorship' as pointed out by Barendt.[14]

Independence of film censors

There is compelling evidence that film censors are not independent in making censorship decisions.[15] This is primarily due to the 'threat' to security of tenure which places censors under some influence of the Minister and the executive branch of government.[16] Additionally, censors are 'paid and accorded such allowances and privileges as may be determined by the Minister'.[17] Thus, there is a strong incentive for censors to strive to conform to the government's wishes and policies. This structural weakness, suggested by the legislative provisions,[18] was confirmed in interviews. Khoo Eng Yow, for example, pointed out that the censors are 'not independent' and 'politicians are affecting the censors too much… the censors just obey for the job's sake. They are not in their own control' while Amir Muhammad observed that:

> The censors' decisions reflect whatever the general political mood of the establishment is. If they feel like being liberal, they will do something liberal. If they feel like clamping down, they will clamp down on something. If they feel like pleasing certain people, they will do just that.

This is clearly inconsistent with the free speech principle's requirement of 'an impartial tribunal'.[19] It is also a weakness that appears to have been avoided in both Hong Kong and Australia. In the former, fieldwork revealed that censors are not subject to political pressure or interference while in the latter, appointments can only be terminated under the circumstances prescribed in the statute and the interviewees raised no concern over this matter.[20]

To ensure the independence of film censors, their tenure must be secured and that can be achieved by setting a specified duration of appointment, with censors being ineligible for reappointment. In addition, there must be provisions in the Film Censorship Act 2002 (which could be enacted based on sections 65 and 83 of the Australian Classification (Publications, Films and Computer Games) Act 1995), stating expressly the circumstances under which members of the Board of Censors and the Appeal Committee can be removed. This would prevent arbitrary termination of appointment and minimize the threat to security of tenure. If these proposals are put in place, censors would have greater independence and ability to carry out their duties based on the law, guidelines and procedure, not according to the wishes or directives of the Minister or government. Although this change would not in itself create an 'impartial tribunal' and completely overcome the 'disturbing vices' of government officials being keen to censor materials critical of government,[21] it would at least guarantee a higher degree of independence of the censors in making film censorship decisions.

Absolute discretionary power to ban films

The Home Minister is empowered under section 26 of the Film Censorship Act 2002 to override decisions made by the Board of Censors and the Appeal Committee and to ban films at his or her absolute discretion.[22] This ability to ban films is inconsistent with free speech principles and stands in stark contrast with the position in Hong Kong and Australia where, as discussed in Chapters 3 and 4, none of the decision-making entities is conferred with such a wide power. The exercise of this power would greatly affect the film practitioners concerned, particularly if the film involved was a local production. This is because a Malaysian film's market is almost completely domestic: films are rarely released commercially overseas. Therefore, a ban under this provision would translate as the 'death' of the film in its commercial sense and this could possibly wipe out the production company as the capital invested to produce the film could not be recouped. The Malaysian interviewees were generally uncomfortable with the Minister wielding such a wide power.[23]

Although the discretion conferred on the Minister by section 26 is not unfettered in light of the Supreme Court judgment in the *Persatuan Aliran Kesedaran Malaysia* case,[24] there could be instances where it would be very difficult for an applicant-film practitioner to challenge the decision because of the need to establish that the Minister had exercised his discretion wrongfully, unfairly, dishonestly or in bad faith.[25] On top of that, as pointed out in Chapter 6, there are a number of other 'hurdles' that an applicant would have to overcome in pursuing an application for judicial review in addition to the necessity of having an independent and robust judiciary in applications challenging the exercise of discretionary powers by the executive. In relation to the discretionary power to ban films, the doctrinal materials, free speech concerns and the fieldwork all suggest that section 26 should be repealed and the power be removed.

The exemption of films from censorship

There are two provisions in the Film Censorship Act 2002 that allow films to be exempted from the censorship process. Section 2(2)(a) provides that the Act is not applicable to any film sponsored by the Malaysian Government while section 28 confers a blanket power on the Home Minister to exempt any film from censorship.

While raising similar free speech issues to those noted above about decision-making entities, and causing dissatisfaction among Malaysian interviewees who questioned the rationale of having these provisions,[26] sections 2(2)(a) and 28 also appear more problematic than the Hong Kong and Australian models. In each case, their systems allow some films to be exempted, but within clearly circumscribed limits.[27] Defined categories of film, which could be expected to raise no issues about censorship, are exempted. They are films of the type such as educational, sporting, travelogue and musical.

All this suggests that sections 2(2)(a) and 28 should be repealed. To achieve fairness within the system, every film intended for exhibition and distribution should be subjected to the same process or requirement, regardless of the entity that produces the film, or is involved with it in other ways. However, for reasons of practicality and efficiency, a new provision may be enacted so films that are innocuous in nature may be exempted from censorship. The types, categories or descriptions of such films must be expressly stated and reference may be made to the second schedule to the Hong Kong Film Censorship Regulations and section 5B(1) of the Australian Classification (Publications, Films and Computer Games) Act 1995 for useful examples of the approach.

Matters to be taken into account by censors

Film censors in Malaysia are not required to take into account two important matters in the course of making censorship decisions. These matters are the artistic merit of the film under examination and current community standards and attitudes toward film censorship, both of which if given due consideration would have significant impact on the decisions made.

Artistic merit of the film

Unlike the Hong Kong and Australian models, the Malaysian film censorship system does not require censors to take into account artistic merits in the censorship process.[28] The omission of such a requirement has caused many critically acclaimed foreign and local films to be banned (or released subject to substantial alteration)[29] and it also discourages local film practitioners from attempting to produce 'serious and critical works' which may at the same time necessarily contain contentious content.

Most of the interviewees (from all three jurisdictions) believed that the consideration of artistic merit does, or would, have significant impact on censorship decisions in that a film with high artistic value may be approved for exhibition and distribution subject to age restrictions although it contains content which otherwise may not be permissible or may be deemed objectionable.[30] Even the Chairman of the Malaysian Board of Censors agrees with the author that the consideration of artistic merit is important but Malaysian fieldwork clearly suggest that the matter is not taken into account at all in the censorship process. Besides the approach adopted by the Hong Kong and Australian film censorship systems, it may be recalled that Anglo-American jurisprudence on obscenity law also emphasizes the consideration of literary or artistic merits in their tests to determine whether a work should be proscribed or otherwise.[31] It is therefore proposed that a new provision be added to the Film Censorship Act 2002 stipulating that: 'film censors, in making a censorship decision, shall take into account the artistic merit of the film under examination and its value for cultural or social reasons' to avoid films with artistic, social or cultural values from being stifled.[32]

Current community standards

Besides the omission of a provision requiring censors to take artistic merit into account, there is also no provision in the law or guidelines stipulating that censors must take into account current community standards while making censorship decisions. Fieldwork revealed that film censorship decisions are made based on censors' subjective views or personal standards (and only partially guided by the censorship guidelines). In addition, as we have seen, the censors as an unvaried group are hardly representative of Malaysian society and no systematic effort is carried out to ensure that the decisions made are reflective of contemporary standards.

As discussed in Chapter 4, Hong Kong censors are required under paragraph 2 of the Film Censorship Guidelines for Censors to take into account current community standards in the censorship process while their Australian counterparts are required to do so under section 11 of the Classification (Publications, Films and Computer Games) Act 1995. In Hong Kong, public opinion surveys on film censorship standards are conducted biennially to gauge community acceptance and tolerance to portrayals of nudity, sex, violence, horror as well as offensive language, behaviour and criminality in films. Besides surveys, film censors are assisted by the Panel of Advisers to ensure that their decisions are in touch with the standards of taste and decency accepted by the community. In Australia, the decision-making entities are staffed with members who are broadly representative of the community.[33] Additionally, the Community Assessment Panel scheme and other research ensures that the decisions made follow closely the expectations of the society.

The majority of the interviewees were in favour of film censorship decisions being made based on current community standards as opposed to censors' subjective views and standards.[34] The interviewees' opinions of this issue echoed each other and it may be sufficient to quote only one from each jurisdiction:

> Film censorship decisions should be made based on current community standards… they shouldn't be made based on censors' personal standards. (Malaysia – Ahmad Puad Onah, 17 December 2008)

> It [a film censorship decision] should be made based on the current atmosphere of the society… I think film censors should pay close attention to the opinion that prevails in the community. (Hong Kong – Mabel Cheung, 28 May 2009)

> Classification decisions should be made based on the standards of the community we live in and their progression. (Australia – Ray Lawrence, 20 August 2009)

Films are made for people to watch, they are meant for the audience. It would therefore be sensible for those making film censorship decisions to take account of the standards of those in the community who are likely to watch them. Since exhibition and distribution of films in Malaysia is concentrated in the larger cities and amongst youth, censorship decisions should take into account the standards of this section of the community and not the standards of the older generation living in rural areas of the country. It is proposed that a new provision be included in the censorship guidelines requiring censors to take into account the standards of the likely audience when making censorship decisions. Contemporary standards are to be considered, not standards of some past age, and therefore surveys should be carried out at regular intervals to ensure that censors are 'in tune' with the standards and expectations of the film-going community. This proposal is slightly different from the Hong Kong and Australian models as the former provides that 'the aim of the censors should be to reflect contemporary public attitudes towards censorship standards'[35] while the latter provides that 'the standards of morality, decency and propriety accepted by reasonable adults'[36] are to be taken into account. These provisions are more general in nature and do not emphasize the 'standards of the likely audience', which is the key point of this proposal.

It may be noted again that the English obscenity test has evolved from focusing on the effect of the publication (charged to be obscene) on the 'most vulnerable members of the society' (as in the *Hicklin* test)[37] to 'persons who are likely, in all circumstances, to read, see or hear the matter' (as provided in the Obscene Publications Act),[38] making the determination of obscenity centred on an assessment of a work's likely effect on its primary audience.[39] It may well be advocated that in film censorship, the standards of the likely audience should be the benchmark, not the most vulnerable members, the elderly and rural members, of Malaysian society who are very unlikely to purchase tickets to (and the DVD of) the film in question.

Censorship guidelines

As noted in Chapter 3, a new set of guidelines known as the *Garis Panduan Penapisan Filem* or Film Censorship Guidelines (hereinafter referred to as 'the 2010 Guidelines') was introduced on 15 March 2010 to replace the Film Censorship Guidelines 1993.[40] The 2010 Guidelines comprises seven parts and in its Introduction, it is stated that the guidelines are to be applied in accordance to the Film Censorship Act 2002, other relevant legislation in force, government policies and international covenants.

Part I of the 2010 Guidelines lays down the general principles of film censorship which are similar to those stated in the Film Censorship Guidelines 1993.[41] In addition to the principles, Part I also provides the definition of 'film', 'film trailer' and 'film publicity material', the matters to be taken into account by censors in the course of censoring films and the time frame within which a censorship decision is to be made. The matters that censors are required to take into account are similar to the eight questions stated under Part D of the Film Censorship Guidelines 1993 as discussed in the section on the process of the Malaysian film censorship system in Chapter 3. Artistic merit of the film and current community standards are *not* prescribed in the guidelines as matters to be taken into account by censors.

Part II, which is the main section of the 2010 Guidelines, contains provisions on the types of film, content and portrayal that *may* not be approved for distribution and exhibition in Malaysia. These provisions are divided into four censorship elements – 'Public safety and public order', 'Religion', 'Socio-culture' and 'Etiquette and decorum'[42] – and they are vague, confusing and indeterminate. An example would be: 'Film containing a religious theme, storyline, scene or dialogue is allowed. However, the following matters must be considered so that it will not cause controversy and raise doubt in the society.'[43] This provision is then followed by a long list of matters, including 'a belief that every religion is the same' and 'a belief in the concept of reincarnation', for censors' consideration.[44] It is not at all clear from the provisions whether a film that portrays the concept of reincarnation that *may* cause controversy or contains a line of dialogue stating that 'Allah and

Jesus are one' that *may* cause confusion amongst audiences, will be banned, or approved but classified in a restricted category, or approved subject to alteration being made. The effect of content that *may* cause controversy and raise doubts on the film's censorship decision is not stated at all in the guidelines. This omission and the crucial determination of whether a particular content or portrayal *may* or *may not* 'cause controversy and raise doubt in the society' leaves too wide a discretion to the censors which could lead to the making of arbitrary and inconsistent censorship decisions. It appears that if the guidelines were read liberally, most content and portrayals in film would be permissible but censors may 'choose' to construe and apply the guidelines restrictively (or worse, irrationally, as they have proven themselves to be capable of) so as to prohibit films from being released in Malaysia.

Part III of the 2010 Guidelines deals with commercial, trailer and film publicity material, stating that prior approval from the Board of Censors must be obtained before it can be released. Part IV follows by providing that 'coarse language is not *encouraged* in any film'.[45] A list of profanity in Malay, English, Tamil, Hindi, Mandarin and Cantonese is appended but there is no instruction to censors as to how films containing coarse language are to be dealt with. The consequence of the use of expletives is also not stated at all, unlike the Hong Kong and the Australian guidelines where there are clear provisions as to how a film containing coarse language will be classified based on the context, type and frequency of the use of such language.

Part V then provides, in very broad terms, the types of film that will be banned and they are:

1 films that contain themes or story lines that are incompatible with the Malaysian socio-cultural values;
2 films that are seditious in nature;
3 films that are anti-religion or insulting to the belief of a particular race or group;
4 films containing content that is against government policies; and
5 films that contain excessive violence and cruelty.

It is also expressly stated in Part V that every film to be released locally must respect Malaysia as a sovereign country. Films that insult Malaysia or are detrimental to its image will be prohibited. These provisions are loosely drafted and can therefore be interpreted in various ways, again leaving very wide discretion to the censors.

Part VI then provides for the submission of film to the Board of Censors. It also provides that any film owner who is dissatisfied with the Board's decision may appeal to the Appeal Committee. Part VII, the final section of the 2010 Guidelines, provides for three classification categories – 'U',[46] 'PG13'[47] and '18'[48] – that are applicable in Malaysia.[49] However, it omits to provide descriptions as to the scope and limits of content that are permissible under each category, as are provided in the Hong Kong and Australian guidelines.[50]

It is claimed in the Introduction section of the 2010 Guidelines that they were introduced with the aim of assisting film practitioners by providing them with a clear and comprehensible set of guidelines so that they are able to consider and pay attention to the censorship elements, content and portrayal that will be scrutinized by censors. Upon careful examination of the guidelines, it is apparent that little improvement has been made. Most of the provisions in the 2010 Guidelines are similar to those in the 1993 version. Very few new provisions have been introduced. Only minor changes have been made to the wordings[51] and sequence of arrangement of provisions under the four censorship elements.[52] The guidelines still lack clarity as there has been no improvement at all in this regard compared to the Film Censorship Guidelines 1993.

An overall problem with the 2010 Guidelines is that provisions under every censorship element are preceded with a general statement which reads: 'Film containing a public safety and public order [or a religious, socio-cultural or etiquette and decorum] theme, storyline, scene or dialogue is allowed. However, the following matters must be considered so that it will not cause controversy and raise doubt in the society'.[53] Thereafter, a list of matters follows suit (under each of the four elements) for censors' consideration. It appears from these provisions (particularly with the use of the phrase 'is allowed') that the Home Ministry attempted to draw up a 'liberal and permissive looking' set of guidelines instead of dictating the types of film, content and portrayal that are prohibited like the Film Censorship Guidelines 1993 did. However, the Ministry has failed and the resulting 2010 Guidelines, that appear to have been put together haphazardly and not well thought out, are far from desirable as they are now even more vague and indeterminate and have further widened the censors' discretion in deciding whether a particular film or content will be approved for exhibition and distribution. The general statement that precedes every censorship element has made the 2010 Guidelines indeterminate as discussed above. It is foreseeable that there will be more inconsistent decisions being made in the future.

The key weaknesses in these guidelines that need to be rectified are in regard to the clarity of the provisions; the omission of provisions stipulating that context, degree, intensity and realism of presentation are to be taken into account; and the non-prescription of limits of the classification categories.

Clarity of provisions

As discussed in Chapters 4 and 5, the provisions in the Film Censorship Guidelines 1993 (and the subsequent 2010 version) are vague, generalized and can be interpreted in many different ways.[54] Indeed, it might appear that the guidelines are intentionally kept sufficiently 'loose' so that they can be utilized to prohibit films. Shuhaimi Baba, for example, commented that the guidelines 'do not give an idea of what you can or cannot do… there is a lot of vagueness… [The guidelines] should describe and provide instances, like for example, [what amounts to a threat to] national security' while Amir Muhammad found the guidelines to be 'very vague' and thus, 'can be interpreted in many ways'.[55] This defect has led to the making of inconsistent censorship decisions and 'shifting grounds', posing challenges to film practitioners unable to gauge how their films will end up being censored. As with obscenity laws in the United States (where the failure to formulate a clear standard that distinguished protected from unprotected speech chilled speech protected under the First Amendment)[56] vague provisions in film censorship guidelines deter filmmakers from producing content that might in fact be allowed under the censorship system.

It is proposed that the guidelines be revised to make the provisions sufficiently clear so that film practitioners can have greater knowledge of what content will run foul of the censors and will be better able to gauge which category their film falls within. Although vagueness is classically a weakness apparent in obscenity and indecency laws, the Hong Kong and Australian film censorship guidelines appear to be able to satisfactorily overcome the issue of vagueness and inconsistencies in censorship decisions.[57] The degree to which this happens in the law and practice in Hong Kong and Australia for the vast majority of films,[58] and the degree to which it fails to happen in Malaysia,[59] is a key finding of this book. The wider literature on obscenity would suggest that ambiguity is an intractable problem. However, in areas like film censorship, the experiences of Hong Kong and Australia show that meaningful specificity and lack of ambiguity can be achieved.

There is no reason why the Malaysian guidelines could not achieve a similar level of clarity and precision. The Hong Kong guidelines, for example, set out quite clearly what content as well as what degree and intensity of presentation will push a film from one classification category to another. The Australian guidelines also provide demarcation for each classifiable element in every classification category and stipulate quite clearly the content and portrayal that will be refused classification. The advantages of having comparatively clear and well-defined guidelines are apparent in Hong Kong and Australia. An equally clear and precise set of guidelines should be produced in Malaysia. It must be stressed that a person who invests resources in film production or acquisition must have clear guidance in advance, in addition to a line of reliable and consistent censorship decisions made in the past. As noted in Chapter 1, the application of 'detailed and precise standards' (along with other arrangements) would 'meet many of the objections to censorship systems'.[60]

Context; degree, intensity and realism of presentation; and limits of the categories

Malaysian censors are not required to consider a film as a whole when they make a censorship decision. Generally, any shot, scene, dialogue or subtitle that is ruled out by the guidelines *shall* be altered (usually by way of excision) although such content is justifiable within context. Censorship decisions in Malaysia are therefore made based on content severed from the context of the film. This was clear through interviews with film practitioners.[61] The guidelines also do not require censors to take into account the degree, intensity and realism of presentation of a censorship element. Additionally, the limits of each classification category are not prescribed. Thus, what content will push a film into the next classification category is not made clear at all. These 'defects' were absent in the Hong Kong and Australian models where their guidelines require the context of a film to be taken into account; the degree, intensity and realism of presentation of a censorship element would affect the censorship decision; and the limit for each censorship element allowed under every applicable classification is clearly spelt out.[62]

It is proposed that provisions requiring censors to consider film as a whole and to allow contents that are justified in the context of the film (if such content is not gratuitous or of a high degree of impact to the extent that even a restricted category could not accommodate) to be included in the revised guidelines. A film must be viewed and examined as a whole. It should be considered in its entirety because context may justify the content that censors find objectionable. Provisions to the effect that the degree, intensity and realism of presentation of censorship elements shall be taken into account should also be included in the guidelines to play a decisive part in the decision-making process. The limit of each classification category must be expressly set out so that Malaysian film practitioners will have a clear idea (as their Hong Kong and Australian counterparts do) how their films will be classified.[63]

A very high number of prohibited types of film, content and portrayal are found in the Malaysian censorship guidelines. As a result, most of the interviewees felt constrained in their work. Such 'prohibition' impedes film practitioners' creative expression and thus is an affront to the 'free speech and autonomy' principle.[64] It may be argued that Malaysian film practitioners' 'self-determination and fulfilment' are inhibited because they are not free to express their ideas.[65]

It is proposed that the number of prohibited types of film, content and portrayals be reduced and at the same time, the classification approach of the Hong Kong and Australian models be adopted. In the two comparative jurisdictions, most of the censorship elements and content described in their guidelines are not prohibited outright, rather, they are there mainly for the purpose of classifying films into appropriate categories. Only certain types of film are prohibited and, as described in Chapter 4, they are rather limited in number. Such minimal prohibition may not be viewed as an encroachment on free speech rights: as Barendt observed, 'most proponents of strong free speech guarantees concede that its exercise may be restricted in some circumstances'.[66]

Alteration to films and determination of classification category

Although the Malaysian film censorship system has a restricted classification category,[67] films approved for exhibition are still subject to alteration and may not necessarily be released in their entirety even when classified as suitable for viewing by audiences aged 18 and above only. The majority of films released in Malaysia have undergone some form of alteration, most commonly by way of excision. In addition, there is no formal channel for film practitioners to discuss with censors the classification category to be given to their film. These issues are closely related in that most of the interviewees were of the opinion that when a film is classified in a restricted category, it should not be subjected to any alteration. The interviewees were also of the view that there is a need for an opportunity to discuss the classification category to be given to their film with censors because the classification a film receives affects its commercial viability.

Alteration to films and restricted category

Film censors in Malaysia are empowered under section 10(1)(b) of the Film Censorship Act 2002 to require alteration to be made before a film is approved for exhibition. As noted in Chapter 4, the word 'alteration' is defined as to include excision, addition and reconstruction of scenes, dialogues, sound or subtitles.[68]

Although in practice consent from the film practitioner concerned is sought before any alteration is made, this procedure does not in any way provide film practitioners with a choice because if consent to alter is withheld, approval for exhibition will not be granted. Producer Ahmad Puad Onah recounted his experience in dealing with the censors over a film he co-produced and distributed entitled *Kami* (Effendee Mazlan, 2008) where alterations were required to be made to the film by the Board of Censors. The producer noted that he finally had to cave in (after an appeal to the Appeal Committee which affirmed the alterations required by the Board) because 'we had to release the movie [as] we had already invested so much money in it'. As discussed earlier, a non-approval of a local film for exhibition would be a disaster for the film commercially and film practitioners cannot afford to let this happen.

The exercise of the power conferred under section 10(1)(b) could affect the film's artistic integrity (in terms of narration, presentation and aesthetics) and the film's commercial appeal.[69] It also encroaches on the filmmakers' right to freedom of expression which the Federal Constitution guarantees[70] and which the interviewees described, amongst other things, as 'very important'.[71] Additionally, excision (or alteration) could destroy a film's purpose or distort its intended message, for example, by making violence seems less revolting or condemnable, and thus more acceptable, when a violent film (with an anti-violent message) is 'toned down' by the censors. Alteration to films also falls foul of the 'free speech and autonomy' rationale which sees speech or expression as having an inherent value and being an integral aspect of every individual's right to self-determination and fulfilment.[72]

All of the Malaysian interviewees were of the opinion that once a film is classified in a restricted category, the film should not be subjected to any alteration. For example, Amir Muhammad noted that 'what we need now is age classification and then just leave the film alone' while Lorna Tee was of the opinion that 'when an adult pays to go to the cinema, he or she is making a conscious decision as to what to see… so it is not up to the government to claim that "we are doing this to protect the people."' The film censorship authorities could do better by only classifying films and providing consumer advice so that the public can be informed of the content and nature of the film and, as adult audiences, they should have the autonomy to choose what they want to see.

It is proposed that section 10(1)(b) which reads: 'Having viewed a film submitted to it for censorship, the Board may approve the film for exhibition with such alteration as it may require' be repealed and replaced with a new provision that allows film practitioners to elect whether to have their film classified in a restricted category (if the film contains content which warrants such classification) but released in its complete version, or to make the necessary alteration so that the film can be approved under a non-restricted category. What is preferable is an appropriate age classification, not alteration to a film's content which will affect its artistic integrity and commercial appeal. The option as to whether or not to make an alteration should rest squarely with the film practitioner concerned. If a film contains content that pushes it into a restricted category, the film practitioner (who stands to be affected the most by the outcome) may choose whether such content ought to be removed so that the film could obtain a lower classification, or to retain such content but have the film classified in a restricted category. The proposed provision is not meant to advocate the possibility of releasing every film uncut if classified for audiences aged 18 and above. It is considered that there are certain types of content and portrayal that should be prohibited like those proscribed under the Hong Kong and Australian systems, for example, detailed depiction of sexual acts accompanied by offensive perversion (like necrophilia or bestiality); depiction that promotes, incites or instructs in the use of dangerous drugs; and depiction that instructs in, or promotes, matters of crime.[73] Such proscriptions are reconcilable with free speech principles because even strong free speech proponents themselves concede that the exercise of free speech 'may be restricted in some circumstances, for example, when it is likely to lead to imminent violence'.[74]

What is envisaged by this proposal is the possibility of the film practitioner concerned being able to elect whether to excise parts of the film to secure a lower rating, or to release their film in its entirety with a restricted classification category. It is essentially for the benefit of film practitioners to best market their films. Under this proposed provision, censors may suggest excision that could be made if they are of the opinion that this would result in the film being classified differently, which is the usual practice in Hong Kong. It is very rare for Hong Kong censors to require excision to be made to a film before approval for exhibition is granted, although they are empowered to do so. Normally, where a film falls between two classification categories, the censor will leave the option as to whether to excise a certain part of the film (so that it could obtain the lower classification) to the film practitioner concerned.[75] In Australia, classifiers are not empowered to require alteration to be made to a film. However, they may refuse classification if a film contains content which is prohibited by the law or guidelines, though this very rarely occurs to films meant for public commercial release.

Discussion with censors on classification category

Film practitioners in Malaysia have no formal channel through which to discuss with censors the classification category to be given to their film. It is proposed that a provision that enables film practitioners to indicate the classification sought and then discuss it with the censors (if necessary) be included in the Film Censorship Act 2002. This new provision could be modelled along the lines of section 8(2) of the Hong Kong Film Censorship Ordinance and paragraphs 10 and 60 of the Hong Kong Film Censorship Guidelines for Censors.[76] It could be worded as follows:

> When a film is submitted for censorship purposes, the film owner may state the classification category which is sought for the film and censors assigned

> to examine the film should, as far as possible, accommodate the classification sought. If that classification cannot be accommodated, the film practitioner concerned is to be given an opportunity to discuss with the censors as to the minimum alteration that should be made in order for the film to secure the desired classification.

This procedure is important as all of the Malaysian, Hong Kong and Australian interviewees agree that the classification category a film receives affects its commercial viability.[77] For example, if the targeted market of a film is audiences in their early teens but the film is classified in a restricted category, the core audience will be 'cut-off', thereby severely affecting the box office takings of the film.

It is important that an express provision be included in the legislation because if the opportunity to discuss the decision is not guaranteed, it would be up to the censors' discretion as to whether or not they will discuss it with the film practitioner concerned. As one of the interviewees puts it:[78]

> It will be safer [if the opportunity to discuss the decision with censors is guaranteed under the law].... Most of the matters are up to their discretion and that is not good... but if they have to see you and discuss it when you are not happy [with their decision], that will be much better.

Fieldwork conducted in Malaysia revealed that some film practitioners were able to confer with censors while others were denied the opportunity to do so. Therefore, an express statutory provision is needed in order for every film practitioner to have the opportunity to discuss the classification category of their film with censors. This proposal provides equality of treatment between film practitioners and also natural justice – the right to be heard – to each of them.

The provision of reasons for decisions

Although section 10(3) of the Film Censorship Act 2002 provides that when the Board of Censors requires alteration to be made to a film or refuses to approve a film for exhibition the Board must furnish its reasons in writing, fieldwork revealed that the Board very rarely provides film practitioners with reasons for the decisions they make. It was also disclosed that Malaysian film practitioners encounter difficulties in obtaining reasons for censorship decisions from the Board. On the rare occasion where reasons were provided, the reasons were found to be not sensible, irrational and inadequate to address why the decision was taken.[79] Additionally, section 10(3) does not stipulate that the Board shall also provide reasons for classifying a film with a particular category. Neither does it require the Appeal Committee or the Home Minister to provide reasons for the decisions they make under the Act. In contrast, fieldwork conducted in the two comparative jurisdictions revealed that their film practitioners did not encounter any difficulty in obtaining reasons for the decisions made on their films.[80]

It is proposed that section 10(3) be amended, by expanding its scope, to provide that every censorship decision made by the Board, the Committee and the Minister under the Act must be accompanied by written reasons. Failure to do so would give rise to a ground for judicial review.[81] Written reasons from the Board are important to film practitioners who want to appeal against the decision to the Committee while reasons from the Committee or the Minister are important if the decision is to be challenged in court as decisions are challengeable on the reasons provided by the decision-maker. It is pertinent to stress that administrative decisions (particularly those that affect fundamental rights) must always be justified on the basis of sound reasons. However, it may also be suggested here that the reasons required to be provided to film practitioners need not be very elaborate or minutely detailed (therefore the Film Control Division would not be able to argue that they were too understaffed to provide reasons, or that they were not always provided for the sake of efficiency of the censorship process), but they must not be so brief (the most common one-liner being 'this film is not suitable for Malaysian audiences')[82] as to fail to explain and justify the censors' decision.

Appeal against censorship decisions

There are two issues of concern in regard to appeal against film censorship decisions. First, whether members of the public should be given the right to appeal and second, whether film practitioners should have the right to make oral representations during the appeal process.

Appeal by members of the public

Members of the public have no express right under the Film Censorship Act 2002 to appeal against decisions made by the Board of Censors. The law only provides that the owner of a film who is aggrieved by the censorship decision may appeal to the Appeal Committee.[83] Be that as it may, there have been numerous instances where public complaints have caused approved films to be re-examined, oftentimes resulting in the banning of those films.[84] Although these instances are not appeals in the proper sense, it is an issue of concern amongst Malaysian film practitioners,[85] who question whether such 'complaints' should be looked into by the Appeal Committee (or the Home Minister) to the extent of reversing the initial decision. Film director Saw Teong Hin noted: 'the problem is that when a film goes out there, all it needs is for one member of the public to write in and they [the censors] will pull the film back and review it' while James Lee observed that 'it takes very little effort to sabotage a film in Malaysia, you just need one or two people to complain and that's it'. Therefore, there is a real danger of films being easily sabotaged when unsubstantiated complaints are given undue weight by the censors who appear to be 'anxious about public criticisms', which is one of the 'characteristic vices of prior restraints' as noted by Barendt.[86]

It is suggested that once a censorship decision is made, complaints from the public should not automatically lead to a re-examination of the film concerned as in the Hong Kong and Australian models. Only the film practitioners concerned should have the right to appeal because they are the parties who are affected the most by the decision. Film censors should also be confident of their decisions if they were founded on rational reasoning. The foundation of their decisions should not be easily shaken by some disgruntled voices of the public. This, again, underlines the importance of appointing suitable and competent individuals to be the decision-makers as discussed earlier in the chapter. Additionally, there are pitfalls in opening up censorship decisions to appeal by members of the public as it will create more problems for film practitioners. For example, complaints that lead to the pulling back of a film would disrupt its release and any subsequent banning or reclassification of the film with a higher classification category would adversely affect the film's box office receipts. The artistic integrity of the film might also be affected if the re-examination resulted in a decision where alteration was required to be made to the film. If this happened often, individuals, lobby groups, campaigners or politicians would become disproportionately powerful in influencing censorship decisions, thus challenging the overall functioning of the film censorship system.[87]

The right to make oral representations

Film practitioners in Malaysia do not have an express right to make oral representations at the appeal stage of a censorship process. In appealing to the Appeal Committee, a written notice of appeal must be lodged and that notice may contain the applicant-film practitioner's representation.[88] Therefore, film practitioners are limited to making written representations only. This procedure lacks sufficient protections. Drastic decisions, such as the banning of a film or subjecting a film to alteration, must only be made after careful consideration of all relevant arguments and representations from parties affected by the decision. This is in contrast with the situation in Hong Kong where the Film Censorship Ordinance confers film practitioners with an express right to make both written and oral representations.[89] Although the Australian law does not specifically provide the right to make oral representations, the Classification Review Board declared it would hear, and in practice has heard, submissions from the applicant and parties with an interest in the decision.

It is proposed that a provision guaranteeing the right to make oral representations be added to the Film Censorship Act 2002. The provision should, in addition to guaranteeing such a right, also stipulate that the representations to be made may not be restricted (as had happened under the Australian system)[90] so that film practitioners are able to make a comprehensive argument. This provision is important because the omission of a statutory right would deprive some film practitioners of the opportunity to effectively articulate their arguments to justify the content in their film that censors found objectionable. If the right is not expressly guaranteed in the law, it will be up to the discretion of the Committee as to whether to allow the film practitioner concerned to submit orally or otherwise and, even if film practitioners are allowed to do so, the Committee could then go on to determine what can and cannot be submitted before them.[91] This discretion is not desirable as it may be abused to privilege certain parties and exclude others.[92]

All of the Malaysian interviewees were of the opinion that the right to make oral representations should be guaranteed in law so that it can be exercised when the need arises. The interviewees were also of the opinion that the opportunity to have access to the Appeal Committee to present their arguments was vital because it would affect the outcome of an appeal.[93] For example, Shuhaimi Baba who had the opportunity to make oral representations noted that 'I can see such a marked difference when you actually go there and discuss it with the Committee.' It is noteworthy that all of the Hong Kong interviewees were of the opinion that the right to make oral representations was very important as it would have a positive effect on the outcome of an appeal. The Australian interviewees were also of similar opinion.[94]

Availability of judicial review

There are two ouster clauses in the Film Censorship Act 2002, sections 23(2) and 48, which seek to bar judicial review application challenging decisions made under the Act.[95] If these provisions are given their intended effect of shutting out the possibility of review, film practitioners will be left with no avenue to seek legal redress. As noted earlier, it would be disastrous to Malaysian film practitioners whose productions have been banned if that decision could not be challenged in court, because there appears to be no other outlet for them to recoup their investments, as local films are yet to be able to penetrate foreign markets.

It is therefore proposed that sections 23(2) and 48 be repealed as the rationale of having them is doubtful in the first place[96] and second, their retention in the statute is a retrograde step for a country with a written constitution guaranteeing its citizens the right to freedom of expression.[97] As discussed in Chapter 6, although the Malaysian courts have adopted the proposition laid down in the *Anisminic* case on the scope of judicial review in the face of an ouster clause, it is still advisable to have sections 23(2) and 48 repealed because the judicial trend tends to swing like a pendulum. The independence of the judiciary was a concern to the interviewees who were of the opinion that the courts were biased in favour of the executive and hence, the censorship authorities.[98] There is the risk that the courts may revert back to interpreting ouster clauses widely (as the courts did once before in the 1980s) and rule that an applicant-film practitioner is effectively barred from challenging a film censorship decision by way of judicial review.

There are no ouster clauses in the Hong Kong and Australian film censorship laws. All of the Hong Kong and Australian interviewees were of the opinion that the availability of judicial review was very important in a film censorship system, especially one which operated under the purview of the government.[99] Additionally, most of the Hong Kong and Australian interviewees were certain that they would have recourse to judicial review in the (unlikely) event where they were dissatisfied with the censorship decision passed on their film. All of the Malaysian interviewees were also of the opinion that the availability of judicial review was crucial and that they should have the right to challenge film censorship decisions in court. Some interviewees even noted that they would be prepared to pursue a judicial review application if dissatisfied with the decision made on their film.[100] Judicial review should be made available to serve as a 'safety net' to film practitioners in the event censorship authorities take the drastic step of banning their films, as has happened twice before to Amir Muhammad, where his films *Lelaki Komunis Terakhir* and *Apa Khabar Orang Kampung* were banned – the former by the Home Minister and the latter by both the Board of Censors and the Appeal Committee.

As elaborated in Chapter 6, judicial review can provide appropriate, adequate and effective remedies to a successful applicant. In addition, the availability of judicial review, even if not put into action, could also act as a 'threat' to the unaccountability and arbitrariness of the censors. Amir Muhammad's experience could serve as an illustration here as the filmmaker's documentary *Malaysian Gods* (2008) was approved by the Board of Censors but at the same time slapped with an order prohibiting its exhibition. This arbitrary and illegal decision goes to substantiate the importance of having judicial review to seek redress. As Amir Muhammad noted, 'we need it [judicial review], otherwise there will be these little Napoleons!' The availability of judicial review and the shadow that it would cast on the decision-makers would encourage censorship decisions to be made properly, legally and rationally.

The areas of concern in the Hong Kong and Australian film censorship systems for further research

Even though the main focus of the book is to improve the Malaysian film censorship system, the research located five areas of concern in the Hong Kong and Australian models. In the former they are the double standards applied to treatment of coarse language between local and foreign films and the single-censor panel arrangement, while in the latter, they are in regard to restrictions in film advertising, the inability to reference previous classification decisions during appeal and the power to reclassify films. These areas of concern merit further research and will now be discussed in turn.

The Hong Kong film censorship system

Censorship element: language

Although all of the Hong Kong interviewees were satisfied with the clarity of the provisions in the Film Censorship Guidelines for Censors and were generally happy with its application, three interviewees did point out that there appeared to be a double standard when it came to the censorship element of language.[101] One of these interviewees is Lo Chi Leung who questioned 'why are foreign films containing the F words usually classified Category IIB while Hong Kong films with the word '*tiu*' (meaning 'fuck' in Cantonese) end up being classified Category III? I think there is double standard as regards this treatment'.[102] Besides the allegation of such double standard, two Hong Kong interviewees expressed hope that the standard on the use of coarse language, in general, would be further relaxed. For example, Mabel Cheung was of the opinion that censors should be more liberal because 'language is the expression of characters, it makes them real and three dimensional... if you are depicting a triad boss or prostitute, I mean, they speak differently. So I think the standard [of the use of coarse language] had to be readjusted'.

Censorship panels

In Hong Kong, a submitted film is dealt with by a single censor assigned to examine the film by the Film Censorship Authority. In addition to assigning a censor, the Authority may also assign not less than two advisers to the film.[103] Although the censor is obliged to consult the assigned advisers (if any) before making his or her decision, the censor is not bound by the advisers' opinions.[104] Therefore, censorship decisions appear to be made essentially by the censor alone and this could lack the benefit of deliberations between numerous censors which occur in Malaysia and Australia. The arrangement where only one censor is examining a film and subsequently making the censorship decision could pose problems to film practitioners as that particular censor could be a problematic one and, as such, will find many things that are objectionable about the film.

In contrast, under the Malaysian system, film censorship decisions are made by panels and, typically, a panel consisting of three or more members from the Board of Censors will be assigned to examine a film.[105] There was no complaint amongst Malaysian interviewees over the prescribed number of censors to examine a film. In Australia, the Director of the Classification Board is empowered under section 57 of the Classification (Publications, Films and Computer Games) Act 1995 to give directions as to the constitution of the Board (in the form of a panel) to classify a film. Section 58 then provides that five members shall constitute the quorum for a meeting of the Board[106] and matters arising therein will be determined by the majority vote.[107] It is also provided that only members who have seen the film are allowed to vote.[108] This procedure allows decisions to be made after deliberations between members of the panel and there were no concerns raised by the Australian interviewees regarding the panel arrangements, nor about its actual day-to-day practice.

Most of the Hong Kong interviewees were in favour of having more than one censor assigned to examine a film. Patrick Tam, for example, was of the opinion that the more censors assigned to make a censorship decision the better because then there could be 'exchange of ideas where different perspectives or judgments will come through instead of having just one individual censor deciding'. Lo Chi Leung shares the same opinion and added that 'when there is only one censor, [the decision made] could be subjective and biased' while Mabel Cheung suggested that the number of censors 'should be increased to at least three... or let the two advisers have voting power as well so that you will have the majority decision'. However, three interviewees held different views. They were of the opinion that the single-censor panel arrangement contributed to a more efficient and speedy censorship process.[109] Wellington Fung, for example, noted that time was of the essence for

Hong Kong film practitioners as they would normally have scheduled the release dates of their films in advance of their hectic production schedules. Fung added: 'it all comes back to speed and efficiency... time is really important for us. We send the film in [for censorship] and hope it will be done within a few days and get the business going… if it is a collective decision, then more time will be needed'.

The Australian film classification system

Film advertising

There is dissatisfaction amongst Australian interviewees (in particular the distributors and exhibitors) when it comes to film advertising. A film trailer is categorized on the basis of the film's classification, not on the content of the trailer itself. Additionally, a trailer can only be screened together with a film which is of similar or a higher classification category. That is, if the trailer is for a film classified as MA15+, that trailer can only be screened with a film which is classified MA15+ or R18+.[110] It cannot be screened with a G, PG or M rated film even if the trailer itself does not contain content that warrants a restricted classification. This rule has caused marketing and promotional challenges to film practitioners. Joel Pearlman, Managing Director of Roadshow Films, for example, described it as 'constraints' on film advertising, particularly for films classified in restricted categories.

An executive of a major exhibition and distribution company (who prefers to remain anonymous) described this issue as 'the main area of concern in film publicity and marketing'. This interviewee pointed out that the Australian way of classifying trailers differs from most countries where a trailer is classified based on the content of the trailer itself, rather than on the feature film's classification. Peter Campbell, a distributor, characterizes the approach as 'nonsensical' because the trailer itself does not necessarily contain content that is objectionable while Greg Denning of Icon Film Distribution was of the opinion that classifying a trailer based on its content 'would be a fairer system'. Denning added: 'If you have a PG rated family movie that you can cut a G rated trailer for it so that you can run it on other G rated products… I don't see why we should be restricted in doing that'.

In regard to where a trailer can be screened, Campbell and Denning's colleague in the distribution sector James Hewison commented:

> What is limiting the marketing and therefore the visibility of a film before it goes into release is where a trailer can screen. If a film is rated R, then the trailer can only be screened with other films rated R and given that there are virtually no other films rated R released in the cinemas, then obviously the opportunity [of exposure] for that film will be very limited.

Richard J. Frankland whose film *Stone Bros.* (2009) was classified MA15+ said that because of this approach, his film's trailer was not well circulated in cinemas, therefore limiting the film's visibility.

In contrast, film trailers in Malaysia and Hong Kong are approved (or otherwise) based on the trailer's content and there is no rule stipulating that a trailer can only be screened with a film which is of similar or a higher classification category. The Malaysian interviewees have not encountered any problem in obtaining approval for the publicity materials of their films and, hence, no concern was raised. Like their Malaysian counterparts, the Hong Kong interviewees have also not encountered any difficulty in obtaining film advertising approvals.

Appeal against classification decisions

Although film practitioners may make oral representations before the Classification Review Board during an appeal process, they are not allowed to reference other classification decisions. Greg Denning, who finds this procedure to be 'flawed', noted that film practitioners are 'not allowed to reference any previous decisions or any other films that have been classified in the past'. He added:

> If I got a horror film that got up to appeal that I think it should be [classified] MA but is given an R, I would love to be able to go in with a list of previous horror films that contain similar content that were [classified] MA. You are essentially asked to consider every previous decision irrelevant! We are not allowed to specifically reference any of those films. It doesn't really enable you to bring a concise case before the Appeal Board. I guess what that means to a distributor is that there is a high degree of uncertainty when you go to appeal. My frustration comes from not being able to be specific and say "OK, the scene where X character chops off the head of Y character is [classified] R, but here are four other films with the same contents but they received an MA and why are you giving us an R?" …to not be able to reference previous decisions just seems to be unfair.

Reclassification of films

In Australia, a classified film may be reclassified by the Classification Board after a period of two years commencing on the day on which the classification was made.[111] The Board may reclassify a film at the request of the Minister or on its own initiative.[112] If the Board intends to reclassify a film, its director must issue a notice of that intention to invite submissions about the matter.[113]

Since films may be reclassified, it is possible for a Refused Classification (RC) film to be classified (approved for exhibition and distribution) and vice versa.[114] It is also possible for films to be reclassified with a different classification category. Therefore, depending on the classification a film receives, reclassification may work for the benefit or to the detriment of the film practitioners concerned. The opinions of the Australian interviewees were split on this area of concern. It appears that those who viewed reclassification as necessarily leading to a lower classification category were in favour of it[115] while those who thought that reclassification would essentially result in restricting the classification were against it. Interviewees who did not object to reclassification of films were generally of the opinion that 'it makes sense if you classify films based on community standards because community standards change and there are films that were classified R in the past which aren't really R films now'[116] and '[the practice of reclassification of films] is a sound one because community standards do change'.[117] Interviewees who objected, like Peter Campbell, for example, was of the opinion that:

> Once a film is classified, it should stay.[118] It is ludicrous because if it has already been out there, why go back and try to ban it? All they are doing is just forcing a desire for others to buy it offshore… forcing sales away from the local market and making it harder for Australian distributors. They have just got to wake up to the fact that when people want it, they can still get it elsewhere.

Producer Jan Chapman was of the opinion that the Classification Board should only reclassify a film if the application to do so was made by the film practitioner concerned: 'I don't think they [the Board] should be able to do it if they change their minds [about their initial decision]'.

There is no provision in the Malaysian or the Hong Kong laws that provides for reclassification of films. Reclassification is therefore unique to the Australian system.

Conclusion

The proposals for reform to the Malaysian film censorship system that are discussed above involve important amendments to the law, further revision to the guidelines and changes to the censorship process. In light of the comparative experience in Hong Kong and Australia, it appears that the reformed system would be much more capable of promoting the artistic vibrancy and commercial viability of the Malaysian film industry. It will be more transparent and responsive to the needs of film practitioners as well as the audience, and at the same time reconcilable with the basic common law approach to free speech.

A reformed film censorship system would help to address the concerns of Malaysian film practitioners as encapsulated by Aziz M. Osman – 'in every film that I wanted to make, I would always think "would the censorship board allow it to be shown to the public?"'; Ruhani Abdul Rahman – 'we get short of ideas because we cannot do this, we cannot do that'; and U-Wei Haji Saari – 'it is difficult for me to get foreign producers to invest in my work because they know that it can be butchered, it can be censored!'. The proposals would help to create a better environment suitable for filmmakers to develop and the industry to grow, for a greater variety of films to be produced locally and for fostering a more open, critical and cultured film-going public.

Notes

1 Introduction

1 Motion Picture Association of America (MPAA) (2010) *History of the MPAA*, Online. Available: http://www.mpaa.org/about/history (accessed 10 May 2010).
2 British Board of Film Classification (2010) *About the BBFC*, Online. Available: http://www.bbfc.co.uk/about (accessed 10 May 2010).
3 In Australia, for example, a system of co-regulation operates for television broadcasting where broadcasters are responsible for the classification of their programmes in compliance with the standards developed by the Australian Communications and Media Authority under the Broadcasting Services Act 1992. In Malaysia, the broadcasting of films on television is regulated under the Communications and Multimedia Act 1998 while the Broadcasting Ordinance is the law applied in Hong Kong for the same purpose.
4 Interview with Tsai Ming-liang, film director and producer (Kuala Lumpur, 1 February 2009).
5 For example, Tsai's *Vive L'Amour* was awarded the Golden Lion (Best Film) at the Venice Film Festival in 1994, *What time is it there?* garnered the Grand Jury Prize and the Best Director award at the Chicago International Film Festival in 2001, and *The Wayward Cloud* won three awards at the 2004 Berlin International Film Festival including the Berlin Bear for Outstanding Artistic Achievement while Tsai himself was conferred the distinction of *Chevalier des Arts et Lettres* by the French government in 2002.
6 'Freedom of expression' and 'freedom of speech' or 'free speech' are terms capable of conveying different meanings depending on the context, but they were often used interchangeably in the literature. See D. Rolph, M. Vitins and J. Bannister, *Media Law: Cases, Materials and Commentary*, Melbourne: Oxford University Press, 2010, p. 22.
7 L. McNamara, 'Free Speech' in D. Butler and S. Rodrick, *Australian Media Law* (3rd edn), Sydney: Lawbook Co., 2007, p. 3. See also G. Robertson and A. Nicol, *Media Law* (5th edn), London: Sweet & Maxwell, 2007, pp. 1–7.
8 For a concise outline of the development of free speech and the emergence of a free press in England, see L. McNamara, 'Free Speech' in D. Butler and S. Rodrick, *Australian Media Law* (3rd edn), Sydney: Lawbook Co., 2007, pp. 4–6.
9 A. T. Kenyon, 'What Conversation? Free Speech and Defamation Law', *Modern Law Review*, 73(5) 2010, 697–720. Kenyon observed that these rationales are 'generally shared across jurisdictions even though the laws regulating speech in them differ markedly'.
10 D. Rolph, M. Vitins and J. Bannister, *Media Law: Cases, Materials and Commentary*, Melbourne: Oxford University Press, 2010, p. 23.
11 Ibid.
12 See, for example, Justice Holmes' dissenting judgment in *Abrams v United States* 250 US 616 (1919) as well as Justice Brandies' judgment in *Whitney v California* 274 US 357 (1927).
13 G. Robertson and A. Nicol, *Media Law* (5th edn), London: Sweet & Maxwell, 2007, p. 3.

14 D. Rolph, M. Vitins and J. Bannister, *Media Law: Cases, Materials and Commentary*, Melbourne: Oxford University Press, 2010, p. 24. For criticisms on the free speech and truth rationale, see F. Schauer, 'Free Speech in a World of Private Power' in T. Campbell and W. Sadurski (eds), *Freedom of Communication*, Aldershot: Dartmouth, 1994, p. 6, where Schauer asserted that inequalities in the 'marketplace' justify regulation to enhance the public discourse.

15 See A. Meiklejohn, *Political Freedom: The Constitutional Powers of the People*, New York: Harper, 1960 and R. Post, 'Reconciling Theory and Doctrine in First Amendment Jurisprudence' *California Law Review*, 88, 2000, 2353.

16 D. Rolph, M. Vitins and J. Bannister, *Media Law: Cases, Materials and Commentary*, Melbourne: Oxford University Press, 2010, p. 28.

17 E. Barendt, *Freedom of Speech* (2nd edn), New York: Oxford University Press, 2005, p. 13. See also C. E. Baker, *Human Liberty and Freedom of Speech*, New York: Oxford University Press, 1989, where the free speech and autonomy rationale is articulated based on the concept of human liberty.

18 D. Rolph, M. Vitins and J. Bannister, *Media Law: Cases, Materials and Commentary*, Melbourne: Oxford University Press, 2010, p. 28.

19 L. McNamara, 'Free Speech' in D. Butler and S. Rodrick, *Australian Media Law* (3rd edn), Sydney: Lawbook Co., 2007, p. 6.

20 Lord Goff in *Attorney General v Guardian Newspapers Ltd (No 2)* observed that Article 10 of the *ECHR* 'recognizes freedom of expression as a general right, but allows exceptions. In other words, freedom of expression is the rule and regulation of speech is the exception requiring justification': [1990] 1 AC 109. See also D. Watkins, 'Freedom of Artistic Expression and the Human Rights Act 1998', *Art, Antiquity and Law*, 2005, pp. 147–73.

21 Article 19(3) of the *ICCPR*. Qualifications on the right to freedom of expression were also found in Article 10(2) of the *ECHR*. See the cases of *Otto-Preminger Institute v Austria* (1994) 19 EHRR 34 and *Wingrove v United Kingdom* (1997) 24 EHRR 1.

22 E. Barendt, *Freedom of Speech* (2nd edn), New York: Oxford University Press, 2005, p. 7.

23 Cinema has enjoyed the First Amendment protection since the decision of *Burstyn Inc. v Wilson* where Justice Clark in delivering the unanimous judgment of the Supreme Court states that 'the expression by means of motion pictures is included within the free speech and free press guarantee of the First and Fourteenth Amendments': 343 US 495 (1952) 502.

24 See for example, *Schenk v United States* 249 US 47 (1919) and *Brandenburg v Ohio* 395 US 444 (1969). See also S. Fish, 'There's No Such Thing as Free Speech, and It's a Good Thing Too' in H. A. Veeser (ed.), *The Stanley Fish Reader*, Oxford: Blackwell Publishers, 1999, pp. 145 – 64, where it was asserted that free speech is not an absolute and inviolable principle under the First Amendment.

25 In *Roth v United States* and *Alberts v California* 354 US 476 (1957), the Supreme Court held that obscenity fell outside of the First Amendment protection because it was 'utterly without redeeming social importance'. See also the earlier case of *Chaplinsky v New Hampshire* 315 US 568 (1942) where Justice Murphy, in delivering the unanimous judgment of the Supreme Court, observed that: 'It is well understood that the right to free speech is not absolute at all times and under all circumstances. There are certain well-defined and narrowly limited classes of speech, the prevention and punishment of which have never been thought to raise any constitutional problem. These include the lewd and obscene, the profane, the libellous, and the insulting or 'fighting' words – those which by their very utterance inflict injury or tend to incite an immediate breach of the peace. It has been well observed that such utterances are no essential part of any exposition of ideas, and are of such slight social value as a step to truth that any benefit that may be derived from them is clearly outweighed by the social interest in order and morality' (1942, 571–2).

26 See also S. M. Easton, *The Problem of Pornography: Regulation and the Right to Free Speech*, London: Routledge, 1994, pp. 122–44 and E. Barendt, *Freedom of Speech* (2nd edn), New York: Oxford University Press, 2005, pp. 355 – 63.

27 For example, the disputes between liberals (who generally argued that the consumption of pornography falls within 'self-regarding' or 'private sphere' and thus, the individual adult has the right and 'moral independence' to decide) and some feminists, most notably Catharine MacKinnon and Andrea Dworkin (who, in general, argued against pornography in relation to humiliation and harm against woman). See R. M. Dworkin, 'Is there a Right to Pornography?' *Oxford Journal of Legal Studies*, 1, 1981, 177 where the right to consume pornography is defended on the basis of freedom to moral independence; C. MacKinnon, 'Pornography, Civil Rights and Speech', *Harvard Civil Rights – Civil Liberties Law Review*, 20, 1985, 1; A. Dworkin, 'Against the Male Flood: Censorship, Pornography and Equality' *Harvard Women's Law Journal*, 8, 1985, 1; and F. Schauer, *The Law of Obscenity*, Washington: Bureau of National Affairs, 1976.

28 See *Nationwide News Pty Ltd v Wills* (1992) 177 CLR 1 and *Australian Capital Television v Commonwealth* (1992) 177 CLR 106. See also *Lange v Australian Broadcasting Corporation* (1997) 189 CLR 520, 559 and *Coleman v Power* [2004] 220 CLR 1, 48–9.

29 See G. Robertson and A. Nicol, *Media Law* (5th edn), London: Sweet & Maxwell, 2007, pp. 194–7 and S. M. Easton, *The Problem of Pornography: Regulation and the Right to Free Speech*, London: Routledge, 1994, pp. 124–9. For the historical origins of American obscenity law, see generally F. Schauer, *The Law of Obscenity*, Washington: Bureau of National Affairs, 1976.

30 S. Coldham, 'Reports of the Committee on Obscenity and Film Censorship', *Modern Law Review*, 43, 1980, pp. 306–7.

31 'Obscenity' (or 'obscene') rather than 'pornography' is the usual term used in legislation. The former is wider in scope as it covers not only sexually explicit materials (as the latter does) but extends to materials encouraging violence and drug abuse. Robertson and Nicol observed that the obscenity laws and the arrangements for film censorship in England are directed against explicit sexual materials but the tests applied are wide enough to include materials that advocate violence or encourage the use of dangerous drugs. For example, 'Video-nasties' that combine pornography with strong rape or terrifying scenes have been successfully prosecuted in England under obscenity laws. See G. Robertson and A. Nicol, *Media Law* (5th edn), London: Sweet & Maxwell, 2007, p. 192.

32 See E. Barendt, *Freedom of Speech* (2nd edn), New York: Oxford University Press, 2005; G. Robertson and A. Nicol, *Media Law* (5th edn), London: Sweet & Maxwell, 2007; F. Schauer, *The Law of Obscenity*, Washington: Bureau of National Affairs, 1976; D. Butler and S. Rodrick, *Australian Media Law* (3rd edn), Sydney: Lawbook Co, 2007; N. Strossen, 'A Feminist Critique of "The" Feminist Critique of Pornography', *Virginia Law Review*, 79, 1993, 1103; and H. White, *Anatomy of Censorship: Why the Censors Have it Wrong*, Lanham: University Press of America, 1997.

33 G. Robertson and A. Nicol, *Media Law* (5th edn), London: Sweet & Maxwell, 2007, p. 191.

34 Ibid. p. 221. See also *Knuller (Publishing, Printing and Promotions) Ltd v Director of Public Prosecutions* [1973] AC 435.

35 N. Strossen, 'A Feminist Critique of "The" Feminist Critique of Pornography', *Virginia Law Review*, 79, 1993, 1103.

36 F. Schauer, *The Law of Obscenity*, Washington: Bureau of National Affairs, 1976, p. 109.

37 H. White, *Anatomy of Censorship: Why the Censors Have it Wrong*, Lanham: University Press of America, 1997, p. 11. See also S. Bronitt and B. McSherry, *Principles of Criminal Law* (2nd edn), Sydney: Lawbook Co., 2005, pp. 616–7.

38 In this case, the Supreme Court defined 'obscenity' as 'material which deals with sex in a manner appealing to prurient interest': *Roth v United States* 354 US 476 (1957) 487, per Brennan, J.

39 Ibid. 491.

40 *Paris Adult Theatre v Slaton* 413 US 49 (1973).

41 Ibid. 83.

42 *Ginzberg v United States* 383 US 463 (1966) 480.
43 *Jacobellis v Ohio* 378 US 184 (1964) 197. See Chief Justice Warren's judgment at page 199 where it was noted that: 'although the Federal Government and virtually every state has had laws proscribing obscenity since the Union was formed, and although this Court has recently decided that obscenity is not within the protection of the First Amendment, neither courts or legislatures have been able to evolve a truly satisfactory definition of obscenity'.
44 See paragraphs 9.20 and 9.21 of the *Report of the Committee on Obscenity and Film Censorship* (Cmnd 7772), London: HMSO, 1979.
45 P. Tackaberry and J. Hewitt, 'Towards a New Definition of Obscenity for Canada: Did *Butler* really do it?', *Entertainment Law Review*, 4(5), 1993, 152–5. In *R v Butler* [1992] 89 DLR (4th) 449, the Supreme Court of Canada held the obscenity provisions of the Canadian Criminal Code constitutional and formulated a new definition of obscenity by emphasizing the concept of 'harm'. Although the court conceded that a direct link between obscenity and harm to society may be difficult, if not impossible, to establish, it focused on the harmful effects obscene contents may have on society as the justification to proscribe such materials.
46 G. J. Hawkins, 'The Problem of Pornography', *Sydney Law Review*, 5(2), 1966, 221–3. See also H. Whitmore, 'Obscenity in Literature: Crime or Free Speech', *Sydney Law Review*, 4(2), 1963, 179.
47 See T. A. O. Endicott, 'The Impossibility of the Rule of Law', *Oxford Journal of Legal Studies*, 19, 1999, 1 where it was noted that 'vagueness is ineliminable from a legal system' and that 'legal systems necessarily have vague laws'.
48 See A. Ashworth, *Principles of Criminal Law* (6th edn), Oxford: Oxford University Press, 2009, pp. 63–6.
49 *Jacobellis v Ohio* 378 US 184 (1964).
50 Ibid. 199. Emphasis added.
51 For an exposition of the indecency test, see G. Robertson and A. Nicol, *Media Law* (5th edn), London: Sweet & Maxwell, 2007, pp. 239–41 and *R v Stanley* [1965] 2 QB 327.
52 *R v Hicklin* (1868) LR 3 QB 360, 371.
53 In general, there are three principal grounds on which pornography is proscribed: first, the mass availability of pornographic material might affect moral attitudes of society; second, pornography causes harm to society; and third, pornography offends people. See E. Barendt, *Freedom of Speech* (2nd edn), New York: Oxford University Press, 2005, pp. 370–81 for a discussion of the specific harms (sexual crimes, harm to children and harm to women) said to be caused by pornography.
54 D. Butler and S. Rodrick, *Australian Media Law* (3rd edn), Sydney: Lawbook Co., 2007, p. 365.
55 Under this test, the defence of literary or artistic merit is not available to the defendant-publisher.
56 S. M. Easton, *The Problem of Pornography: Regulation and the Right to Free Speech*, London: Routledge, 1994, p. 125.
57 G. Robertson and A. Nicol, *Media Law* (5th edn), London: Sweet & Maxwell, 2007, p. 201. In *Director of Public Prosecutions v Whyte* [1972] 3 All ER 12, the House of Lords held that the magistrate or jury have to first ascertain who are the likely audience before considering whether the article in question is likely to deprave or corrupt them.
58 *R v Calder & Boyars Ltd* [1969] 1 QB 151.
59 E. Barendt, *Freedom of Speech* (2nd edn), New York: Oxford University Press, 2005, pp. 370–1.
60 Section 4 of the Obscene Publications Act in part, reads: 'A person shall not be convicted of an offence … if it is proved that publication of the article in question is justified as being for the public good on the grounds that it is in the interest of science, literature, art or learning, or of other objects of general concern'.
61 S. M. Easton, *The Problem of Pornography: Regulation and the Right to Free Speech*, London: Routledge, 1994, p. 125.

62 E. Barendt, *Freedom of Speech* (2nd edn), New York: Oxford University Press, 2005, p. 382.
63 Ibid. 383.
64 Ibid. 382.
65 The test approved earlier by the Supreme Court for identifying obscenity was 'whether to the average person, applying contemporary community standards, the dominant theme of the material taken as a whole appeals to prurient interest'. See *Roth v United States* 354 US 476 (1957) 489.
66 *Miller v California* 413 US 15 (1973) 24. Thus, for a speech to be 'obscene' it has to satisfy the 'tripartite test' set out in this case. See B. Harris, 'Censorship: A Comparative Approach Offering a New Theoretical Basis for Classification in Australia', *Canberra Law Review*, 8, 2005, 25, 27.
67 F. Schauer, 'The Ontology of Censorship' in R. C. Post (ed.), *Censorship and Silencing*, Los Angeles: Getty Research Institute for the History of Art and the Humanities, 1998, p. 162.
68 Ibid. 163.
69 See E. Barendt, *Freedom of Speech* (2nd edn), New York: Oxford University Press, 2005, p. 122.
70 Barendt argued that 'the executive is not only determining conclusively whether an individual is free to speak, but it is also in effect deciding that that person is guilty of an offence if he publishes without the required permit. Under the constitutional principles of the separation of powers, these decisions should be taken by the courts'. See E. Barendt, *Freedom of Speech* (2nd edn), New York: Oxford University Press, 2005, p. 122. See also M. I. Meyerson, 'The Neglected History of the Prior Restraint Doctrine: Rediscovering the Link between the First Amendment and Separations of Powers', *Indiana Law Review*, 34, 2001, 295.
71 E. Barendt, *Freedom of Speech* (2nd edn), New York: Oxford University Press, 2005, p. 124

2 The film industries in Malaysia, Hong Kong and Australia in their socio-legal context

1 It is extremely difficult, if not impossible, to satisfactorily compress the long and illustrious histories of the film industries into a mere few pages. Hence, for more detailed expositions of these industries and the films they produced, reference may be made to the following publications: H. A. Khan, *The Malay Cinema*, Selangor: National University of Malaysia Press, 1997 and W. van der Haide, *Malaysian Cinema, Asian Film: Border Crossings and National Cultures*, Amsterdam: Amsterdam University Press, 2002 for the Malaysian film industry; S. Teo, *Hong Kong Cinema: The Extra Dimension*, London: BFI Publishing, 1997, D. Bordwell, *Planet Hong Kong: Popular Cinema and the Art of Entertainment*, Massachusetts: Harvard University Press, 2000 and K. Law and F. Bren, *Hong Kong Cinema: A Cross-Cultural View*, Lanham: Scarecrow Press, 2004 for the Hong Kong film industry; and D. Collins, *Hollywood Down Under: Australians at the Movies – 1896 to the Present Day*, North Ryde: Angus & Robertson, 1987; S. Dermody and E. Jacka, *The Screening of Australia: Anatomy of a Film Industry*, Sydney: Currency Press, 1987, S. Murray (ed.) *Australian Cinema*, Sydney: Allen & Unwin, 1994; and T. O'Regan, *Australian National Cinema*, London: Routledge, 1996 for the Australian film industry.
2 The country is nominally headed by a King (known as the *Yang di-Pertuan Agong*) who, in the exercise of most of his constitutional functions, acts in accordance with the advice of the Cabinet.
3 Great Britain began to establish colonies and protectorates in the peninsular from the late eighteenth century.
4 Singapore subsequently seceded from the Federation in 1965 and became an independent city-state.
5 For a concise history of Malaysia, see B. W. Andaya and L. Andaya, *A History of Malaysia* (2nd edn), London: Macmillan, 2001 and C. M. Turnbull, *A History of Malaysia, Singapore and Brunei*, Sydney: Allen & Unwin, 1989.

6 See A. Harding, *Law, Government and the Constitution in Malaysia*, Selangor, Malaysia: Lexis Nexis, 1996.
7 It is worth noting that 'censorship' falls within federal legislative powers. See item 22 of the Ninth Schedule to the Federal Constitution.
8 United Nations Human Rights Council, Government of Malaysia (2009) *National Report Submitted in Accordance with Paragraph 15(A) of the Annex to Human Rights Council Resolution 5/1: Malaysia*, Online. Available: http://lib.ohchr.org/HRBodies/UPR/Documents/Session4/MY/AHRC_WG6_4_MYS_1_E. PDF (accessed 29 October 2010).
9 See articles 5 to 13 of the Federal Constitution.
10 For detailed discussion of the Malaysian legal system, see M. A. Wu, *The Malaysian Legal System* (3rd edn), Selangor: Longman Malaysia, 2005 and W. A. Hamzah, *Malaysian Legal System*, Selangor: Oxford Fajar, 2009.
11 These include marriage and divorce, inheritance, custody of children and apostasy.
12 Article 122B of the Federal Constitution.
13 For further discussion of the jurisdiction of these Islamic courts, see F. S. Shuaib, *Powers and Jurisdiction of Syariah Courts in Malaysia*, Kuala Lumpur: Lexis Nexis, 2003.
14 Malaysia, Commission of Enquiry on the Video Clip Recording of Images of a Person Purported to be an Advocate and Solicitor Speaking on the Telephone on matters regarding the Appointment of Judges, *Final Report* (2008), p. 175.
15 See Kuala Lumpur Bar Committee, 'The Administration of Justice in Malaysia' (2001) 2 *INSAF: The Journal of the Malaysian Bar*, pp. 39–63.
16 Economic Planning Unit, Prime Minister's Department Malaysia (2012) *Population by Sex, Ethnic Group and Age*, Online. Available: http://www.epu.gov.my/html/themes/epu/images/ common/eco.stat/1.2.5pdf (accessed 12 January 2012).
17 See for example article 89 (reservation of land for Malays) and article 153 (reservation of quota in respect of civil service, permit, and etcetera for Malays and natives of Sabah and Sarawak) of the Federal Constitution. The National Economic Policy (NEP) was launched following the 13 May 1969 riot to increase the *bumiputra*'s share/equity in the country's economy (to provide them with preferential treatment in education, employment and business, amongst others) and to eradicate poverty. See A. Whiting, 'Desecularising Malaysian Law?' in Penelope Nicholson and Sarah Biddulph (eds), *Examining Practice, Interrogating Theory: Comparative Legal Studies in Asia*, Leiden: Martinus Nijhoff Publishers, 2008, p. 224 and C. C. Gan, 'Administrative Law and Judicialized Governance in Malaysia' in T. Ginsburg and A. H. Y. Chen (eds), *Administrative Law and Governance in Asia: Comparative Perspectives*, London: Routledge, 2009, p. 257.
18 Central Intelligence Agency, United States of America (2012) *The World Factbook: Malaysia*, Online. Available: http://www.cia.gov/library/publications/the-world-factbook/geos/my.html (accessed 1 June 2012).
19 Other religions and faiths made up the remaining 5.0 per cent: Central Intelligence Agency, United States of America (2010) *The World Factbook: Malaysia*, Online. Available: http://www.cia.gov/library/publications/the-world-factbook/geos/my.html (accessed 27 October 2010).
20 See the landmark Supreme Court case of *Che Omar Che Soh v Public Prosecutor* [1988] 2 MLJ 55.
21 The Pan-Malaysian Islamic Party has occasionally complained and called for film censorship decisions to be re-evaluated. A recent example is the complaint and allegation by the party that *Hantu Bonceng* (Ahmad Idham, 2011), a film approved for exhibition by the Board of Censors without cuts, contained elements that insulted Islam and the Prophet Mohammed.
22 Article 152 of the Federal Constitution. See also the National Language Act 1963 (Act 32).
23 Central Intelligence Agency, United States of America (2010) *The World Factbook: Malaysia*, Online. Available: http://www.cia.gov/library/publications/the-world-factbook/geos/my.html (accessed 27 October 2010).

24 Central Intelligence Agency, United States of America (2012) *The World Factbook: Malaysia*, Online. Available: http://www.cia.gov/library/publications/the-world-factbook/geos/my.html (accessed 1 June 2012).
25 Hamzah Hussin as quoted by W. van der Heide, *Malaysian Cinema, Asian Film: Border Crossings and National Cultures*, Amsterdam: Amsterdam University Press, 2002, p. 105.
26 Ibid. p.118.
27 The same company that played a major role in Hong Kong as discussed in the overview of the Hong Kong film industry.
28 B. van der Heide, 'Malaysian Movies: The Shaw Brothers Meet the Pandava Brothers in the Land Below the Wind' in B. Bennett, J. Doyle and S. Nandan (eds), *Crossing Cultures: Essays on Literature and Culture of the Asia-Pacific*, London: Skoob Books, 1996, p. 101.
29 See H. Muthalib and T. C. Wong, 'Malaysia: Gentle Winds of Change' in A. Vasudev, L. Padgaonkar and R. Doraisamy (eds), *Being and Becoming: The Cinemas of Asia*, 2002, pp. 301–28.
30 G. C. Khoo, *Reclaiming Adat: Contemporary Malaysian Film and Literature*, Vancouver: UBC Press, 2006, p. 90.
31 B. van der Heide, 'Malaysian Movies: The Shaw Brothers Meet the Pandava Brothers in the Land Below the Wind' in B. Bennett, J. Doyle and S. Nandan (eds), *Crossing Cultures: Essays on Literature and Culture of the Asia-Pacific*, London: Skoob Books, 1996, p. 102.
32 Shaw Brothers/MFP was founded by brothers Run Run Shaw and Runme Shaw while Cathay-Keris was formed by the partnership of Loke Wan Tho and Ho Ah Loke.
33 See generally, H. A. Khan, *The Malay Cinema*, Selangor: National University of Malaysia Press, 1997 and G. C. Khoo, *Reclaiming Adat: Contemporary Malaysian Film and Literature*, Vancouver: UBC Press, 2006.
34 W. van der Heide, *Malaysian Cinema, Asian Film: Border Crossings and National Cultures*, Amsterdam: Amsterdam University Press, 2002, pp. 134–6.
35 M. Ahmad, 'Colonial Policies, the Marketplace and the Malaysian Film Industry' in L. Feilberg (ed.), *Film Industries in Asia and Europe: A Platform for Experiences Sharing*, Singapore: Asia-Europe Foundation, 2005, p. 17.
36 W. van der Heide, *Malaysian Cinema, Asian Film: Border Crossings and National Cultures*, Amsterdam: Amsterdam University Press, 2002, p. 117.
37 Ibid.
38 H. Muthalib and T. C. Wong, 'Malaysia: Gentle Winds of Change' in A. Vasudev, L. Padgaonkar and R. Doraisamy (eds), *Being and Becoming: The Cinemas of Asia*, 2002, p. 306.
39 B. van der Heide, 'Malaysian Movies: The Shaw Brothers Meet the Pandava Brothers in the Land Below the Wind' in B. Bennett, J. Doyle and S. Nandan (eds), *Crossing Cultures: Essays on Literature and Culture of the Asia-Pacific*, London: Skoob Books, 1996, p. 107.
40 M. Ahmad, 'Colonial Policies, the Marketplace and the Malaysian Film Industry' in L. Feilberg (ed.), *Film Industries in Asia and Europe: A Platform for Experiences Sharing*, Singapore: Asia-Europe Foundation, 2005, p. 19.
41 W. van der Heide, *Malaysian Cinema, Asian Film: Border Crossings and National Cultures*, Amsterdam: Amsterdam University Press, 2002, p. 117.
42 The mushrooming of these production companies is attributable to the New Economic Policy introduced in 1971 to implement affirmative action for the benefit of the Malay-Bumiputeras.
43 H. Muthalib and T. C. Wong, 'Malaysia: Gentle Winds of Change' in A. Vasudev, L. Padgaonkar and R. Doraisamy (eds), *Being and Becoming: The Cinemas of Asia*, 2002, p. 314.
44 Ibid., pp. 301–28.

45 For example, *Sepet* won the Best Asian Film award at the Tokyo International Film Festival in 2005 while *Mukhsin* won the Crystal Bear at the Berlin International Film Festival in 2007.

46 See W. van der Heide, *Malaysian Cinema, Asian Film: Border Crossings and National Cultures*, Amsterdam: Amsterdam University Press, 2002, p. 117.

47 Section 22 of the National Film Development Corporation of Malaysia Act 1981.

48 Compiled and adapted from National Film Development Corporation of Malaysia (2011) *Message from the Director General*, Online. Available: http://finas.gov.my/index.php?mod=finas&sub=perutusan (accessed 21 March 2011) and National Film Development Corporation of Malaysia (2011) *Industry: Malaysian Film Industry Statistics*, Online. Available: http://finas.gov.my/index.php?mod=industry&sub= filemmalaysia (accessed 21 March 2011).

49 National Film Development Corporation of Malaysia (2011) *List of Cinemas*, Online. Available: http://finas.gov.my/index.php?mod=wajibtayang&sub=pawagam (accessed 21 March 2011).

50 N. Balaraman, 'The Legislative System to Support Cinema: Instruments and Policies' in L. Feilberg (ed.), *Film Industries in Asia and Europe: A Platform for Experiences Sharing*, Singapore: Asia-Europe Foundation, 2005, p. 13.

51 Adapted from National Film Development Corporation of Malaysia (2011) *Industry: Malaysian Film Industry Statistics*, Online. Available: http://finas.gov.my/index.php?mod=industry&sub=filemmalaysia (accessed 21 March 2011).

52 G. C. Khoo, *Reclaiming Adat: Contemporary Malaysian Film and Literature*, Vancouver: UBC Press, 2006, p. 91.

53 The term 'film industry' was defined in section 2 of the 1981 Act as to include 'the activities of film production, distribution and exhibition carried out in Malaysia'.

54 N. Balaraman, 'The Legislative System to Support Cinema: Instruments and Policies' in L. Feilberg (ed.), *Film Industries in Asia and Europe: A Platform for Experiences Sharing*, Singapore: Asia-Europe Foundation, 2005, p. 13.

55 FINAS is, at present, operating under the purview of the Ministry of Information, Communication and Culture, while film censorship is placed under the control of the Home Ministry.

56 Emphasis added. See section 6(1) of the National Film Development Corporation of Malaysia Act 1981. Section 2 defined 'film production' as to include 'all activities related to the production or processing of films, or the recording or duplicating of video tapes, for viewing by the public or any class of the public'; 'film distribution' as to include 'the renting, hiring and loaning of films produced abroad and the distribution of films produced locally'; and 'film exhibition' as 'the screening of films for viewing by the public or any class of the public'.

57 National Film Development Corporation of Malaysia (2009) *Wajib Tayang: Compulsory Screening Scheme*, Online. Available: http://finas.gov.my.index.php?mod=wajibtayang (accessed 28 April 2009).

58 Ibid.

59 Ibid.

60 National Film Development Corporation of Malaysia (2009) *Funding: Feature Film Loan Scheme*, Online. Available: http://finas.gov.my/index.php?mod=dana&sub=pinjaman (accessed 28 April 2009).

61 National Film Development Corporation of Malaysia (2011) *Message from the Director General*, Online. Available: http://finas.gov.my/index.php?mod=finas&sub=perutusan (accessed 21 March 2011).

62 The British formally occupied the territories (of what is today the HKSAR) through a series of treaties entered into with China as results of the Opium Wars. For a concise history of Hong Kong, see Information Services Department of the Hong Kong Special Administrative Region, *Hong Kong Yearbook 2009*, Hong Kong: Information Services Department of the HKSAR, 2010, pp. 418–28; S. Tsang, *A Modern History of Hong*

Kong, New York: I.B. Tauris, 2004; and C. Courtauld and M. Holdsworth, *The Hong Kong Story*, Hong Kong: Oxford University Press, 1997.

63 United Nations Human Rights Council, People's Republic of China (2009) *National Report Submitted in Accordance with Paragraph 15(A) of the Annex to Human Rights Council Resolution 5/1: China*, Online. Available: http://lib.ohchr.org/HRBodies/UPR/Documents/Session4/CN/AHRCWG64CHN1E.pdf (accessed 29 October 2010).

The transfer of sovereignty in 1997 officially ended 156 years of British rule in Hong Kong.

64 Information Services Department of the Hong Kong Special Administrative Region, *Hong Kong Yearbook 2009*, Hong Kong: Information Services Department of the HKSAR, 2010, p. 1.

65 Government of the Hong Kong Special Administrative Region (2010) *Government Structure*, Online. Available: http://www.gov.hk/en/about/govdirectory/govstructure.htm (accessed 27 October 2010). The HKSAR government has the autonomy over film censorship and the PRC will not interfere or control the territory's film industry.

66 See A. H. Chen, 'The Concept of "One Country, Two Systems" and Its Application to Hong Kong' in C. S. Hsu (ed.), *Understanding China's Legal System*, New York: New York University Press, 2003, pp. 353–73.

67 See Chapter III of the Basic Law of the Hong Kong Special Administrative Region.

68 Government of the Hong Kong Special Administrative Region (2010) *Government Structure*, Online. Available: http://www.gov.hk/en/about/govdirectory/govstructure.htm (accessed 27 October 2010).

69 See Information Services Department of the Hong Kong Special Administrative Region, *Hong Kong Yearbook 2009*, Hong Kong: Information Services Department of the HKSAR, 2010, p. 3.

70 Information Services Department of the Hong Kong Special Administrative Region, *Hong Kong Yearbook 2009*, Hong Kong: Information Services Department of the HKSAR, 2010, p. 27.

71 Department of Justice of the Hong Kong Special Administrative Region (2009) *The Legal System in Hong Kong*, Online. Available: http://www.doj.gov.hk/eng/legal/index.htm (accessed 27 October 2010). For further discussion of the Hong Kong legal system, see P. Wesley-Smith, *An Introduction to the Hong Kong Legal System* (3rd edn), Hong Kong: Oxford University Press, 1998. Reference may also be made to C. Shum, *General Principles of Hong Kong Law*, Hong Kong: Longman, 1992, in particular the first chapter entitled 'The Nature and Sources of Hong Kong Law'. The laws of the PRC do not apply in HKSAR except those relating to defence and foreign affairs that are listed in Annex III to the Basic Law of the Hong Kong Special Administrative Region.

72 Government of the Hong Kong Special Administrative Region (2010) *Government Structure*, Online. Available: http://www.gov.hk/en/about/govdirectory/govstructure.htm (accessed 27 October 2010).

73 Department of Justice of the Hong Kong Special Administrative Region (2009) *The Legal System in Hong Kong*, Online. Available: http://www.doj.gov.hk/eng/legal/index.htm (accessed 27 October 2010).

74 Central Intelligence Agency, United States of America (2010) *The World Factbook: Hong Kong*, Online. Available: http://www.cia.gov/library/publications/the-world-factbook/geos/hk.html (accessed 1 June 2012).

75 Asian Development Bank, *Key Indicators for Asia and the Pacific 2010* (41st edn), Manilla: Asian Development Bank, 2010, p. 132.

76 Census and Statistics Department, Government of the Hong Kong Special Administrative Region, (2007) *2006 By-census*, Online. Available: http://www.bycensus2006.gov.hk/en/data/data3/ statisticaltables/index.htm#F1 (accessed 3 November 2010).

77 US Department of State (2010) *Diplomacy in Action: International Religious Freedom Report 2010 (China)*, Online. Available: http://www.state.gov/drl/rls/irf/2010/148863.htm#hong-kong (accessed 19 September 2011).

78 Article 32 of the Basic Law of the Hong Kong Special Administrative Region.

79 Information Services Department of the Hong Kong Special Administrative Region, *Hong Kong Yearbook 2009*, Hong Kong: Information Services Department of the HKSAR, 2010, p. 22.

80 Department of Justice of the Hong Kong Special Administrative Region (2009) *The Legal System in Hong Kong*, Online. Available: http://www.doj.gov.hk/eng/legal/index.htm (accessed 27 October 2010).

81 Census and Statistics Department, Government of the Hong Kong Special Administrative Region (2010) *The Four Key Industries in the Hong Kong Economy*, Online. Available: http://www.censtatd.gov.hk/hongkongstatistics/four_key_industries/index.jsp (accessed 3 November 2010).

82 Central Intelligence Agency, United States of America (2012) *The World Factbook: Hong Kong*, Online. Available: http://www.cia.gov/library/publications/the-world-factbook/geos/hk.html (accessed 1 June 2012).

83 Ibid.

84 K. Law and F. Bren, *Hong Kong Cinema: A Cross-Cultural View*, Lanham: Scarecrow Press, 2004, pp. 6 and 19.

85 The origins of Hong Kong film production are still being debated among film historians today.

86 F. Dannen and B. Long, *Hong Kong Babylon: An Insider's Guide to the Hollywood of the East*, London: Faber and Faber, 1997, p. 9 and M. Scott, '100 Years of Hong Kong Cinema', *Screen International*, Hong Kong, 20 March 2009, p. 14.

87 E. Yau, 'China' in W. Luhr (ed.), *World Cinema Since 1945*, New York: Ungar, 1987, p. 132.

88 M. Scott, '100 Years of Hong Kong Cinema', *Screen International*, Hong Kong, 20 March 2009, p. 15.

89 K. Law and F. Bren, *Hong Kong Cinema: A Cross-Cultural View*, Lanham: Scarecrow Press, 2004, p. xvi.

90 Ibid. p. xvii.

91 E. Yau, 'China' in W. Luhr (ed.), *World Cinema Since 1945*, New York: Ungar, 1987, p. 132.

92 Ibid. p. 133.

93 Ibid.

94 K. Law and F. Bren, *Hong Kong Cinema: A Cross-Cultural View*, Lanham: Scarecrow Press, 2004, p. 281.

95 E. Yau, 'China' in W. Luhr (ed.), *World Cinema Since 1945*, New York: Ungar, 1987, p. 133.

96 M. Curtin, *Playing to the World's Biggest Audience: The Globalization of Chinese Films and TV*, Berkeley: University of California Press, 2007, pp. 24 and 60. This set-up is often referred to as the 'vertical integration system' or the 'fully integrated operations' of production, distribution and exhibition of films.

97 Ibid. p. 270.

98 F. Dannen and B. Long, *Hong Kong Babylon: An Insider's Guide to the Hollywood of the East*, London: Faber and Faber, 1997, p. 12.

99 S. Chaudhuri, *Contemporary World Cinema: Europe, the Middle East, East Asia and South Asia*, Edinburgh: Edinburgh University Press, 2005, p. 120.

100 For example, Wong Kar Wai won the Best Director Award (for *Happy Together*) at the Festival de Cannes in 1997, Tsui Hark won the Future Film Digital Award (for *Time and Tide*) at the Venice Film Festival in 2000 and Ann Hui won the Jury Grand Prize (for *Summer Snow*) at the Berlin International Film Festival in 1995.

101 M. Curtin, *Playing to the World's Biggest Audience: The Globalization of Chinese Films and TV*, Berkeley: University of California Press, 2007, p. 65.

102 Ibid. p. 62.

103 F. Dannen and B. Long, *Hong Kong Babylon: An Insider's Guide to the Hollywood of the East*, London: Faber and Faber, 1997, p. 8.

104 See, for example, M. Curtin, *Playing to the World's Biggest Audience: The Globalization of Chinese Films and TV*, Berkeley: University of California Press, 2007, F. Dannen and B. Long, *Hong Kong Babylon: An Insider's Guide to the Hollywood of the East*, London: Faber and Faber, 1997, and K. Law and F. Bren, *Hong Kong Cinema: A Cross-Cultural View*, Lanham: Scarecrow Press, 2004.

105 M. Curtin, *Playing to the World's Biggest Audience: The Globalization of Chinese Films and TV*, Berkeley: University of California Press, 2007, pp. 48–71.

106 Ibid. pp. 68–84.

107 Ibid. pp. 74–8.

108 Ibid. p. 78. See also S. Chaudhuri, *Contemporary World Cinema: Europe, the Middle East, East Asia and South Asia*, Edinburgh: Edinburgh University Press, 2005, p. 115.

109 See M. Curtin, *Playing to the World's Biggest Audience: The Globalization of Chinese Films and TV*, Berkeley: University of California Press, 2007, p. 83 for a discussion of the effects of video piracy on film distribution.

110 K. Law and F. Bren, *Hong Kong Cinema: A Cross-Cultural View*, Lanham: Scarecrow Press, 2004, p. xviii.

111 See S. Chaudhuri, *Contemporary World Cinema: Europe, the Middle East, East Asia and South Asia*, Edinburgh: Edinburgh University Press, 2005, p. 129.

112 M. Curtin, *Playing to the World's Biggest Audience: The Globalization of Chinese Films and TV*, Berkeley: University of California Press, 2007, p. 251.

See also C. T. Li, 'Journal: Hong Kong' (2004) *Film Comment (September/October 2004)*, Online. Available: http://www.filmlinc.com/fcm/9-10-2004/hongkongjournal.htm (accessed 14 May 2009).

113 See Tables 2.1 to 2.4.

114 Screen Australia (2012) *Australia and the World: International Comparisons*, Online. Available: http://www.screenaustralia.gov.au/research/statistics/acompinvestment.asp (accessed 1 June 2012).

115 Film Services Office (2011) *The Hong Kong Film Industry*, Online. Available: http://www.fso-create hk.gov.hk/accessibility/eng/guidetofilming0201.cfm (accessed 6 May 2011).

116 Ibid.

117 Film Services Office (2008) *About Us*, Online. Available: http://www.fso-tela.gov.hk/accessibility/eng/aboutus.cfm (accessed 13 May 2009).

118 Film Services Office (2009) *Establishment of the Hong Kong Film Development Council*, Online. Available: http://www.fso-tela.gov.hk/accessibility/eng/FDC_02.cfm (accessed 13 May 2009).

119 Hong Kong Film Development Council (2009) *Hong Kong Film New Action*, Online. Available: http://www.fdc.gov.hk/NewAction/en/background/background.htm (accessed 13 May 2009).

120 Film Services Office (2009) *Film Development Fund*, Online. Available: http://www.fso- tela.gov.hk/accessibility/eng/filmdevelopmentfund.cfm (accessed 13 May 2009).

121 An application for funds to finance film production can be made by persons who have produced at least two films for theatrical release in the preceding ten years. A film director or producer with such experience may be engaged if the applicant himself does not meet this requirement. Additionally, the project in question must: (1) be a feature film intended for commercial exhibition in Hong Kong with a production budget not exceeding HKD$ 15 million; (2) be identifiable as commercially viable; (3) have secured third-party financing; (4) be able to obtain approval under the Film Censorship Ordinance for public exhibition; and (5) 50 per cent of its main cast and crew are Hong Kong residents.

122 Film Services Office (2009) *Film Guarantee Fund Scheme*, Online. Available: http://www.fso-tela.gov.hk/accessibility/eng/filmguaranteefund.cfm (accessed 13 May 2009).

123 Ibid.

124 The land of Australia was inhabited by indigenous people (the Aboriginal and Torres Straits Islander peoples) long before the arrival of European settlers. Britain's settlement of the land was initially through transportation of convicts to the penal colony in the late eighteenth century. For a concise history of Australia, see generally D. Denoon, P. Mein-Smith and M. Wyndham, *A History of Australia, New Zealand and the Pacific*, Massachusetts: Blackwell Publishers, 2000 and S. Macintyre, *A Concise History of Australia*, Melbourne: Cambridge University Press, 2000.

125 Australian Government Attorney-General's Department (2010) *Universal Periodic Review – National Report Part II*, Online. Available: http://www.ag.gov.au/www/agd/nsf/Page/Humanrightsandantidiscrimination/InternationalHumanRightsUniversalPeriodicReview/DraftNationalReport-PartII (accessed 27 October 2010).

126 Australia is also a Commonwealth realm where the Queen is represented by the Governor-General.

127 Australian Government Attorney-General's Department (2010) *Universal Periodic Review – National Report Part II*, Online. Available: http://www.ag.gov.au/www/agd/nsf/Page/Humanrightsandantidiscrimination/InternationalHumanRightsUniversalPeriodicReview/DraftNationalReport-PartII (accessed 27 October 2010).

128 It is worth noting that film censorship is not listed under section 51 which provides for the legislative powers of the Commonwealth Parliament. See the discussion about the law in the Australian system discussed in Chapter 3.

129 For a thorough discussion of the Australian legal system, reference may be made to P. Vines, *Law and Justice in Australia* (2nd edn), Melbourne: Oxford University Press, 2009; R. Hinchy, *The Australian Legal System: History, Institutions and Method*, Sydney: Pearson Australia, 2008; and D. J. Gifford, *Understanding the Australian Legal System*, Sydney: Cavendish, 1997.

130 Australian Government Attorney-General's Department (2009) *The Courts*, Online. Available: http://www.ag.gov.au/www/agd/agd.nsf/Page/LegalsystemandjusticeThe Courts (accessed 27 October 2010).

131 Ibid.

132 *Coleman v Power* [2004] 220 CLR 1, 81 (Kirby J).

133 *Lange v Australian Broadcasting Corporation* (1997) 189 CLR 520, 561.

134 *Coleman v Power* [2004] 220 CLR 1.

135 See *Lange v Australian Broadcasting Corporation* (1997) 189 CLR 520, 567–8.

136 The phrase 'in a manner' was inserted by the High Court in *Coleman v Power* to substitute the phrase 'the fulfilment of' in the test laid down in *Lange v Australian Broadcasting Corporation* to make the test clearer and to note that the court has a role to review whether the approach used in the legislation is reasonably appropriate and adapted.

137 *Lange v Australian Broadcasting Corporation* (1997) 189 CLR 520, 567.

138 Australian Bureau of Statistics (2010) *Australian Demographic Statistics*, Online. Available: http://www.abs.gov.au/ausstats/abs@nsf/mf/3101.0 (accessed 15 December 2010).

139 Asian Development Bank, *Key Indicators for Asia and the Pacific 2010* (41st edn), Manilla: Asian Development Bank, 2010, p. 132.

140 See section 116 of the Australian Constitution.

141 Australian Bureau of Statistics (2007) *2006 Census QuickStats: Australia*, Online. Available: http://www.censusdata.abs.gov.au/ABSNavigation/prenav/LocationList?newgeography=Australia&level1=0&submitbutton=View+QuickStats+ (accessed 4 November 2010).

142 J. L. Bianco, *Pluralist Nations: Pluralist Language Policies?*, Australian Government Department of Immigration and Citizenship (2010), Online. Available: http://www.immi.gov.au./media/publications/multicultural/confer/04/speech18b.htm (accessed 4 November 2010). It was noted that: 'In Australia, English has no *de jure* status but it is so entrenched as the common language that it is *de facto* the official language as well as the national language'.

143 The service sector of the economy includes education, tourism and financial services.

144 Central Intelligence Agency, United States of America (2012) *The World Factbook: Australia*, Online. Available: http://www.cia.gov/library/publications/the-world-factbook/geos/as.html (accessed 1 June 2012).

145 Screen Australia, *Information for Filmmakers*, Sydney: Screen Australia, 2008, p. 3.

146 N. Rattigan, *Images of Australia: 100 Films of the New Australian Cinema*, Dallas: Southern Methodist University Press, 1991, p. 4 and J. Rayner, *Contemporary Australian Cinema*, Manchester: Manchester University Press, 2000, p. 4.

147 Screen Australia, *Information for Filmmakers*, Sydney: Screen Australia, 2008, p. 3.

148 Ibid.

149 N. Rattigan, *Images of Australia: 100 Films of the New Australian Cinema*, Dallas: Southern Methodist University Press, 1991, p. 4.

150 Ibid. p. 5.

151 Screen Australia, *Information for Filmmakers*, Sydney: Screen Australia, 2008, p. 4.

152 See T. F. Sheckels, *Celluloid Heroes Down Under: Australian Film, 1970–2000*, Westport, CT: Praeger, 2002, pp. 1–9, J. Rayner, *Contemporary Australian Cinema*, Manchester: Manchester University Press, 2000, pp. 166–79, D. Gonski, *Review of Commonwealth Assistance to the Film Industry*, Canberra: Department of Communications and the Arts Australia, 1997, pp. 5–6. See also House of Representatives Standing Committee on Environment, Recreation and the Arts, Parliament of the Commonwealth of Australia, *Report of the Moving Pictures Inquiry* (1992) p.4 and House of Representatives Standing Committee on Communications, Information Technology and the Arts, Parliament of the Commonwealth of Australia, *From Reel to Unreal: Future Opportunities for Australia's Film, Animation, Special Effects and Electronic Games Industries* (2004) p. xxvii.

153 Screen Australia, *Information for Filmmakers*, Sydney: Screen Australia, 2008, p. 4.

154 See generally N. Rattigan, *Images of Australia: 100 Films of the New Australian Cinema*, Dallas: Southern Methodist University Press, 1991.

155 Screen Australia, *Information for Filmmakers*, Sydney: Screen Australia, 2008, p. 5.

156 See N. McDonald, 'Australia' in W. Luhr (ed.) *World Cinema Since 1945*, New York: Ungar, 1987, pp. 35–61.

157 The name of the scheme came from the relevant tax provisions – Division 10BA of Part III of the Income Tax Act 1936.

158 J. Rayner, *Contemporary Australian Cinema*, Manchester: Manchester University Press, 2000, p. 168.

159 Screen Australia, *Information for Filmmakers*, Sydney: Screen Australia, 2008, p. 5.

160 For example, *Shine* grossed more than US$ 89 million at the international box office. For more examples, see M. A. Reid, *More Long Shots: Australian Cinema Successes in the 90s*, Sydney: Australian Film Commission, 1999, p. 18.

161 T. F. Sheckels, *Celluloid Heroes Down Under: Australian Film, 1970–2000*, Westport, CT: Praeger, 2002, p. 223.

162 J. Rayner, *Contemporary Australian Cinema*, Manchester: Manchester University Press, 2000, p. 178.

163 Screen Australia, *Information for Filmmakers*, Sydney: Screen Australia, 2008, p. 6.

164 Figures include Australian co-productions with overseas partners (averaging two co-productions per year): Adapted from Screen Australia (2010) *Number of Feature Films Produced, Total Production Budgets and Spend in Australia, 1990/91 – 2008/09*, Online. Available: http://www.screenaustralia.gov.au/gtp/mpfeaturessummary.html (accessed 20 April 2011) and Screen Australia (2010) *Australian Content: Box Office, 1977–2009*, Online. Available: http://www.screenaustralia.gov.au/research/statistics/boxofficeaustralianshare.asp (accessed 20 April 2011).

165 Screen Australia, *Information for Filmmakers*, Sydney: Screen Australia, 2008, p. 6.

166 R. Jones, 'The Australian Film Distribution and Exhibition Industry and Competition Law and Policy' in M. Alderson (ed.), *Current Issues in Film Law*, Sydney: Prospect Media, 2007, pp. 121–2.

167 Compiled and adapted from Screen Australia (2010) *Number of Australian Cinema Admissions and Gross Box Office*, Online. Available: http://www.screenaustralia.gov.au/gtp/ wcboadmission.html (accessed 20 April 2011) and Screen Australia (2010) *Total Screens, Seating Capacity and Theatres in Australia, 1980–2009*, Online. Available: http://www.screenaustralia.gov.au/gtp/wcsttotal.html (accessed 20 April 2011).

168 Screen Australia (2011) *Australian Films at the Local Box Office in 2010*, Online. Available:http://www.screenaustralia.gov.au/newsandevents/2011/mr110120boxoffice.aspx (accessed 15 November 2010).

169 R. Jones, 'The Australian Film Distribution and Exhibition Industry and Competition Law and Policy' in M. Alderson (ed.), *Current Issues in Film Law*, Sydney: Prospect Media, 2007, p. 129.

170 See B. Hodsdon, *Straight Roads and Crossed Lines: The Quest for Film Culture in Australia?*, Shenton Park, WA: Bernt Porridge Group, 2001, pp. 43–50.

171 *The Economics of Films and Television in Australia* (published by the AFC in 1993) highlighted that 'apart from the US, at least in the English-speaking world, no significant national film industries would exist without government support' while the *Review of Commonwealth Assistance to the Film Industry* noted that 'Commonwealth assistance has been critical to the building and development of the industry to this level of expertise and quality': D. Gonski, *Review of Commonwealth Assistance to the Film Industry*, Canberra: Department of Communications and the Arts Australia, 1997, p. 5.

For a discussion of the government's initiatives to support the film industry from the 1970s to 1990s, see I. Bertrand, 'Finance' in B. McFarlane, G. Mayer and I. Bertrand (eds), *The Oxford Companion to Australian Film*, Melbourne: Oxford University Press, 1999, pp. 156–9.

172 These incentives include tax rebates and location cash grants.

173 See Screen Australia (2010) *Production Financing Programs*, Online. Available: http://www.screenaustralia.gov.au/industry_support/Production.asp for details on eligibility, requirements and the selection criteria of Screen Australia's production financing.

174 See Screen Australia (2011) *Industry Support*, Online. Available: http://www.screenaustralia.gov.au/industrysupport/GWOverview.asp and Screen Australia (2011) *Development Programs*, Online, Available: http://www.screenaustralia.gov.au/industrysupport/Development.asp for details of the four main development support programs provided and Screen Australia (2011) *Marketing Support Programs*, Online. Available: http://www.screenaustralia.gov.au/industry_support/Marketing-Support.asp for information on the marketing support provided by the agency.

175 Screen Australia works with its overseas counterparts to ensure efficient administration in co-production projects. A film approved as an official co-production is regarded as a national production of each of the co-producing countries and is therefore eligible for the incentives available in each of them. Australia had entered into co-production treaties with the United Kingdom, Canada, Italy, Israel, Germany, China and Singapore to facilitate screen productions.

176 Screen Australia (2011) *Producer Offset*, Online. Available: http://www.screenaustralia.gov.au/produceroffset/default.asp (accessed 1 June 2012).

177 The Division 10BA scheme was introduced to encourage private investment in film projects. Under this scheme, investors will acquire an interest in the copyright of the film they invested in as well as write off 150 per cent (subsequently reduced to 100 per cent) of capital expenditures in the film production.

178 Under this scheme, investors will receive a 100 per cent tax concession for buying shares in a FLIC company which will in turn invest in a slate of film productions.

179 See Screen Australia, *Information for Filmmakers*, Sydney: Screen Australia, 2008, p. 14.

180 Ibid.

181 Screen Australia (2011) *Production Incentives Overview*, Online. Available: http://www.afc.gov.au/gtp/mptax.html (accessed 1 June 2012).

182 Ibid.

183 Ibid.
184 Ibid.
185 Malaysian films, if ever commercially distributed and exhibited abroad, are confined to the Singaporean and Indonesian markets only.
186 Screen Australia (2010) *Domestic Films' Share of Box Office in Australia and Selected Other Countries, 2000–2009*, Online. Available: http://www.screenaustralia.gov.au/gtp/acompboxofficeozshare.html (accessed 16 November 2010).
187 Screen Australia (2010) *Top 20 Countries Ranked by Box Office Revenues, 2005–2009*, Online. Available: http://www.screenaustralia.gov.au/research/statistics/acompboxoffice.asp (accessed 6 May 2011).
188 Screen Australia (2010) *Top 20 Countries by Number of Cinema Admissions, 2005–2009*, Online. Available: http://www.screenaustralia.gov.au/research/statistics/acompadmissions.asp (accessed 6 May 2011).
189 There are film market sidebars at Australian film festivals but their scale is comparatively modest compared to the ones held at the Hong Kong International Film Festival.
190 FINAS occasionally funds nationalistic film projects, for example *1957: Hati Malaya* (*1957: Heart of Malaya*, Shuhaimi Baba, 2007) was made to commemorate the 50th anniversary of the nation's independence.

3 Film censorship systems in Malaysia, Hong Kong and Australia: the laws, guidelines and processes

1 For a concise history of the BBFC and the unique origins of the British film censorship system, see G. Robertson and A. Nicol, *Media Law* (5th edn), London: Sweet & Maxwell, 2007, pp. 817–63, N. M. Hunnings, *Film Censors and the Law*, London: Allen & Unwin, 1967 and Appendix III (entitled 'The Development of the Film Censorship System') of the *Report of the Committee on Obscenity and Film Censorship* (Cmnd 7772), London: HMSO, 1979, pp. 190–5.
2 See E. Barendt, *Freedom of Speech* (2nd edn), New York: Oxford University Press, 2005, pp. 130–1 and G. Robertson and A. Nicol, *Media Law* (5th edn), London: Sweet & Maxwell, 2007, pp. 34–5. The BBFC classifies films for cinema release on behalf of the local authorities which license cinemas and classifies videos and DVDs under the Video Recordings Act 1984.
3 For example, in the predominantly Muslim Malaysia, the Malaysian guidelines prohibit films which give an anti-God message that may affect the religious faith of its adherers, whereas the Hong Kong guidelines prohibit films glorifying the power of triads and membership of triad society.
4 See section 53 of the Film Censorship Act 2002. Early legislation on the control of film exhibition and distribution were in the form of ordinances and enactments, enacted by the British Colonial Government. These regulations were enacted as the Cinematograph Films Ordinance No. 76 of 1952. This nomenclature was subsequently changed to Film (Censorship) Act 1952 and was enforced in West Malaysia (then Malaya) from 1 May 1954. It was later revised and published as Laws of Malaysia (Act 53) on 1 August 1971 and extended to East Malaysia. See S. S. Faruqi and S. Ramanathan, *Mass Media Laws and Regulations in Malaysia*, Singapore: Asian Media Information and Communication Centre, 1998, p. 67.
5 Malaysia, *Parliamentary Debates*, House of Representatives, 6 December 2001, p. 106 (Chor Chee Heung, Deputy Minister of Home Affairs).
6 Sections 1 to 3 of the Film Censorship Act 2002.
7 Sections 7 to 10, 15, 19 and 20 of the Film Censorship Act 2002.
8 Section 11 of the Film Censorship Act 2002.
9 Sections 14, 16 and 17 of the Film Censorship Act 2002.
10 Section 18 of the Film Censorship Act 2002.
11 Sections 21 to 24 of the Film Censorship Act 2002.
12 Section 25 of the Film Censorship Act 2002.

13 Section 26 of the Film Censorship Act 2002.
14 Section 28 of the Film Censorship Act 2002.
15 Section 27 of the Film Censorship Act 2002.
16 The offences include possessing, exhibiting or distributing any film that has not been approved by the Board of Censors.
17 Section 43 of the Film Censorship Act 2002.
18 Sections 53 to 56 of the Film Censorship Act 2002.
19 Ministry of Home Affairs, Malaysia (2008) *Explanatory Statement of the Film Censorship Act 2002*, Online. Available: http://www.moha.gov.my/eng/3rdLevel.asp?tt=32&parentid=587&content ID (accessed 11 March 2009).
20 See Chapter 7 for a discussion of, and criticism on, the new guidelines.
21 It is not uncommon in Malaysia for plans to be announced and projects launched that do not lead to any subsequent concrete actions and enforcement.
22 The Pan-Malaysian Islamic Party, the Malaysian Youth Council and the Federation of Malaysian Consumers Associations were among those that objected to the self-regulation scheme proposed by the Home Ministry. They argued that the country is not ready for self-censorship.
23 Section 19C reads: 'The Minister may from time to time give the Board, the Committee of Appeal and the Assessment Committee directions of a general character not inconsistent with the provisions of this Act as to the exercise of their powers and duties which appears to him may affect the government policy relating to public exhibition of films and the Board, the Committee of Appeal and the Assessment Committee shall give effect to all such directions', whereas section 28(2)(c) reads:

'Without prejudice to the generality of subsection (1), such regulations may provide for all or any of the following matters – (c) the procedure of the Board, Committee of Appeal and Assessment Committee in relation to the censoring and review of films'.

24 It should be noted that the Guidelines were drawn up in Malay and there is no official English version. Therefore, quotations from the Guidelines are the author's translation. The Guidelines are not available to the public, but are kindly provided by the Home Ministry with an understanding that the provisions will not be reproduced or published elsewhere in full.
25 The *Rukunegara* is Malaysia's national ideology, proclaimed on 31 August 1970. The five principles enunciated therein are: Belief in God; Loyalty to the King and Country; Upholding the Constitution; Sovereignty of the Law; and Good Behaviour and Morality.
26 The appendix to the Guidelines also states that censors must understand the provisions of the Sedition Act 1948 to avoid films from being manipulated to cause racial disharmony in Malaysia.
27 See Chapter 5 for the film practitioners' comments on censorship guidelines.
28 Interview with Hussain Shafie, Chairman of the Board of Censors (Putrajaya, 6 January 2009).
29 See also sections 12 and 13 of the Film Censorship Act 2002 for provisions on retention and return, and disposal of films that have been refused approval for exhibition.
30 Section 10(2) of the Film Censorship Act 2002.
31 Section 10(3) of the Film Censorship Act 2002.
32 Section 11(2) provides that if any film is delivered to its owner for the purpose of making alteration, the owner must return the film to the Board within the time specified together with the excised parts of the film if the alteration is by way of excision.
33 Films classified 18SG, 18SX, 18PA and 18PL are legally restricted to persons of 18 years of age and over.
34 If the film owner intends to make duplicate copies of a film that has been certified under section 14, the owner must submit a statutory declaration to the Board of Censors in accordance with section 16 stating the intention to do so, the number of duplicate copies to be made, and that the duplicate copies are to be made from the film approved by the Board. A censorship certificate will be issued under section 17 to each of the duplicate copies of the film.

35 See sections 14 and 18 of the Film Censorship Act 2002.
36 'Film publicity material' is defined under section 3 of the Film Censorship Act 2002 as to include 'the original or duplicate of the whole or any part of a picture, photograph, poster, figure, handbill, slide, newspaper advertisement and other form of advertisement printed or recorded on any material and intended to publicize a film'.
37 Section 19(1) of the Film Censorship Act 2002.
38 Section 19(2) of the Film Censorship Act 2002.
39 Section 10(3) of the Film Censorship Act 2002.
40 Section 21(2) of the Film Censorship Act 2002.
41 Paragraph 9 of the Schedule to the Film Censorship Act 2002.
42 Section 23 of the Film Censorship Act 2002.
43 Judicial review of film censorship decisions is explored in Chapter 6.
44 Prior to the enactment of the Film Censorship Ordinance, censorship of films was regulated under the Places of Public Entertainment Ordinance (Cap. 172) under which the Film Censorship Regulations 1953 were made. The principles of film censorship were stated in the Film Censorship Standards, published by the Hong Kong Government.
45 J. Chan, 'Film Censorship Ordinance 1988', *Hong Kong Law Journal*, 18, 1988, 457.
46 See F. Ching, 'Hong Kong Plays Political Censor for China', *Asian Wall Street Journal* (Hong Kong), 17 March 1987, p. 1.
47 See A. H. Y. Chen, 'Some Reflections on the 'Film Censorship Affair'', *Hong Kong Law Journal*, 17, 1987, 352 and J. Chan, 'Freedom of Expression: Censorship and Obscenity', in R. Wacks (ed.) *Civil Liberties in Hong Kong*, Hong Kong: Oxford University Press, 1988, p. 208.
48 Pending the enactment of the Ordinance, a new set of Film Censorship Regulations which revokes and replaced the existing deficient Film Censorship Regulations 1953 was gazetted.
49 Section 10(2)(c) requires censors to consider when determining the suitability of a film for exhibition, whether there is a likelihood that the exhibition of the film would seriously damage good relations with other territories. This provision justified what is referred to as 'political censorship' in Hong Kong and it is seen as applicable mainly to films which could offend or embarrass the People's Republic of China. See J. Chan, 'Freedom of Expression: Censorship and Obscenity', in R. Wacks (ed.) *Civil Liberties in Hong Kong*, Hong Kong: Oxford University Press, 1988, p. 216. Section 10(2)(c) was repealed in 1994 by the Film Censorship (Amendment) Ordinance 1994.
50 For further discussion of this point, see J. Chan, 'Film Censorship Ordinance 1988', *Hong Kong Law Journal*, 18, 1988, 457. Section 10(3)(d) was later repealed in 1994 by the Film Censorship (Amendment) Ordinance 1994.
51 Sections 1 and 2 of the Film Censorship Ordinance.
52 Section 3 of the Film Censorship Ordinance.
53 Sections 4 and 5 of the Film Censorship Ordinance.
54 Section 6 of the Film Censorship Ordinance.
55 Sections 8 to 11 of the Film Censorship Ordinance.
56 Sections 12 to 14 of the Film Censorship Ordinance.
57 Section 12 of the Film Censorship Ordinance.
58 Section 13 of the Film Censorship Ordinance.
59 Sections 15A to 15J of the Film Censorship Ordinance.
60 Section 15K of the Film Censorship Ordinance.
61 Section 16 of the Film Censorship Ordinance.
62 Sections 17 to 19 of the Film Censorship Ordinance.
63 Sections 20 to 33 of the Film Censorship Ordinance.
64 Section 20 of the Film Censorship Ordinance.

Films classified as Category III are approved for exhibition and distribution only to persons who have attained the age of 18 years. This provision makes the Category III classification legally enforceable and not merely advisory in nature.

65 Sections 21 and 22 of the Film Censorship Ordinance.
66 Paragraph 2 of the Film Censorship Guidelines for Censors.
67 See the discussion of the censorship processes in the Hong Kong system for the provisions.
68 Paragraph 7 of the Film Censorship Guidelines for Censors.
69 Paragraph 10 of the Film Censorship Guidelines for Censors.
70 Paragraph 25 of the Film Censorship Guidelines for Censors.
Such acknowledgement coupled with the fact that most contentious contents are not prohibited if they can be justified in the context of the film would encourage filmmakers to depict the reality of everyday life (and be critical of existing social problems) as well as to strive for realism in their films.
71 See the discussion of the Hong Kong censorship guidelines in Chapter 4 for the list of prohibited film content.
72 The classes of film suitable for exemption include cultural, educational, promotional, sports, travel, musical and religious films.
73 Paragraph 48 of the Film Censorship Guidelines for Censors.
A film title may be rejected if it: (a) is likely to cause deep shock or disgust; (b) is likely to corrupt morals; (c) is likely to promote, incite or encourage crime, violence and drug use; (d) contains insulting or sexually suggestive wording or symbols; (e) contains coarse language, expressions with sexual connotations or sexual references; (f) contains triad expressions or signs; or (g) is likely to incite hatred or denigration on grounds of racial, religious, national or sexual differences.
74 Paragraphs 52 and 53 of the Film Censorship Guidelines for Censors.
75 Paragraph 59 of the Film Censorship Guidelines for Censors.
76 Paragraph 60 of the Film Censorship Guidelines for Censors.
77 See the section on the Hong Kong system in Chapter 4 for a discussion of the exemption of films from censorship.
78 The statement and declaration are to be made in the Film Submission Form. The Authority may refuse to accept a submission if the film has been classified under the Control of Obscene and Indecent Articles Ordinance (COIAO) or if any submission requirement is not complied with.
79 Section 10(1) of the Film Censorship Ordinance.
80 Censors are statutorily bound to consider the matters stated under section 10(2) and to take into account the matters stated under section 10(3). Failure to do so may be a ground to quash the resulting censorship decision by way of judicial review.
81 Section 10(6)(a) of the Film Censorship Ordinance.
What normally transpires is that the censor will view the submitted film with the assigned advisers. Thereafter, the censor will highlight the contentious contents and censorship elements that appeared in the film to the advisers before they fill in a form which consists of three basic questions: 'Is the film suitable for public exhibition?'; 'If yes, under which category it should be classified in?'; and 'Does the film needs to undergo any excision before it is released in that classification category?' Further discussion with the advisers will be held, if necessary, before the censor proceeds to make his or her decision: Interview with Rose May Li, Principal Entertainment Standards Control Officer (Film), Television and Entertainment Licensing Authority (Hong Kong, 24 March 2009). It is important to note that on 1 April 2012, the Office for Film, Newspaper and Article Administration of the Government of the Hong Kong Special Administrative Region was established to take over the functions of the Television and Entertainment Licensing Authority in relation to film censorship, control of obscene and indecent articles and newspaper registration.
82 Section 10(6)(a) of the Film Censorship Ordinance.
83 Section 10(6)(b) of the Film Censorship Ordinance.
The most common entity consulted by censors is the Hong Kong police force where advice is sought in relation to films portraying triad activities: Interview with Rose May Li, Principal Entertainment Standards Control Officer (Film), Television and Entertainment Licensing Authority (Hong Kong, 24 March 2009).

84 See section 10(6) of the Film Censorship Ordinance.
85 Section 13(2) of the Film Censorship Ordinance.
86 Section 13(3) of the Film Censorship Ordinance.
87 Section 13(4)(a) of the Film Censorship Ordinance.
88 Section 15A of the Film Censorship Ordinance.
89 'Advertising material' is defined under section 2 of the Film Censorship Ordinance as 'a display, figure, film, poster, picture or text used or intended to be used for the purpose of advertising – (a) a film which is exhibited or intended for exhibition; (b) a videotape or a laserdisc which is published or intended for publication'.
90 Section 15K (5) of the Film Censorship Ordinance.
91 Section 15K (6) of the Film Censorship Ordinance.
92 Paragraph 54 of the Film Censorship Guidelines for Censors.
93 Paragraph 55 of the Film Censorship Guidelines for Censors. For the list of contents not permitted in film advertising materials, see the same paragraph of the Film Censorship Guidelines for Censors.
94 Section 10(6) of the Film Censorship Ordinance.
95 See sections 16(3), 17(6), 18(7) and 19(8) of the Film Censorship Ordinance.
96 Section 17(3) of the Film Censorship Ordinance.
97 Section 18(2)(b) of the Film Censorship Ordinance.
99 Section 18(8) of the Film Censorship Ordinance.
100 Section 18(4) of the Film Censorship Ordinance.
101 Section 19(2A) of the Film Censorship Ordinance.
102 Sections 17(3)(c), 18(4)(c) and 19(5)(c) of the Film Censorship Ordinance.
103 Sections 17(4), 18(5) and 19(6) of the Film Censorship Ordinance.
104 See Classification (Publications, Films and Computer Games) (Enforcement) Act 1995 (Vic), Classification (Publications, Films and Computer Games) (Enactment) Act 1995 (ACT), Classification (Publications, Films and Computer Games) Enforcement Act 1995 (NSW), Classification of Publications, Films and Computer Games Act (NT), Classification (Publications, Films and Computer Games) Enforcement Act 1995 (SA), Classification (Publications, Films and Computer Games) Enforcement Act 1995 (Tas) and Censorship Act 1996 (WA).

Every state and territory with the exception of South Australia has adopted the classification arrangement. The South Australian Classification (Publications, Films and Computer Games) Enforcement Act 1995 established the South Australian Classification Council, which has the power to reclassify films and override decisions made by the Classification Board and the Classification Review Board. See section 3 of the Classification (Publications, Films and Computer Games) Enforcement Act 1995 (SA).

In 2005, the South Australian Classification Council reclassified *9 Songs* (Michael Winterbottom) from R18+ (given by the Classification Review Board) to X18+, thereby banning the film in the state.

105 This cooperative scheme is underpinned by an Intergovernmental Agreement on Censorship made between the Commonwealth and all states and territories.
106 For a detailed history of film censorship in Australia from the 1900s to the 1970s, see I. Bertrand, *Film Censorship in Australia*, Queensland: University of Queensland Press, 1978.
107 The Customs (Cinematograph Films) Regulations were repealed by section 98 of the Classification (Publications, Films and Computer Games) Act 1995.
108 Daryl Williams, 'From Censorship to Classification' (Speech delivered at Murdoch University, Western Australia, 31 October 1997).

The 'mess' can be illustrated by this example – each censorship decision was made under up to 13 separate pieces of legislation in the various jurisdictions and there were numerous differences between each of these pieces of legislation, one of which is the matters to be considered in making a decision. Therefore, a film could be banned in some states and not in the others.

109 Australian Law Reform Commission, *Censorship Procedure*, Report No.55, Sydney: Australian Law Reform Commission, 1991, 2.13.
110 Commonwealth, *Parliamentary Debates*, House of Representatives, 22 September 1994, p. 1381 (Michael Lavarch, Attorney-General).
111 Sections 1 to 6A of the Classification (Publications, Films and Computer Games) Act 1995.
112 Sections 7 and 8 of the Classification (Publications, Films and Computer Games) Act 1995 respectively.
113 Section 14 of the Classification (Publications, Films and Computer Games) Act 1995.
114 Sections 29 to 37 of the Classification (Publications, Films and Computer Games) Act 1995.
115 Sections 38 to 41 of the Classification (Publications, Films and Computer Games) Act 1995.
116 Sections 42 to 44B of the Classification (Publications, Films and Computer Games) Act 1995.
117 Section 42 of the Classification (Publications, Films and Computer Games) Act 1995.
118 Section 43 of the Classification (Publications, Films and Computer Games) Act 1995.
119 Section 44 of the Classification (Publications, Films and Computer Games) Act 1995.
120 Sections 45 to 51 of the Classification (Publications, Films and Computer Games) Act 1995.
121 Sections 72 to 76 of the Classification (Publications, Films and Computer Games) Act 1995.
122 Sections 87A and 87B of the Classification (Publications, Films and Computer Games) Act 1995.
123 Section 93 of the Classification (Publications, Films and Computer Games) Act 1995. See for example the Classification (Publications, Films and Computer Games) Regulations 2005 which primarily deal with fees for classification and review applications. In addition, the regulations also provide for the maximum number of members of the Classification Board and the computation of time within which the Classification Board and the Classification Review Board are to make their decisions.
124 Sections 94 to 98 of the Classification (Publications, Films and Computer Games) Act 1995.
125 It is noteworthy that the ALRC does not make recommendations on exactly how the provisions of the proposed Classification of Media Content Act should be drafted.
126 Australian Law Reform Commission, *Classification – Content Regulation and Convergent Media (ALRC Report 118)*, Sydney: Australian Law Reform Commission, 2012.
127 It is recommended that the new scheme based upon the Classification of Media Content Act should be enacted pursuant to the legislative power of the Parliament of Australia and not as part of any new cooperative scheme. It is also recommended that the Australian Government should be responsible for the enforcement of classification laws and a regime of offences and penalties.
128 It may be noted that the review is sparked by the greater scale of media convergence and the volume of media content available to, and consumed by, the public. The review emphasizes technological change, particularly regarding the internet. It is worth noting that in Australia, a film may be subject to up to four different regulatory requirements: as it is exhibited in cinemas (films are classified separately for 2D and 3D versions), sold or rented in DVD format, accessed online and broadcast on television.
129 The ALRC recommends that feature films for cinema release must be classified by the Classification Board while feature films not for cinema release (for example, films on DVD) may be classified by the Board or by authorized industry classifiers.
130 The ALRC recommends that the current prohibition of the two following contents be reviewed: the depiction of sexual fetishes in films and 'detailed instruction in the use of proscribed drugs'. It is also recommended that the prohibition on content that 'promotes, incites or instructs in matters of crime' be confined to 'serious crime'.

131 The ALRC recommends that the Classification Board, rather than the Classification Review Board, be responsible for reviewing classification decisions, that is, to make a new classification decision in response to an application for review.
132 Sections 12(2) and 12(3) of the Classification (Publications, Films and Computer Games) Act 1995.
133 Des Clark, 'A Practical Response to Classification of Convergent Media in the Australian Context: The Combined Guidelines for Films and Computer Games', (Speech delivered at the International Ratings Conference 2003: Classification in a Convergent World, Sydney, 23 September 2003). The OFLC was abolished on 1 July 2007. Its functions were transferred to the new Classification Policy Branch and Classification Operations Branch of the Attorney-General's Department.
134 Guidelines for the Classification of Films and Computer Games.
135 Emphasis added.
136 See Chapter 4 for a discussion of the exemption of films from classification in the Australian system.
137 Besides submitting a film for classification under section 14, an application may be made under section 28A for a certificate that the film is an exempt film.
138 One of the indications would be the controversy that the film had caused in other countries. A panel will normally consist of three classifiers but for controversial films, a larger panel of five or seven classifiers will be set up to examine the film: Interview with Greg Scott, Deputy Director of the Classification Board (telephone interview, 20 July 2010).
139 Section 57(3) of the Classification (Publications, Films and Computer Games) Act 1995.
140 Section 8 of the Classification (Publications, Films and Computer Games) Act 1995.

Section 21 provides that if a classified film is subsequently modified, the film becomes unclassified when the modification is made.
141 Section 9 of the Classification (Publications, Films and Computer Games) Act 1995.
142 The Code also contains a table which sets out each of the classification categories and a corresponding description of the types of content that will fall within those categories.
143 The insertion of the qualification 'as far as possible' recognizes that there are situations when other community concerns or considerations take priority over the general freedom of adults to 'read, hear and see what they want'. See Chapter 4 for the types of film content that are prohibited in Australia.
144 Films classified X18+ can only be exhibited and distributed in the Northern Territory and the Australian Capital Territory. Additionally, depiction of violence, sexual violence, sexualized violence or coercion is not allowed in X18+ films. For high level sex scenes, the dividing criteria between the R18+ and X18+ classifications is that, if it is a real depiction of sexual intercourse or other sexual activity, it should be classified X18+ whereas if the sex scene is simulated, it will be classified R18+. It is provided in the R18+ section of the Guidelines for the Classification of Films and Computer Games that: 'Sexual activity may be realistically simulated. The general rule is "simulation, yes – the real thing, no"'.

The case of *Adultshop.Com Ltd v Members of the Classification Review Board and anor.* [2008] 169 FCR 31 disclosed that the Classification Review Board considers that most reasonable adults would accept an exception to the general rule so as to permit an R18+ classification for explicit sexual activity where the film has artistic or other merits (see section 11 of the Classification (Publications, Films and Computer Games) Act 1995) and the *actual sex* is not prolonged or detailed, having regard to the context of the film. For example, *The Piano Teacher* (Michael Haneke, 2001) which contains scenes of actual sexual activity was classified R18+ instead of X18+ because of the artistic merits of the film: Interview with Greg Scott, Deputy Director of the Classification Board (telephone interview, 20 July 2010). Other examples include *Romance* (Catherine Breillat, 1999) which was classified R18+ by the Classification Review Board (the Classification Board initially classified it RC) although it contains actual depictions of fellatio and masturbation.

The Classification Review Board made an exception to the general rule of 'simulation, yes – the real thing, no' due to the consideration of the film's artistic merits. See B. Harris, 'Censorship: A Comparative Approach Offering a New Theoretical Basis for Classification in Australia', (2005) 8 *Canberra Law Review*, 8, 2005 pp. 51–2.

The BBFC also accepts that films with artistic merit would be classified 18 although they contain actual rather than simulated sex. Two examples that can be highlighted here are Michael Winterbottom's *9 Songs* and John Cameron Mitchell's *Shortbus.* See G. Robertson and A. Nicol, *Media Law* (5th edn), London: Sweet & Maxwell, 2007, p. 856.

145 Section 20 of the Classification (Publications, Films and Computer Games) Act 1995. Consumer advice will describe the strongest elements in the film and indicates the intensity of those elements.

146 Section 25(1) of the Classification (Publications, Films and Computer Games) Act 1995.

147 Section 25(2) of the Classification (Publications, Films and Computer Games) Act 1995.

148 A classification marking has three components – the classification symbol, classification description, and consumer advice.

149 Australian Government – Classification (2009) *How to apply for classification of public exhibition films*, Online. Available: http://www.classification.gov.au/special.html?n=278&p=83 (accessed 15 February 2009).

150 Sections 29 to 37 of the Classification (Publications, Films and Computer Games) Act 1995. See also section 5 for the definition of 'advertisement'.

151 Section 29(3) of the Classification (Publications, Films and Computer Games) Act 1995.

152 Section 29(6) of the Classification (Publications, Films and Computer Games) Act 1995.

153 Section 32(1) of the Classification (Publications, Films and Computer Games) Act 1995.

The Board may grant a certificate of exemption under section 33 if it is of the opinion that if the film is classified, it would not be classified RC, X18+ or R18+. See section 33(2) of the Classification (Publications, Films and Computer Games) Act 1995.

154 Section 42(2) of the Classification (Publications, Films and Computer Games) Act 1995 provides that if a participating state or territory minister asks the Commonwealth Minister to apply for a review of a decision, the Commonwealth Minister must make the application. The Commonwealth Minister in this case is the Commonwealth Attorney-General while the participating ministers are the Attorneys-General for New South Wales, South Australia, Tasmania, Victoria, Western Australia, Queensland and the Australian Capital Territory and the Minister for Justice and Attorney-General for the Northern Territory.

Two recent examples where decisions made by the Classification Board were reviewed by the Classification Review Board in response to applications made by this category of persons are the decisions on *Serbian Film* (Srdjan Spasojevic, 2010) and *The Human Centipede II* (Tom Six, 2011). The former was classified R18+ (Restricted) by the Classification Board but a three-member-panel of the Classification Review Board by unanimous decision determined that the film be classified RC (Refused Classification). According to the Review Board's media release dated 19 September 2011, the panel was of the opinion that the film 'could not be accommodated within the R18+ classification as the level of depictions of sexual violence, themes of incest and depictions of child sexual abuse in the film has an impact which is very high and not justified by context'. The film is about a pornographic actor who accepts a job to appear in a snuff movie financed by a reclusive millionaire. It was reported that the film included scenes of sexual violence, child molestation and necrophilia. The latter film was also classified R18+ (Restricted) by the Classification Board but the Classification Review Board later determined that the film be classified RC. The Review Board in its reasons for the decision (published on the Classification website at www.classification.gov.au) noted that *The Human Centipede II* could not be accommodated within the R18+ classification as the level of depictions of violence in the film had an impact which was 'very high' and contained gratuitous, exploitative and offensive depictions of violence (including sexual violence). The Review Board was of the opinion that the contentious scenes were 'lacking in artistic, moral or other values' and they contravened 'the standards of morality, decency and propriety generally accepted by reasonable adults'. In this film, the lead character kidnaps 12 victims to create a 'human centipede' by surgically joining them mouth-to-anus. In the process, the main character tortures his victims with bashing, stabbing and shooting. The film's violent content includes scenes of brutal cutting of throats, mutilation of flesh and rape.

155 Section 43(2) of the Classification (Publications, Films and Computer Games) Act 1995.
156 Section 43(3)(a) of the Classification (Publications, Films and Computer Games) Act 1995.
157 Section 43(3)(b) of the Classification (Publications, Films and Computer Games) Act 1995.
158 Section 43(4) of the Classification (Publications, Films and Computer Games) Act 1995.
159 Section 44 of the Classification (Publications, Films and Computer Games) Act 1995.
160 Australian Government – Classification (2009) *Classification Review Board*, Online. Available: http://www.classification.gov.au/special.html?n=251&p=62 (accessed 15 February 2009).
161 Section 78 of the Classification (Publications, Films and Computer Games) Act 1995.
162 Section 79(1) of the Classification (Publications, Films and Computer Games) Act 1995.
163 Section 26(3) of the Classification (Publications, Films and Computer Games) Act 1995.
164 Section 25(1A) of the Classification (Publications, Films and Computer Games) Act 1995.
165 Section 25(1B) of the Classification (Publications, Films and Computer Games) Act 1995.

4 Film censorship systems in Malaysia, Hong Kong and Australia: the key issues

1 Home Ministry, Malaysia (2009) *Home Ministry Notice*, Online. Available: http://www.moha.gov.my (accessed 12 May 2009).
2 Interview with Hussain Shafie, Chairman of the Board of Censors (Putrajaya, 6 January 2009).
3 Ibid.
4 The four *ex-officio* members are the representative of the Inspector-General of Police, the representative of the Secretary General of the Home Ministry, the representative of the Secretary General of the Ministry of Information and the representative of the Director General of Education.
5 Interview with Hussain Shafie, Chairman of the Board of Censors (Putrajaya, 6 January 2009).
6 Emphasis added.
7 Section 25(2) of the Film Censorship Act 2002.
8 Interview with Amir Muhammad, film director and producer (Kuala Lumpur, 15 December 2008).
9 The word 'film' is defined in the Film Censorship Act 2002 as to include the 'original or duplicate of the whole or any part of a cinematograph film, a videotape, diskette, laser disc, compact disc, hard disc, and other record, of a sequence of visual images, being a record capable of being used as a means of showing that sequence as a moving picture, whether or not accompanied by sound'.

The Act is not applicable to any film published, circulated, exhibited or distributed on the internet. See section 2(3) of the Film Censorship Act 2002.

10 The Board of Censors is empowered to impose conditions subject to which the certificate of exemption is issued. See sections 7 and 8(4) of the Film Censorship Act 2002.
11 The Film Censorship Act 2002 did not provide for classification categories. Section 15 of the Act merely provides that 'the Board may, before issuing a certificate [of approval] under section 14, classify the film in such manner as may be prescribed'.
12 Paragraph 1(vii), section E of the Film Censorship Guidelines 1993.

13 The Film Censorship Guidelines 1993 are issued in Malay and there is no official English version. The provisions quoted in this book are therefore the author's translation.
14 'Alteration' is defined under section 3 of the Film Censorship Act 2002 as to include 'excision, addition, deletion, erasure, reconstruction or removal of scenes, dialogues, or sound, in totality or in part, of a film, and also includes the insertion or amendment of subtitles in a film'.
15 Section 10(1)(b) of the Film Censorship Act 2002.
16 See for example the Supreme Court's decision in *Minister of Labour, Malaysia v Chan Meng Yuen* [1992] 2 MLJ 337. However, when an impugned administrative decision adversely affects a fundamental right such as the right to livelihood, then constitutional review will come into play where articles 5(1) and 8(1) of the *Federal Constitution* may be relied on as the authority to demand for procedural fairness which includes the provision of reasoned decision. See the cases of *Hong Leong Equipment Sdn Bhd v Liew Fook Chuan* [1996] 1 MLJ 481 and *Sivarasa Rasiah v Badan Peguam Malaysia & Anor* [2010] 2 MLJ 333.
17 Section 21(1) of the Film Censorship Act 2002.
18 Section 21(2) of the Film Censorship Act 2002.
19 Malaysia, *Parliamentary Debates*, House of Representatives, 6 December 2001, p.106 (Chor Chee Heung, Deputy Home Minister).
20 Article 5(1) reads: 'No person shall be deprived of his life or personal liberty save in accordance with law', while article 10(1)(a) reads: 'Subject to clauses (2), (3) and (4), every citizen has the right to freedom of speech and expression'. The word 'life' in article 5(1) was interpreted by the courts so as to include the right to livelihood. See *Tan Tek Seng v Suruhanjaya Perkhidmatan Pendidikan* [1996] 1 MLJ 261 and *Lee Kwan Woh v Public Prosecutor* [2009] 5 MLJ 301.
21 The Panel of Censors are therefore not filled with retired government officers.
22 Section 4(2) of the Film Censorship Ordinance.
23 Section 10(6)(a) of the Film Censorship Ordinance.
24 Television and Entertainment Licensing Authority, Government of the Hong Kong Special Administrative Region, Film Censorship Requirements (2009) Available: http://www.tela.gov.hk/english/ about4_org_e.htm (accessed 14 February 2009). Any Hong Kong citizen above the age of 18 and proficient in both Chinese and English languages may apply to be appointed as an adviser.
25 In 2009, this group is made up of two lawyers, two academics, two members from the business and commerce sector, a district councillor, a director of a social welfare organization and a representative from the film industry: Interview with Rose May Li, Principal Entertainment Standards Control Officer (Film), Television and Entertainment Licensing Authority (Hong Kong, 24 March 2009).
26 Section 16(2) of the Film Censorship Ordinance.
27 Rose May Li (2011) 'Members of the Panel of Censors'. E-mail (3 May 2011).
28 Ibid.
29 'Film' is defined under section 2 of the Ordinance as '(a) a cinematograph film and includes any sound-track associated with such film; (b) a videotape or laserdisc and includes any sound-track associated with such videotape or laserdisc; (c) a still film and includes any sound-track associated with such film; (d) any other record of visual moving images that is capable of being used for the subsequent screening of those images and includes any sound-track associated with such record; (e) any combination of the films referred to in paragraphs (a), (b), (c), and (d); or an excerpt or part of a film referred to in paragraph (a), (b), (c), (d) or (e)'.
30 Section 7 of the Film Censorship Ordinance.
31 Section 9(3) of the Film Censorship Ordinance.
32 Section 29(1)(d) of the Film Censorship Ordinance.
33 The provision reads: '(2) The censor shall as soon as practicable view the film and consider the following matters for the purpose of making his decision under subsection

(4): (a) whether the film portrays, depicts or treats cruelty, torture, violence, crime, horror, disability, sexuality or indecent or offensive language or behaviour; and (b) whether the film denigrates or insults any particular class of the public by reference to the colour, race, religious belief or ethnic or national origins or the sex of the members of that class'.

34 Television and Entertainment Licensing Authority, Government of the Hong Kong Special Administrative Region (2009) *Vision, Mission and Values*, Online. Available: http://www.tela.gov.hk/english/ about.htm (accessed 14 February 2009); Office for Film, Newspaper and Article Administration, Government of the Hong Kong Special Administrative Region (2012) *Vision, Mission and Values*, Online. Available: http://www.ofnaa.gov.hk/eng/aboutus/ aboutus1.htm (accessed 1 June 2012).

35 Public opinion surveys on film censorship standards in Hong Kong are conducted biennially. The most recent survey was conducted in 2011 and the reports are available upon request from the Office of Film, Newspaper and Article Administration, Government of the Hong Kong Special Administrative Region.

36 Rose May Li (2010) 'Film Censorship Guidelines for Censors 1999'. E-mail (22 November 2010).

37 Paragraph 31 of the Film Censorship Guidelines for Censors.

38 See paragraphs 2, 30, 31, 32 and 36 of the Film Censorship Guidelines for Censors.

39 See paragraphs 14 to 19, 23, 27, 34 and 37 of the Film Censorship Guidelines for Censors.

40 Emphasis added.

41 Paragraph 38(a) of the Film Censorship Guidelines for Censors.

42 Paragraph 24 of the Film Censorship Guidelines for Censors.

43 Paragraph 31 of the Film Censorship Guidelines for Censors. The term 'hard core pornography' is not defined in the Guidelines. It is renowned as a difficult term to define and indeed in the US Supreme Court case of *Jacobellis v Ohio*, Justice Stewart conceded that he could never succeed in intelligibly defining the term 'obscenity' but went on to note that 'I know it when I see it': 378 US 184 (1964) 197. However, of more importance for this book is the evidence from interviews that suggests there is a clear understanding of the term by film practitioners as it is applied; see Chapter 5 for the interviewees' comments.

44 Paragraph 38(d) of the Film Censorship Guidelines for Censors.

45 Paragraph 41 of the Film Censorship Guidelines for Censors.

46 See the section on the Hong Kong System in Chapter 3 for a discussion of the censorship process.

47 See the section on alteration to films and determination of classification category in Chapter 5 for the Hong Kong interviewees' comments.

48 Section 8(2) of the Film Censorship Ordinance.

49 Section 17 of the Film Censorship Ordinance.

50 Section 18 of the Film Censorship Ordinance

51 Section 19 of the Film Censorship Ordinance.

52 Section 49(1) of the Classification (Publications, Films and Computer Games) Act 1995. There are part-time members as well in the Board, see section 49(2) of the Classification (Publications, Films and Computer Games) Act 1995.

53 Australian Government – Classification (2011) *Classification Board Members*, Online. Available: http://www.classification.gov.au/www/cob/classification.nsf/Page/Classification_Whoweare/ClassificationBoard_ClassificationBoardMembers (accessed 11 May 2011). See also section 47 of the Classification (Publications, Films and Computer Games) Act 1995.

54 Temporary members may be appointed by the Minister for the efficient dispatch of the Board's business. A temporary member is appointed for a maximum period of three months. See section 50 of the Classification (Publications, Films and Computer Games) Act 1995.

55 Section 48(1) of the Classification (Publications, Films and Computer Games) Act 1995.

56 Section 48(2) of the Classification (Publications, Films and Computer Games) Act 1995. Other than the requirement that the membership is 'broadly representative of the

Australian community', the Classification (Publications, Films and Computer Games) Act 1995 places no other requirement upon appointment to the Board. Members are drawn from diverse backgrounds and locality and recruitment advertisements are placed in newspapers to invite the public to apply to be a member/classifier.

57 Section 48(3) of the Classification (Publications, Films and Computer Games) Act 1995.
58 Section 51(1) of the Classification (Publications, Films and Computer Games) Act 1995.
59 Section 51(3) of the Classification (Publications, Films and Computer Games) Act 1995.
60 Section 65(1) of the Classification (Publications, Films and Computer Games) Act 1995.
61 Section 65(2) of the Classification (Publications, Films and Computer Games) Act 1995.
62 Section 73 of the Classification (Publications, Films and Computer Games) Act 1995.
63 Section 74(1) of the Classification (Publications, Films and Computer Games) Act 1995.
64 As is the case with the Board, the law does not stipulate any other requirement for appointment to the Review Board.
65 Section 74(3) of the Classification (Publications, Films and Computer Games) Act 1995.
66 Section 73 of the Classification (Publications, Films and Computer Games) Act 1995.
67 Section 76(1) of the Classification (Publications, Films and Computer Games) Act 1995.
68 Section 76(3) of the Classification (Publications, Films and Computer Games) Act 1995.
69 Australian Government – Classification (2010) *Classification Review Board*, Online. Available: http://www.classification.gov.au/special.html?n=251&p=62 (accessed 15 February 2010).
70 Section 77 of the Classification (Publications, Films and Computer Games) Act 1995.
71 Australian Government – Classification (2011) *Classification Review Board Members*, Online. Available: http://www.classification.gov.au/www/cob/classification.nsf/Page/ClassificationAustralia/whoweare/ClassificationBoardClassificationReviewBoardMembers (accessed 11 May 2011).
72 Section 83(1) of the Classification (Publications, Films and Computer Games) Act 1995.
73 Section 83(2) of the Classification (Publications, Films and Computer Games) Act 1995.
74 Sections 67 and 85 of the Classification (Publications, Films and Computer Games) Act 1995.
75 Australian Law Reform Commission, *Classification – Content Regulation and Convergent Media*, Sydney: Australian Law Reform Commission, 2012, p. 149.
76 'Film' is defined under section 5 of the Classification (Publications, Films and Computer Games) Act 1995 as to include 'a cinematograph film, a slide, video tape and video disc and any other form of recording from which a visual image, including a computer generated image, can be produced (together with its soundtrack), but does not include: (a) a computer game; or (b) an advertisement for a publication, a film or a computer game'.
77 Section 5B(3) provides that a film is not an exempt film if it contains an advertisement that has been refused approval, or an advertisement for a film that has been classified M or a higher classification, or contains material that would be likely to cause the film to be classified M or a higher classification.
78 See section 5B(1) of the Classification (Publications, Films and Computer Games) Act 1995 for the full description of each type of exempt film.
79 Section 28C of the Classification (Publications, Films and Computer Games) Act 1995.
80 See sections 48 and 74 of the Classification (Publications, Films and Computer Games) Act 1995.
81 Australian Government Attorney-General's Department (2010) *Research*, Online. Available: http://www.ag.gov.au/www/agd/agd.nsf/Page/Classificationpolicy_research (accessed 8 October 2010).
82 For example, the 2004 Community Assessment Panel rounds were conducted in Canberra, Alice Springs and Melbourne and the outcome showed 'a high level of agreement between the Community Assessment Panels and the Classification Board': Australian Government Attorney-General's Department (2010) *Research*, Online. Available: http://www.ag.gov.au/www/agd/agd.nsf/Page/Classificationpolicy_research (accessed 8 October 2010).

83 For the Community Assessment Panel and other research and survey reports, see the Attorney-General's Department: Classification Policy Research website at http://www.ag.gov.au/www/agd/agd.nsf/Page/Classificationpolicy_research.

84 The Office of Film and Literature Classification received more than 370 submissions from the film industry and the public.

In *Adultshop.Com Ltd. v Members of the Classification Review Board and anor.* [2008] 169 FCR 31 the Australian Federal Court held the view that the guidelines, 'promulgated by elected Government representatives after community consultation', were 'broadly representative of the current community standards'.

85 See the Guidelines for the Classification of Films and Computer Games for the complete description of all the classifiable elements in the various classification categories.

86 The word 'themes' is defined in the Guidelines as to mean 'social issues such as crime, suicide, drug and alcohol dependency, death, serious illness, family breakdown and racism'.

87 It may be noted that these contents are considered obscene by the standards of the contemporary Australian society and, hence, not suitable to be released.

88 Interview with Greg Scott, Deputy Director of the Classification Board (Telephone interview, 20 July 2010).

89 Ibid.

90 See for example the High Court's decision in *Public Service Board of New South Wales v Osmond* (1986) 159 CLR 656.

91 Section 5 of the Administrative Decisions (Judicial Review) Act 1977 laid down the grounds of judicial review.

92 Section 13(2) of the Administrative Decisions (Judicial Review) Act 1977.

93 This right is subject to the request being made in writing within the prescribed time frame. See section 13(5) of the Administrative Decisions (Judicial Review) Act 1977.

94 See generally the website www.classification.gov.au. However, reasons for decisions made by the Classification Board are not published on the website.

95 By virtue of section 42(2), this category also includes the state and territory ministers.

96 Section 5 of the Classification (Publications, Films and Computer Games) Act 1995 defines 'publish' as to include 'sell, offer for sale, let on hire, exhibit, distribute and demonstrate'.

97 Section 42A of the Classification (Publications, Films and Computer Games) Act 1995.

The Classification website defined 'person aggrieved' as someone who can demonstrate an interest in the subject matter of the film in question that extends beyond that of an ordinary member of the public: Australian Government – Classification (2009) *Classification Review Board*, Online. Available: http://www.classification.gov.au/special.html?n =251&p=62 (accessed 15 February 2009).

An example of application for review initiated under the category 'person aggrieved by the decision' is the application made by three non-profit groups who sought to have the film *Lolita* (Adrian Lyne, 1997) banned in Australia. However, the Review Board declined to deal with the application on several grounds, one of which is that these groups did not qualify as 'aggrieved persons'. For an account of this application, see T. Gutman, 'Lolita's Lesson Learned', *Communications Update*, 155, 1999, 18.

98 Section 42 has caused worries amongst censorship-watch groups and film activists because subsection (3) gave standing to apply for review only to persons or organizations whose activities relate to the contentious aspects of the film's themes or subject matter but shuts out those whose purposes and activities relate to freedom of expression. See D. Marr, 'Censored: Attorney-General vs. "aggrieved persons"', *Art + Law*, 9, 2001, 3.

99 Sections 19 and 44 of the Classification (Publications, Films and Computer Games) Act 1995.

100 Australian Government – Classification (2009) *Classification Review Board*, Online. Available: http://www.classification.gov.au/special.html?n=251&p=62 (accessed 15 February 2009).

101 See Chapter 1 for a discussion of the legal literature about freedom of expression and censorship.
102 F. Schauer, 'The Ontology of Censorship', in R. C. Post (ed.) *Censorship and Silencing*, Los Angeles: Getty Research Institute for the History of Art and the Humanities, 1998, p. 162.
103 E. Barendt, *Freedom of Speech* (2nd edn), New York: Oxford University Press, 2005, p. 122.
104 In Australia, films have been censored on the basis of the views of reasonable adults in the community since the 1970s, while in Hong Kong, films have been censored based on the standards of the community brought to light by public opinion surveys since the late 1980s.
See also *Crowe v Graham* (1968) 121 CLR 375 where the High Court emphasized offence to community standards as a determinant for censorship.
105 For an interesting discussion of the types of content censored under the British system, see G. Robertson and A. Nicol, *Media Law* (5th edn), London: Sweet & Maxwell, 2007, pp. 845–57.
106 See the sections on Malaysian film censorship guidelines in Chapters 4 and 7.
107 See sections 3 and 10 of the Film Censorship Act 2002.
108 See the section on alteration to films and determination of classification category in Chapter 5 for the Hong Kong interviewees' responses.
109 E. Barendt, *Freedom of Speech* (2nd edn), New York: Oxford University Press, 2005, p. 122.

5 Film censorship systems in Malaysia, Hong Kong and Australia: the practitioners' opinions and experiences

1 Interview with Tsai Ming-liang, film director and producer (Kuala Lumpur, 1 February 2009).
2 Interview with U-Wei Haji Saari, film director and producer (Kuala Lumpur, 11 December 2008).
3 Interview with Lorna Tee, film producer and distributor (Hong Kong, 26 March 2009).
4 Besides *Susuk*, *Histeria* (*Hysteria*, James Lee, 2009) a horror film produced by another established mainstream film production company was classified 'U' (suitable for all ages) with very minimal excision, a decision which surprised even the film's director himself who expected more cuts to be required by the censors and the film to be classified in a restricted category. Interview with James Lee, film director and producer (Kuala Lumpur, 19 December 2008).
5 Interview with Amir Muhammad, film director and producer (Kuala Lumpur, 15 December 2008).
6 Interview with Yasmin Ahmad, film director (Kuala Lumpur, 6 January 2009).
7 *Muallaf* (*The Convert*, 2008) was finally released in Malaysia on 24 December 2009 after more than a year of entanglement with the censorship authority and alterations being made to it. Sadly, the director did not live to see her film released theatrically in her country.
8 Interview with Ahmad Puad Onah, film producer and distributor (Kuala Lumpur, 17 December 2008).
9 Interview with Amir Muhammad, film director and producer (Kuala Lumpur, 15 December 2008).
10 Interview with Aziz M. Osman, film director and producer (Kuala Lumpur, 4 September 2009).
11 Interview with Ruhani Abdul Rahman, film producer (Kuala Lumpur, 16 December 2008).
12 Interviews with Khoo Eng Yow, film director and producer (Kuala Lumpur, 18 December 2008) and Tsai Ming-liang (Kuala Lumpur, 1 February 2009).
13 Interviews with Ahmad Puad Onah (Kuala Lumpur, 17 December 2008) and Ruhani Abdul Rahman (Kuala Lumpur, 16 December 2008).

14 Interviews with Leonard Tee, film distributor (Kuala Lumpur, 18 December 2008) and Tsai Ming-liang, film director and producer (Kuala Lumpur, 1 February 2009).

15 Interview with Aziz M. Osman, film director and producer (Kuala Lumpur, 4 September 2009).

Aziz's second film *Fantasia* was banned by the censors for four years and was only subsequently approved for exhibition after substantial alterations were made to the film.

16 Tsai's opinion that the censorship standard is becoming stricter and censors more conservative is shared by Khoo Eng Yow and Leonard Tee.

17 Interviews with Saw Teong Hin, film director (Kuala Lumpur, 10 December 2008), Shuhaimi Baba, film director and producer (Kuala Lumpur, 5 January 2009), Ahmad Puad Onah (Kuala Lumpur, 17 December 2008), Ruhani Abdul Rahman (Kuala Lumpur, 16 December 2008), and U-Wei Haji Saari (Kuala Lumpur, 11 December 2008).

18 Interviews with Amir Muhammad (Kuala Lumpur, 15 December 2008) and Khoo Eng Yow (Kuala Lumpur, 18 December 2008).

19 This view is also shared by Ahmad Puad Onah and Shuhaimi Baba.

20 Interview with Shuhaimi Baba, film director and producer (Kuala Lumpur, 5 January 2009).

21 Four out of the ten top grossing Malaysian films are in the horror genre and they were all produced after 2004. See National Film Development Corporation of Malaysia (2011) *Industry: Top 20 Feature Films*, Online. Available: http://www.finas.gov.my/index.php?mod=industry&sub=top20 (accessed 20 April 2011).

22 Interview with Gordon Chan, film director, producer and President of the Hong Kong Film Directors' Guild (Hong Kong, 25 March 2009).

23 Interviews with Benny Chan, film director and producer (Hong Kong, 23 March 2009); Winnie Tsang, film distributor (Hong Kong, 1 June 2009), Wellington Fung, Secretary General of the Hong Kong Film Development Council (Hong Kong, 26 May 2009); and Bill Kong, film producer and distributor (Hong Kong, 26 March 2009).

24 This response is echoed by Kenneth Bi who noted that 'because the rating system is clear, we can make our choices as to what to keep and what to be taken out. If you want a Category II rating, you can cut a scene or a shot or a line out… so you can decide whether or not to cross that border [into Category III]'. Interview with Kenneth Bi, film director and producer (Hong Kong, 26 May 2009).

25 Terence Chang (2010) 'Film Censorship in Hong Kong'. E-mail (12 October 2010).

26 Interview with Wellington Fung, Secretary General of the Hong Kong Film Development Council (Hong Kong, 26 May 2009).

27 Interviews with Kenneth Bi (Hong Kong, 26 May 2009) and Benny Chan (Hong Kong, 23 March 2009).

28 Interview with Nansun Shi, film producer (Hong Kong, 29 May 2009).

29 Interview with Bill Kong, film producer and distributor (Hong Kong, 26 March 2009).

30 Interview with Gordon Chan, film director, producer and President of the Hong Kong Film Directors' Guild (Hong Kong, 25 March 2009).

31 Interview with Lorna Tee, film producer and distributor (Hong Kong, 26 March 2009).

32 Interview with Lo Chi Leung, film director (Hong Kong, 2 June 2009).

33 Interview with Bill Kong, film producer and distributor (Hong Kong, 26 March 2009).

34 Interview with Gordon Chan, film director, producer and President of the Hong Kong Film Directors' Guild (Hong Kong, 25 March 2009).

35 Interviews with Benny Chan (Hong Kong, 23 March 2009), Gordon Chan (Hong Kong, 25 March 2009), Wellington Fung (Hong Kong, 26 May 2009), Bill Kong (Hong Kong, 26 March 2009), Lo Chi Leung (Hong Kong, 2 June 2009) and Winnie Tsang (Hong Kong, 1 June 2009).

36 Some of the interviewees do not deal with graphic violence and sex in their films for three main reasons: (1) such content is not necessary in their films; (2) personal taste or preference; and (3) commercial considerations.

37 Mabel Cheung's 2001 film *Beijing Rocks* was banned in China.

38 In China, films are either approved for exhibition and distribution (with or without excision) or banned. There are no classification categories and rating system for films there.
39 Only two of the Australian interviewees (Richard J. Frankland and Peter Campbell) expressed disappointment over certain aspects of the system.
40 Interview with Tony Ayres, film director and producer (Melbourne, 9 October 2009).
41 Interview with Rolf de Heer, film director and producer (Telephone interview, 6 October 2009).
42 Interview with Ray Lawrence, film director (Telephone interview, 20 August 2009).
43 Interview with James Hewison, film distributor (Melbourne, 19 August 2009).
44 Interview with Joel Pearlman, film distributor and exhibitor (Melbourne, 4 June 2010).
45 Interview with Peter Campbell, film distributor (Melbourne, 14 August 2009).
46 Ruhani Abdul Rahman's answer suggests that positions in the Board of Censors were being 'handed out' easily to retired senior government officers without much evaluation and consideration as to their suitability and competency to carry out censorship duties.
47 The word means 'may peace be upon you', a common Arabic greeting used amongst the Muslim-Malay community.
48 Interview with Amir Muhammad, film director and producer (Kuala Lumpur, 15 December 2008).
49 The filmmaker discussed in particular, the experiences he had with the censors regarding two films he directed – *Senario* (1999) a slapstick comedy and *Seri Dewi Malam* (2001) a love story of a comatose woman and her husband.
50 Members of the Board of Censors may be reappointed by the Minister after their term of service has expired.
51 See the section on the Malaysian system in Chapter 4 for a discussion of the appointment and removal of censors in Malaysia.
52 The film consists of interviews with the locals who presently live in the places where Chin Peng had lived, punctuated with musical numbers and biographical on-screen texts explaining what Chin did in those places. The film does not contain any image of Chin Peng, nor is there any interview with the man himself. It also has no archive footage or any reconstruction of the battles with the communists.
53 The censors must have made their decision to approve the film based on some reasoning of their own but when the Minister banned the film, the basis supporting their decision suddenly disappeared.
54 See Chapter 4 for a discussion of the appointment of censors in Hong Kong.
55 Interview with Benny Chan, film director and producer (Hong Kong, 23 March 2009).
56 Interview with Gordon Chan, film director, producer and President of the Hong Kong Film Directors' Guild (Hong Kong, 25 March 2009).
57 Interview with Bill Kong, film producer and distributor (Hong Kong, 26 March 2009).
58 Interview with Winnie Tsang, film distributor (Hong Kong, 1 June 2009).
59 Interviews with Gordon Chan (Hong Kong, 25 March 2009), Wellington Fung (Hong Kong, 26 May 2009), Nansun Shi (Hong Kong, 29 May 2009) and Winnie Tsang (Hong Kong, 1 June 2009).
60 See sections 65 and 83 of the Act.
61 Interview with Richard J. Frankland, film director and producer (Melbourne, 7 October 2009).
62 Interview with Peter Campbell, film distributor (Melbourne, 14 August 2009).
63 The profiles of members of the Classification Board and Classification Review Board are published at the Australian Government Classification website at www.classification.gov.au.
64 Interview with Ray Lawrence, film director (Telephone interview, 20 August 2009).
65 Interview with Greg Denning, film distributor (Telephone interview, 13 August 2009).
66 Interview with Jan Chapman, film producer (Telephone interview, 30 April 2010).
67 Interview with Saw Teong Hin, film director (Kuala Lumpur, 10 December 2008).
68 See section 9 of the Film Censorship Ordinance.

69 See section 29 of the Film Censorship Ordinance.
70 Section 10(3)(b) of the Film Censorship Ordinance.
71 Interview with Patrick Tam, film director (Hong Kong, 25 March 2009).
72 Ann Hui is one of the Hong Kong New Wave filmmakers and is highly respected whereas Wong Jing is a commercially successful film director and producer, infamous for his exploitation films.
73 Interview with Greg Scott, Deputy Director of the Classification Board (Telephone interview, 20 July 2010).
74 Interview with U-Wei Haji Saari, film director and producer (Kuala Lumpur, 11 December 2008).
75 G. C. Khoo, *Reclaiming Adat: Contemporary Malaysian Film and Literature*, Vancouver: UBC Press, 2006, p. 108.
76 M. Mahathir, 'Censure the Censor', *The Star* (Kuala Lumpur) 5 February 2003, p.5.
77 Paragraph 2 of the Film Censorship Guidelines for Censors.
78 Interview with Benny Chan, film director and producer (Hong Kong, 23 March 2009).
79 Interview with Amir Muhammad, film director and producer (Kuala Lumpur, 15 December 2008).
80 Interview with Leonard Tee, film distributor (Kuala Lumpur, 18 December 2008).
81 Interview with Shuhaimi Baba, film director and producer (Kuala Lumpur, 5 January 2009).
82 Interview with Ahmad Puad Onah, film producer and distributor (Kuala Lumpur, 17 December 2008).
83 Interview with Lorna Tee, film producer and distributor (Hong Kong, 26 March 2009).
84 Interview with U-Wei Haji Saari, film director and producer (Kuala Lumpur, 11 December 2008).
85 *Berkemban* means a female wearing a *sarong* (cloth) around her midriff. U-Wei Haji Saari's film *Perempuan, Isteri & ...* (*Woman, Wife & Whore*, 1993) had a scene where the lead actress wears only a piece of cloth around her midriff taking her bath and that scene was required to be excised from the film.
86 Interview with U-Wei Haji Saari, film director and producer (Kuala Lumpur, 11 December 2008).
87 See the introduction of this chapter for the interviewees' comments.
88 These interviewees include Kenneth Bi (Hong Kong, 26 May 2009), Benny Chan (Hong Kong, 23 March 2009), Gordon Chan (Hong Kong, 25 March 2009), Wellington Fung (Hong Kong, 26 May 2009), Bill Kong (Hong Kong, 26 March 2009), Lorna Tee (Hong Kong, 26 March 2009) and Winnie Tsang (Hong Kong, 1 June 2009).
89 For example, the word 'fuck' in English language films and its Cantonese equivalent '*tiu*' in Hong Kong films.
90 These interviewees include Tony Ayres (Melbourne, 9 October 2009), Rolf de Heer (Telephone interview, 6 October 2009), Ray Lawrence (Telephone interview, 20 August 2009), Jan Chapman (Telephone interview, 30 April 2010), and Greg Denning (Telephone interview, 13 August 2009).
91 Section 10(1)(b) of the Film Censorship Act 2002. See Chapter 3 for a discussion of the censorship process in Malaysia.
92 Section 3 of the Film Censorship Act 2002.
93 See sections 10(1) and 11 of the Film Censorship Act 2002.
94 Shuhaimi Baba also noted that the censors required many scenes to be excised, forcing her to reshoot scenes as substitutes so that the film would make sense to the audience.
95 With a few exceptions, Malaysian films are not released commercially beyond the country's borders.
96 The word '*Jalang*' or 'whore' in the title had to be deleted and replaced with '…'.
97 The word '*halal*' means in accordance with, or permitted under, the *Syariah* (Islamic Law).

98 For example, the name 'Putrajaya', which is a planned city that serves as the Malaysian federal government's administrative centre, was required to be deleted from the subtitles.
99 T. D. Matthews provides numerous examples of censorship damaging the appeal of British films (and hence resulting in reduced audiences for them) in Chapter 15 of his book *Censored: The Story of Film Censorship in Britain*, London: Chatto & Windus Publishers, 1994.
100 Interview with Ruhani Abdul Rahman, film producer (Kuala Lumpur, 16 December 2008).
101 Interview with U-Wei Haji Saari, film director and producer (Kuala Lumpur, 11 December 2008).
102 See section 10(4)(c) of the Film Censorship Ordinance.
103 For example, even *Lust, Caution* (Ang Lee, 2007) a film with high level and extended sex scenes was released uncut in Hong Kong.
104 One of the examples that came up during the fieldwork is *Baise Moi* (*Rape Me* (also known as *Fuck Me* in some European countries), Virginie Despentes, 2000), a film depicting two young women on a journey of murder and sex, where the censor required a few shots to be excised before the approval for exhibition under Category III classification could be granted. Due to the film director's refusal to excise those shots, the film has not been commercially released in Hong Kong: Interview with Winnie Tsang, film distributor (Hong Kong, 1 June 2009).
105 Terence Chang (2010) 'Film Censorship in Hong Kong'. E-mail (12 October 2010).
106 See for example section 9A of the Classification (Publications, Films and Computer Games) Act 1995 which prohibits, amongst other things, films that advocate the doing of a terrorist act.
107 For examples of these contents, see the section on the Australian film classification guidelines in Chapter 4.
108 To protect the anonymity and confidentiality of the interviewees, no further details can be produced here.
109 This information was obtained from the Malaysian fieldwork conducted from December 2008 to February 2009. Three interviewees and two other film practitioners (who preferred not to be interviewed on record) recounted instances where certain prominent producers were given access to 'negotiate' with film censors.
110 The classification category that attracts the largest audience in the UK is '15' – for audiences aged 15 and above only. See G. Robertson and A. Nicol, *Media Law* (5th edn), London: Sweet & Maxwell, 2007, p. 850.
111 Film practitioners are able to discuss with censors when the classification category they sought can not be provided. Interview with Rose May Li, Principal Entertainment Standards Control Officer (Film), Television and Entertainment Licensing Authority (Hong Kong, 24 March 2009).
112 These interviewees include Tony Ayres (Melbourne, 9 October 2009), Peter Campbell (Melbourne, 14 August 2009), Rolf de Heer (Telephone interview, 6 October 2009), Ray Lawrence (Telephone interview, 20 August 2009) and two others who wish to remain anonymous.
113 Section 10(3) of the Film Censorship Act 2002.
114 Interviews with Ahmad Puad Onah (Kuala Lumpur, 17 December 2008) and U-Wei Haji Saari (Kuala Lumpur, 11 December 2008).
115 Amir Muhammad commented that the reasons for the banning of his film *Apa Khabar Orang Kampung* (*Village People Radio Show*, 2007) were 'very juvenile… and can be demolished easily'.
116 Interview with Aziz M. Osman, film director and producer (Kuala Lumpur, 4 September 2009).
117 Interview with Tsai Ming-liang, film director and producer (Kuala Lumpur, 1 February 2009).

118 Interviews with Tsai Ming-liang (Kuala Lumpur, 1 February 2009) and Leonard Tee (Kuala Lumpur, 18 December 2008).
119 Malaysia has been hit by a smog-like haze almost every year since the late 1990s. It is caused by smoke from forest fires in neighbouring Indonesia. The haze is a public health issue and has resulted in a state of emergency being declared.
120 Tsai Ming-liang said: 'They initially banned the film giving me reasons like there are too many migrant workers portrayed in the film, but in reality there are a lot of them in Malaysia… there is also the reason that there is a lot of haze… I did not purposely film it but in reality there is haze here in Malaysia. I mean, how can you dictate that filmmakers can only film [portray] the glory of the Petronas Twin Towers and the impressive high rise buildings? No other countries stipulate this… this is unreasonable' (Kuala Lumpur, 1 February 2009).
121 See sections 10(4) and 13 of the Film Censorship Ordinance.
122 Director Lo Chi Leung and producer Cheung Chi Kwong, for example, remarked that 'reasons for censorship decisions are always provided by the censors'.
123 For example, Jan Chapman noted that she never had any problem in obtaining reasons for the classification decisions made on the films she produced and remarked that the Boards were 'transparent with the reasons given'.
124 Interviews with Peter Campbell (Melbourne, 14 August 2009), Greg Denning (Telephone interview, 13 August 2009) and Richard J. Frankland (Melbourne, 7 October 2009).
125 Interviews with Ahmad Puad Onah (Kuala Lumpur, 17 December 2008), Khoo Eng Yow (Kuala Lumpur, 18 December 2008), Leonard Tee (Kuala Lumpur, 18 December 2008), Shuhaimi Baba (Kuala Lumpur, 5 January 2009) and U-Wei Haji Saari (Kuala Lumpur, 11 December 2008).
126 Interviews with Amir Muhammad (Kuala Lumpur, 15 December 2008), Ruhani Abdul Rahman (Kuala Lumpur, 16 December 2008), Saw Teong Hin (Kuala Lumpur, 10 December 2008) and Yasmin Ahmad (Kuala Lumpur, 6 January 2009).
127 Section 19 of the Film Censorship Ordinance.
128 The names highlighted by Campbell during the interview include Reverend Fred Nile, the Australian Family Association, Family First and the Festival of Light.
129 Michael Atkinson, the South Australian Attorney General, has a long history in censorship issues and his tendency to intervene in this area is well known to the Australian film industry. See, for example, Samantha Maiden, 'Sex and Santa spark movie complaints' *The Australian*, 31 December 2005, p.3; Paul Kalina, 'Short Cuts', *The Age* (Melbourne), 19 October 2006, p.20; Nick Henderson, 'Sorry, This Film is Banned' *The Advertiser* (Adelaide), 20 August 2005, p.13 and 'SA bans British film 9 Songs', *The Mercury* (Hobart), 20 August 2005, p.10.
130 Interview with Peter Campbell, film distributor (Melbourne, 14 August 2009).
131 Since 2003, there has been only one appeal made to the Board of Review and that is on the decision to classify *Irreversible* (Gaspar Noe, 2002) with Category III subject to minor excisions.
132 Gordon Chan noted that 'if we appeal, we can go to them and explain why we appealed and what our views are… I mean you are killing somebody's creative work and I think filmmakers should have that right to defend themselves'.
133 The Classification (Publications, Films and Computer Games) Act 1995 also does not provide an express right to make written representations to the Classification Review Board.
134 For example, Jan Chapman was of the opinion that it is important for film practitioners to be able to argue and explain 'who they envisaged the film will be seen by and how that can best happen'.
135 Interviews with Peter Campbell (Melbourne, 14 August 2009), Greg Denning (Telephone interview, 13 August 2009), Richard J. Frankland (Melbourne, 7 October 2009) and Joel Pearlman (Melbourne, 4 June 2010).

136 Interview with Greg Denning, film distributor (Telephone interview, 13 August 2009).
137 See the final section of Chapter 6 for the interviewees' comments.
138 Interviews with Ahmad Puad Onah (Kuala Lumpur, 17 December 2008), Ruhani Abdul Rahman (Kuala Lumpur, 16 December 2008), Saw Teong Hin (Kuala Lumpur, 10 December 2008), Shuhaimi Baba (Kuala Lumpur, 5 January 2009), Leonard Tee (Kuala Lumpur, 18 December 2008), Tsai Ming-liang (Kuala Lumpur, 1 February 2009) and U-Wei Haji Saari (Kuala Lumpur, 11 December 2008).
139 Interviews with Ruhani Abdul Rahman (Kuala Lumpur, 16 December 2008) and Ahmad Puad Onah (Kuala Lumpur, 17 December 2008).
140 Interviews with Khoo Eng Yow (Kuala Lumpur, 18 December 2008) and Saw Teong Hin (Kuala Lumpur, 10 December 2008).
141 Interviews with Ahmad Puad Onah (Kuala Lumpur, 17 December 2008), Amir Muhammad (Kuala Lumpur, 15 December 2008), Leonard Tee (Kuala Lumpur, 18 December 2008), Tsai Ming-liang (Kuala Lumpur, 1 February 2009) and U-Wei Haji Saari (Kuala Lumpur, 11 December 2008).
142 Interviews with Peter Campbell (Melbourne, 14 August 2009) and an executive of a major film exhibition and distribution company who requested anonymity.
143 Interviews with Greg Denning (Telephone interview, 13 August 2009) and a film distributor who wished to remain anonymous.

6 Judicial review of film censorship decisions

1 These three chapters made up the first part of the book.
2 M. Groves, 'Substantive Legitimate Expectations in Australian Administrative Law', *Melbourne University Law Review*, 32, 2008, 470. Groves also emphasized that a point established by empirical research is that 'matters remitted to decision-makers after a successful application for judicial review often reach a different outcome when reconsidered in the light of the reasons for decision provided by the courts'. See also R. Creyke and J. McMillan, 'Executive Perceptions of Administrative Law – An Empirical Study', *Australian Journal of Administrative Law*, 9, 2009, 163.
3 See J. Morgan, 'Policy Reasoning in Tort Law: The Courts, the Law Commission and the Critics', *Law Quarterly Review*, 125, 2009, 215; T. Poole, 'Of Headscarves and Heresies: The Denbigh High School Case and Public Authority Decision-making under the Human Rights Act', *Public Law*, 2005, 685; M. Sunkin and K. Pick, 'The Changing Impact of Judicial Review: The Independent Review Service of the Social Fund', *Public Law*, 2001, 736; S. Halliday, 'The Influence of Judicial Review on Bureaucratic Decision-making', *Public Law*, 2000, 110; and G. Richardson and M. Sunkin, 'Judicial Review: Questions of Impact', *Public Law*, 1996, 79.
4 See the section on availability of judicial review in Chapter 5 for the interviewees' responses.
5 A. S. Anand, 'Protection of Human Rights through Judicial Review', in M. Andenas (ed.) *Judicial Review in International Perspectives*, Boston, US: Kluwer Law International, 2000, p. 381. See also P. Cane, 'Understanding Judicial Review and Its Impact', in M. Hertogh and S. Halliday (eds) *Judicial Review and Bureaucratic Impact: International and Interdisciplinary Perspectives*, New York: Cambridge University Press, 2004, p. 15.
6 M. Supperstone, 'The Ambit of Judicial Review', in M. Supperstone and J. Goudie (eds), *Judicial Review*, London: Butterworths, 1992, p. 24.
7 *Council of Civil Service Unions v Minister for the Civil Service* [1985] AC 374, 408.
8 Ibid.
9 Ibid., 409.
10 Ibid.
11 M. P. Jain, *Administrative Law of Malaysia and Singapore* (3rd edn), Kuala Lumpur: Butterworths, 1997, p. 625 and Woolf, J. Jowell and A. P. Le Sueur, *Principles of Judicial Review*, London: Sweet & Maxwell, 1999, pp. 89–90.

12 Woolf, J. Jowell and A. P. Le Sueur, *Principles of Judicial Review*, London: Sweet & Maxwell, 1999, p. 95.
13 M. P. Jain, *Administrative Law of Malaysia and Singapore* (3rd edn), Kuala Lumpur: Butterworths, 1997, p. 697.
14 A 'public element' suggests a governmental or quasi-governmental involvement extending to indirect governmental connections.
15 The *GCHQ* case (*Council of Civil Service Unions v Minister for the Civil Service*) [1985] AC 374, 409.
16 [1987] QB 815, 847.
17 [1982] 1 WLR 1155.
18 [1982] 1 WLR 1155, 1174. See also *Re Amin [On appeal from Regina v Entry Clearance Officer, Bombay, Ex parte Amin]* [1983] 2 AC 818, 829.
19 M. Supperstone, 'The Ambit of Judicial Review', in M. Supperstone and J. Goudie (eds), *Judicial Review*, London: Butterworths, 1992, pp. 24–6.
20 See, for example, the cases of *Harpers Trading (M) Sdn Bhd v National Union of Commercial Workers* [1991] 1 MLJ 417 and *Hotel Equatorial (M) Sdn Bhd v National Union of Hotel, Bar and Restaurant Workers* [1984] 1 MLJ 363.
21 See for example the case of *Rohana bte Ariffin v Universiti Sains Malaysia* [1989] 1 MLJ 487.
22 M. Supperstone, 'Judicial Review after the Human Rights Act', *European Human Rights Law Review*, 3, 1993, pp. 301, 328.
23 [1996] 1 MLJ 261.
24 *Tan Tek Seng v Suruhanjaya Perkhidmatan Pendidikan* [1996] 1 MLJ 261, 290.
25 See also the cases of *Hong Leong Equipment Sdn Bhd v Liew Fook Chuan* [1996] 1 MLJ 481 and *Sivarasa Rasiah v Badan Peguam Malaysia & Anor* [2010] 2 MLJ 333.
26 [1997] 1 MLJ 145.
27 *Council of Civil Service Unions v Minister for the Civil Service* [1985] AC 374.
28 *Council of Civil Service Unions v Minister for the Civil Service* [1985] AC 374, 410 – 1.
29 These grounds of judicial review have been accepted *in toto* by the highest court in Malaysia as part of Malaysian law. See the cases of *Rama Chandran R v The Industrial Court of Malaysia* [1997] 1 MLJ 145, 188 – 90 and *Kumpulan Perangsang Selangor Bhd v Zaid bin Hj Mohd Noh* [1997] 1 MLJ 789, 798 – 799.
30 The rules of natural justice at common law refer to the *audi alterem partem* rule (right to fair hearing) and the *nemo judex in causa sua* rule (rule against bias).
31 Woolf, J. Jowell and A. P. Le Sueur, *Principles of Judicial Review*, London: Sweet & Maxwell, 1999, p. 447.
32 See the case of *R v Secretary of State for the Environment, Ex parte Nottinghamshire County Council* [1986] AC 240, 249.
33 For example, the principle that discretion should not be fettered may fall under 'illegality' as well as 'irrationality' and 'procedural impropriety'. See the discussion in Woolf, J. Jowell and A. P. Le Sueur, *Principles of Judicial Review*, London: Sweet & Maxwell, 1999, p. 148.
34 It is necessary to point out that a brief survey of the subject matter is attempted here, with its scope limited to film censorship only. For detailed analyses and discussions, reference may be made to W. Wade and C. Forsyth, *Administrative Law* (10th edn), Oxford: Oxford University Press, 2009; R. Douglas, *Administrative Law* (6th edn), Sydney: The Federation Press, 2009; P. Leyland and G. Anthony, *Administrative Law* (6th edn), Oxford: Oxford University Press, 2009; M. Aronson, B. Dyer and M. Groves, *Judicial Review of Administrative Action* (3rd edn), Sydney: Lawbook Co., 2004; and M. P. Jain, *Administrative Law of Malaysia and Singapore* (3rd edn), Kuala Lumpur: Butterworths, 1997.
35 Woolf, J. Jowell and A. P. Le Sueur, *Principles of Judicial Review*, London: Sweet & Maxwell, 1999, p. 151.
36 Ibid.

37 Interview with Amir Muhammad, the producer and director of *Malaysian Gods* (Kuala Lumpur, 15 December 2008).
38 Woolf, J. Jowell and A. P. Le Sueur, *Principles of Judicial Review*, London: Sweet & Maxwell, 1999, p. 195.
39 Interview with U-Wei Haji Saari, film director and producer (Kuala Lumpur, 11 December 2008).
40 Interview with James Lee, film director and producer (Kuala Lumpur, 19 December 2008).
41 Interview with Leonard Tee, film distributor (Kuala Lumpur, 18 December 2008).
42 See section 26 of the Film Censorship Act 2002.
43 C. C. Gan, *Disciplinary Proceedings Against Public Officers in Malaysia*, Selangor, Malaysia: Lexis Nexis, 2007, p. 203.
44 Woolf, J. Jowell and A. P. Le Sueur, *Principles of Judicial Review*, London: Sweet & Maxwell, 1999, p. 210.
45 In the case of *R v Secretary of State for Trade and Industry, Ex parte Lonrho Plc* [1989] 1 WLR 525, 539, Lord Keith stated that where reasons for a decision were absent and 'if all other known facts and circumstances appear to point overwhelmingly in favour of a different decision, the decision-maker… cannot complain if the court draws the inference that he had no rational reason for his decision'.
46 Woolf, J. Jowell and A. P. Le Sueur, *Principles of Judicial Review*, London: Sweet & Maxwell, 1999, p. 211.
47 Ibid.
48 Amir Muhammad (2006) *Ban This: Kampung Komunis*, Online. Available: http://www.lastcommunist.blogspot.com (accessed 15 April 2009). See also Dennis Lim, 'Your Film is Banned. There's Not Enough Violence', *The New York Times*, Online. Available: http://www.nytimes.com/2006/07/09/movies/09lim.html?r1 (accessed 17 July 2009).

   This is the first time that the author has heard of a film being banned because there is not enough violent content in it.
49 C. C. Gan, *Disciplinary Proceedings Against Public Officers in Malaysia*, Selangor, Malaysia: Lexis Nexis, 2007, p. 208.
50 See Variety (2003) *Malaysian cleric looks to smite 'Almighty': Minister for Religious Affairs calls for pic's ban*, Online. Available: http://www.variety.com/article/VR1117890259.html?categoryid=1236&CS=1 (accessed 25 November 2009); BBC News (2003) *Malaysia delays Carrey movie*, Online. Available: http://news.bbc.co.uk/go/pr/fr/-/2/hi/entertainment/3134589.stm (accessed 25 November 2009); BBC News (2003) *Carrey comedy 'offends' Malaysians*, Online. Available: http://news.bbc.co.uk/go/pr/fr/-/2/hi/ entertainment/3102585.stm (accessed 25 November 2009); Guardian News and Media Limited (2003) *Malaysian Minister urges ban on Bruce Almighty*, Online. Available: http://www.guardian.co.uk/film/2003/jul/29/news (accessed 25 November 2009).
51 [1948] 1 KB 223.
52 [1948] I KB 223, 229.
53 [1986] AC 240.
54 Woolf, J. Jowell and A. P. Le Sueur, *Principles of Judicial Review*, London: Sweet & Maxwell, 1999, p. 488.
55 Ibid.
56 Ibid, p. 459.
57 Reference may be made to the case of *Ketua Pengarah Kastam v Ho Kwan Seng* [1977] 2 MLJ 152 for a classic restatement of the principles of natural justice.
58 Lord Diplock in the case of *O'Reilly v Mackman* [1983] 2 AC 237, 275 stated that the rules of natural justice 'means no more than the duty to act fairly'.
59 Woolf, J. Jowell and A. P. Le Sueur, *Principles of Judicial Review*, London: Sweet & Maxwell, 1999, p. 275.
60 Ibid, p. 282.

61 Ibid, p. 286.
62 For example, the procedure of appeal against a censorship decision provided under the Hong Kong law where the parties affected by the decision under appeal are entitled to make written and oral representations to the Board of Review.
63 See for example, sections 17(2)(c), 18(3)(c) and 19(4)(c) of the Hong Kong Film Censorship Ordinance.
64 Woolf, J. Jowell and A. P. Le Sueur, *Principles of Judicial Review*, London: Sweet & Maxwell, 1999, p. 330.
65 See Chapter 5 for the interviewees' comments on appealing against censorship decisions.
66 Woolf, J. Jowell and A. P. Le Sueur, *Principles of Judicial Review*, London: Sweet & Maxwell, 1999, p. 347.
67 Ibid pp. 34 –52.
68 Section 10(4) of the Hong Kong Film Censorship Ordinance provides that censors must provide reasons for all the types of censorship decision they make under the provision.
69 See C. C. Gan, 'Administrative Law and Judicialized Governance in Malaysia', in T. Ginsburg and A. H. Y. Chen (eds) *Administrative Law and Governance in Asia: Comparative Perspectives*, London: Routledge, 2009, p. 257.
70 *Council of Civil Service Unions v Minister for the Civil Service* [1985] AC 374.
71 See P. Walker, 'Irrationality and Proportionality', in M. Supperstone and J. Goudie (eds) *Judicial Review*, London: Butterworths, 1992, pp. 119–37 and W. Wade and C. Forsyth, *Administrative Law* (9th edn), Oxford: Oxford University Press, 2004, pp. 366–9.
72 Woolf, J. Jowell and A. P. Le Sueur, *Principles of Judicial Review*, London: Sweet & Maxwell, 1999, p. 503. See also the arguments against proportionality by Lord Lowry in the case of *R v Secretary of State for the Home Department, Ex parte Brind* [1991] 1 AC 696, 766 – 7.
73 [1952] 1 All ER 122.
74 [1976] 3 All ER 452.

For a discussion of the application of the doctrine of proportionality in England since the introduction of the Human Rights Act 1998, see P. Leyland and G. Anthony, *Administrative Law* (6th edn), Oxford: Oxford University Press, 2009, pp. 294–309. See also the case of *Huang v Secretary of State for the Home Department* [2007] 2 AC 167 for the four-stage process of the review.

75 [1996] 1 MLJ 261.
76 In this case, articles 5 and 8 of the Federal Constitution.
77 See the case of *Badan Peguam Malaysia v Kerajaan Malaysia* [2008] 2 MLJ 285 where the Federal Court accepted the omnipresence of article 8 when interpreting other provisions in the Federal Constitution.
78 [2006] 6 MLJ 213.
79 Ibid., 219 – 20. See also the case of *Lee Kwan Woh v Public Prosecutor* [2009] 5 MLJ 301 where the Federal Court reaffirmed the principle.
80 See the case of *Om Kumar v Union of India* (2001) 2 SCC 386 for the Indian Supreme Court's elucidation of the principle of proportionality.
81 In addition to the time limitation prescribed by legislation, the court may also refuse to exercise its jurisdiction where there is undue delay (*laches*) in the application and where the relief sought is futile.
82 In Malaysia, the courts have in the course of time created an area of unreviewable discretionary powers and non-justiciable issues through judicial pronouncements. They include the prerogative of mercy, the doctrine of pleasure in public service matters, the constitutional position of Malay rulers in matters of succession, the power of the Attorney-General to institute, conduct or discontinue any proceedings for an offence other than proceedings before a *Syariah* court, a native court or a court martial and preventive detentions.
83 M. Aronson, B. Dyer and M. Groves, *Judicial Review of Administrative Action* (3rd edn), Sydney: Lawbook Co., 2004, p. 144.

84 Section 23(2) reads: 'The decision of the Appeal Committee shall be final and shall not be questioned in any court of law'.
85 Section 48 reads: 'No decision of the Minister, the Board or the Appeal Committee under this Act or any regulations made under this Act shall be subject to appeal or review by any court on any ground'.
86 [1969] 2 AC 147.
87 Ibid., 171.
88 See also the case of *R v Hull University Visitor, Ex parte Page* [1993] AC 682.
89 [1980] 2 MLJ 165.
90 C. C. Gan, 'Privative Clauses: Post-*Fire Bricks* Development and Trend', *Journal of Malaysian and Comparative Law*, 18, 1991, p. 109.
91 M. P. Jain, *Administrative Law of Malaysia and Singapore* (3rd edn), Kuala Lumpur: Butterworths, 1997, p. 785.
92 Ibid., p. 791.
93 [1995] 2 MLJ 336.
94 Ibid., 342.
95 [1997] 1 MLJ 789.
96 [1995] 3 MLJ 378.
97 Woolf, J. Jowell and A. P. Le Sueur, *Principles of Judicial Review*, London: Sweet & Maxwell, 1999, pp. 29–31. See also M. J. Beloff, 'Who Whom? Issues in *Locus Standi* in Public Law', in M. Andenas (ed.), *Judicial Review in International Perspective*, Boston, US: Kluwer Law International, 2000, pp. 275–7.
98 See for example the cases of *Lim Cho Hock v Government of the State of Perak* [1980] 2 MLJ 148, *Mohamed bin Ismail v Tan Sri Haji Othman Saat* [1982] 2 MLJ 133 and *George John v Goh Eng Wah Bros Filem Sdn Bhd* [1988] 1 MLJ 319 where the courts accepted 'sufficient interest' as the basis of *locus standi* and moved away from the early English concept of 'aggrieved person'. In contrast, see *United Engineers (M) Bhd v Lim Kit Siang* [1988] 2 MLJ 12 where the Supreme Court applied a strict *locus standi* rule by insisting that the test applicable is whether the applicant was an 'aggrieved person' or not.
99 [1988] 1 MLJ 319.
100 The approval was granted under the now repealed Film (Censorship) Act 1952.
101 *George John v Goh Eng Wah Bros Filem Sdn Bhd* [1988] 1 MLJ 319, 326.
102 [2006] 3 MLJ 164.
103 Ibid., 171–2.
104 Article 5 guarantees the right to life (which has been judicially interpreted so as to encompass the right to livelihood) while article 10 guarantees freedom of speech.
105 W. A. Ahmad and A. A. Badri, *Judicial Review Handbook*, Kuala Lumpur: Lexis Nexis, 2003, p. 22.
106 *Haji Laugan Tarki bin Mohd Noor v Mahkamah Anak Negeri Penampang* [1988] 2 MLJ 85.
107 *Katherine Lim KH Sr v Ketua Pengarah Perkhidmatan Perubatan Malaysia* [1997] 2 MLJ 538.
108 [2006] 3 MLJ 164.
109 *Majlis Perbandaran Pulau Pinang v Syarikat Berkerjasama-sama Serbaguna Sungai Gelugor dengan Tanggungan* [1999] 3 MLJ 1.
110 *Robin Tan Pang Heng v Ketua Pengarah Kesatuan Sekerja Malaysia* [2002] 1 MLJ 466.
111 *Majlis Perbandaran Pulau Pinang v Syarikat Berkerjasama-sama Serbaguna Sungai Gelugor dengan Tanggungan* [1999] 3 MLJ 1.
112 *Government of Malaysia v Jagdis Singh* [1987] 2 MLJ 185.
113 C. C. Gan, 'Administrative Law and Judicialized Governance in Malaysia', in T. Ginsburg and A. H. Y. Chen (eds) *Administrative Law and Governance in Asia: Comparative Perspectives*, London: Routledge, 2009, p. 261.

114 Section 25 and the Schedule to the Act.
115 Orders 15 and 53 of the Rules.
116 Chapters VI, VIII, IX and X of the Act.
117 M. P. Jain, *Administrative Law of Malaysia and Singapore* (3rd edn), Kuala Lumpur: Butterworths, 1997, p. 665.
118 Ibid. p. 653.
119 An order in the nature of *mandamus* (mandatory order) may also be granted by the court under section 44 of the Specific Relief Act 1950 to enforce the performance of a public duty imposed by law against any person holding a public office.
120 M. P. Jain, *Administrative Law of Malaysia and Singapore* (3rd edn), Kuala Lumpur: Butterworths, 1997, p. 725.
121 The provision reads: 'Without prejudice to the generality of subsection (1), the High Court shall have the additional powers set out in the Schedule. Provided that all such powers shall be exercised in accordance with any written law or rules of court relating to the same.'
122 Paragraph 1 of the Schedule to the Courts of Judicature Act 1964. Freedom of expression and the right to life are guaranteed under Part II of the Constitution.
123 [1997] 1 MLJ 145.
124 See also *Minister of Finance, Government of Sabah v Petrojasa Sdn Bhd* [2008] 4 MLJ 641, 652 where the Federal Court held that the additional powers 'can only be more than, not limited to, what has already been provided by other laws'.
125 Paragraph 1, in its material part, is in *pari materia* with article 226 of the Indian Constitution. For the full potential of the invocation of this provision, see M. P. Jain, *Indian Constitutional Law* (5th edn), New Delhi: Wadhwa and Co., 2003 and M. P. Jain and S. N. Jain, *Principles of Administrative Law* (4th edn), Bombay, India: NM Tripathi Private Ltd., 1986. The Indian courts have relied on article 226 (as well as article 32) as the source of their judicial powers in granting relief to judicial review applicants.
126 See the case of *Ramachandran R v The Industrial Court of Malaysia* [1997] 1 MLJ 145, Rule 76 of the Rules of the Court of Appeal 1994 and Rules 106 and 137 of the Rules of the Federal Court 1995.
127 See the case of *Kerajaan Negeri Selangor v Sagong Tasi* [2005] 4 CLJ 169.
128 [1996] 1 MLJ 481.
129 Ibid., 543.
130 Although *Adultshop.Com Ltd v Members of the Classification Review Board* [2008] 169 FCR 31 is an application for judicial review challenging the decision of the Classification Review Board in classifying a film entitled *Viva Erotica* with the X18+ category, this case (and other similar applications) is not directly relevant to the book because the film in question is not a feature film for commercial public release but contains only sexually explicit materials. For a description of the film's content, see *Adultshop.Com Ltd v Members of the Classification Review Board* [2008] 169 FCR 31, 36.
131 (1987) 17 FCR 324.
132 [2011] FCA 1014.

Judicial review of administrative decisions can be made at the High Court and the Federal Court of Australia. It is worth noting that the Administrative Appeals Tribunal only has jurisdiction to review a decision if the relevant legislation provides so. See generally the Administrative Decisions (Judicial Review) Act 1977 and section 25 of the Administrative Appeals Tribunal Act 1975.

133 The applicant submitted that it had a very substantial interest in the outcome of the matter as reclassification of the film to the 'M' category (meaning that it could be viewed by persons aged 15 years and above) was expected to result in additional box office receipts of two to three million dollars.
134 The film has a complex, controversial and long history of censorship in Australia. It was initially banned in 1975, then approved for screening in 1993 and then banned again in 1998 before the 2010 Classification Review Board's decision to classify it

R18+ for DVD release. Set in an Italian villa in Salo, Northern Italy in 1944, the film follows four fascist men (representing the four pillars of the Italian establishment: the Church, Politics, Nobility and Judiciary) who detain 18 young people and subject them to inhumane treatment and torture before killing some of them. The film is loosely based on Marquis de Sade's novel, *120 Days of Sodom or the School of Licentiousness* and directed by Pier Paolo Pasolini, one of the great names in the history of Italian Cinema.

135 The controversial film contains scenes of rape, sodomy, characters leashed and made to bark like dogs before being forced to compete for food, a character forced to eat pastry containing nails with blood running out from the character's mouth as she screams, a character forced to eat excrement and scenes of execution.

136 Classification Review Board, Decision and Reasons for Decision: *Salo o le 120 Giornate di Sodoma* (*Salo*), Surrey Hills: Australian Government, 2010.

The film was classified R18+ based on the fact that its DVD release contained additional material (of about 176 minutes). Therefore, the screening of the film in cinema without the additional material (that facilitates 'wider consideration of the context of the film which results in the impact of the film no more than high') would constitute a breach of the classification law.

137 Interview with Ruhani Abdul Rahman, film producer (Kuala Lumpur, 16 December 2008).

138 Interview with U-Wei Haji Saari, film director and producer (Kuala Lumpur, 11 December 2008).

139 Interview with Khoo Eng Yow, film director and producer (Kuala Lumpur, 18 December 2008).

140 Interview with Leonard Tee, film distributor (Kuala Lumpur, 18 December 2008).

141 Interview with Aziz M. Osman, film director and producer (Kuala Lumpur, 4 September 2009).

142 Aziz M. Osman's *Fantasia* was banned in 1992 by the Board of Film Censors and was only granted approval for exhibition four years later after substantial alterations were made to the film and the title changed to *Fantasi.* Aziz's *XX Ray 2* also faced censorship problems in 1995 where several scenes had to be excised before the film was approved for exhibition.

143 For example, Gordon Chan noted that it is very unlikely that he would have resort to judicial review because the film censorship system is transparent and works very well. Chan remarked that he does not even need to appeal (against a censorship decision) to the Board of Review: Interview with Gordon Chan, film director, producer and President of the Hong Kong Film Director's Guild (Hong Kong, 25 March 2009).

144 Interview with Mabel Cheung, film director and producer (Hong Kong, 28 May 2009).

145 Interview with Patrick Tam, film director (Hong Kong, 25 March 2009).

146 Interview with Kenneth Bi, film director (Hong Kong, 26 May 2009).

147 Interview with Wellington Fung, Secretary General of the Hong Kong Film Development Council (Hong Kong, 26 May 2009).

148 Interview with Rolf de Heer, film director and producer (Telephone interview, 6 October 2009).

Joel Pearlman also noted that it is unlikely that he would need to apply for judicial review because he had never received a decision that he thought was 'unjustified' in his career: Interview with Joel Pearlman, film distributor and exhibitor (Melbourne, 4 June 2010).

149 Interview with Ray Lawrence, film director (Telephone interview, 20 August 2009).

150 Interview with Tony Ayres, film director and producer (Melbourne, 9 October 2009).

151 Interview with Greg Denning, film distributor (Telephone interview, 13 August 2009).

152 Interview with Peter Campbell, film distributor (Melbourne, 14 August 2009).

7 Conclusion: proposals for the reform of the Malaysian film censorship system and further research

1 See Chapter 5 for the interviewees' comments.
2 See the section on the Malaysian system in Chapter 4 for a discussion of the composition of the Board and the Committee.
3 Interviews with Ahmad Puad Onah, film producer and distributor (Kuala Lumpur, 17 December 2008); Amir Muhammad, film director and producer (Kuala Lumpur, 15 December 2008); Shuhaimi Baba, film director and producer (Kuala Lumpur, 5 January 2009); and Tsai Ming-liang, film director and producer (Kuala Lumpur, 1 February 2009).
4 Interviews with Aziz M. Osman, film director and producer (Kuala Lumpur, 4 September 2009); Khoo Eng Yow, film director and producer (Kuala Lumpur, 18 December 2008); Ruhani Abdul Rahman, film producer (Kuala Lumpur, 16 December 2008); and Yasmin Ahmad, film director (Kuala Lumpur, 6 January 2009).
5 Interviews with Ahmad Puad Onah, film producer and distributor (Kuala Lumpur, 17 December 2008); Tsai Ming-liang, film director and producer (Kuala Lumpur, 1 February 2009); and U-Wei Haji Saari, film director and producer (Kuala Lumpur, 11 December 2008).
6 Positions in the Hong Kong Panel of Censors and Panel of Advisers and the Australian Classification Board are open to the public and recruitment advertisements are placed to invite them to apply to be a member. For further discussion of the recruitment and appointment processes see Chapter 4.
7 Section 4(2) of the Film Censorship Ordinance.
8 In Australia, the names and biographies of classifiers are published on the Classification website.
9 Ray Lawrence also opined that 'censorship boards should consist of intelligent people who are able to see the difference between something that has artistic, social and cultural merits rather than just slop'(Telephone interview, 20 August 2009).
10 A view echoed by fellow director Khoo Eng Yow (Kuala Lumpur, 18 December 2008).
11 Leonard Tee (Kuala Lumpur, 18 December 2008) noted that 'we don't know who makes the decision' while Shuhaimi Baba (Kuala Lumpur, 5 January 2009) remarked that 'I don't know who sits on the Board'.
12 See the section on legal literature in Chapter 1 for further discussion of this point.
13 Interview with Rose May Li, Principal Entertainment Standards Control Officer (Film), Television and Entertainment Licensing Authority (Hong Kong, 24 March 2009).
For example, these members include Ann Hui and Peter Yung, two acclaimed veteran filmmakers of the Hong Kong New Wave Cinema movement.
14 E. Barendt, *Freedom of Speech* (2nd edn), New York: Oxford University Press, 2005, p. 122.
15 See Chapter 5 for some of the instances indicating the lack of independence of censors.
16 See Chapter 4 for a discussion about the appointment, tenure and termination of appointment of censors.
17 Paragraph 12 of the Schedule to the Film Censorship Act 2002.
18 Sections 4 and 22 and paragraphs 4 and 6 of the Schedule to the Film Censorship Act 2002.
20 See Chapter 5 for the Hong Kong interviewees' comments on the independence of film censors and Chapter 4 for the circumstances under which the appointment of Australian classifiers may be terminated.
21 E. Barendt, *Freedom of Speech* (2nd edn), New York: Oxford University Press, 2005, p. 122.
22 For an actual incident of the exercise of this power, see the section on the Malaysian decision-making entities in Chapter 4.
23 See Chapter 5 for the interviewees' opinion of this power.
24 *Minister of Home Affairs v Persatuan Aliran Kesedaran Malaysia* [1990] 1 MLJ 351.
In this case, the respondent had applied for a permit under the Printing Presses and Publications Act 1984 to publish a magazine. The respondent's application was rejected

by the appellant, the Minister of Home Affairs. The respondent then applied for an order of *certiorari* to quash the Minister's decision and for an order of *mandamus* directing the Minister to determine its application according to law. The High Court granted the orders sought and the appellant appealed to the Supreme Court. In allowing the appeal, the Supreme Court noted that section 12(2) of the 1984 Act gives the Minister 'absolute discretion' to refuse an application for a permit and held that the High Court may not intervene to question the Minister's discretion and set aside the decision made 'unless it can be clearly established that the Minister had in any way exercised his discretion wrongfully, unfairly, dishonestly or in bad faith'.

25 *Minister of Home Affairs v Persatuan Aliran Kesedaran Malaysia* [1990] 1 MLJ 351, 355.

26 See Chapter 5 for the interviewees' reactions and comments on these provisions.

27 See Chapter 4 for the classes of film that are eligible to be exempted from censorship in Hong Kong and for the list of 13 types of film designated as exempt films in Australia.

28 See Chapter 4 for a discussion of the consideration of the artistic merit of film in the Hong Kong and Australian systems.

29 Some notable examples include *Schindler's List* (Steven Spielberg, 1993), *Happy Together* (Wong Kar Wai, 1997), *Jogho* (*Champion*, U-Wei Haji Saari, 1997), *Saving Private Ryan* (Steven Spielberg, 1999), *Lan Yu* (Stanley Kwan, 2001), *Brokeback Mountain* (Ang Lee, 2005), *I Don't Want to Sleep Alone* (Tsai Ming-liang, 2006) and *Lust, Caution* (Ang Lee, 2007).

30 See Chapter 5 for the interviewees' opinion of the importance of censors taking into account the artistic merit of the films they examine.

31 See the section on legal literature in Chapter 1 for a discussion of the obscenity tests applied in England and the United States.

32 For the provisions in the Hong Kong and Australian laws stipulating artistic merit as a matter to be taken into account by censors, see the sections on those jurisdictions in Chapter 4.

33 See the section on the Australian system in Chapter 4 for a discussion of the Classification Board and the Classification Review Board.

34 See Chapter 5 for the interviewees' opinions of the standards to be applied.

35 See paragraph 2 of the Film Censorship Guidelines for Censors.

36 See section 11 of the Classification (Publications, Films and Computer Games) Act 1995.

37 See *R v Hicklin* (1868) LR 3 QB 360, 371.

38 See section 1 of the Obscene Publications Act.

39 See the section on legal literature in Chapter 1 for a discussion of the obscenity tests in the Anglo-American jurisprudence.

40 The 2010 Guidelines were drawn up in Malay and there is no official English language version. Therefore, quotations in the text are the author's translation. Like the Film Censorship Guidelines 1993, the 2010 Guidelines are also not published in the *Gazette* and copies are not made available to the public.

41 See the part of Chapter 3 on the Malaysian system for a description of the censorship principles.

42 The four censorship elements provided in the Film Censorship Guidelines 1993 are 'Ideology and Politics', 'Religion', 'Socio-culture' and 'Order and Decorum'.

43 Paragraph 2.2.1 of the Film Censorship Guidelines (2010).

44 'Religion' is the most detailed censorship element in the 2010 Guidelines, containing 55 matters for censors' consideration, 53 of which are in regard to the Islamic faith.

45 Paragraph 1, Part IV of the Film Censorship Guidelines (2010).

46 Films classified U are suitable for viewing by all levels of society.

47 Films classified PG13 are not recommended for viewing by persons under 13 years of age without guidance from a parent or guardian.

48 Films classified 18 are restricted to persons aged 18 and above only. They contain elements of violence, horror or sex that are not excessive and may also contain religious or political elements.

49 Prior to the introduction of the 2010 Guidelines, there were five classification categories: U, 18SG, 18SX, 18PA and 18PL. See Chapter 3 for a summary description of these categories.
50 See Chapter 4 for discussions of the Hong Kong and Australian censorship guidelines.
51 For example, most of the provisions that appear under the censorship element of 'Religion' are verbatim reproductions of those found in the Film Censorship Guidelines 1993.
52 For example, some of the provisions that appear under the 'Socio-culture' section in the Film Censorship Guidelines 1993 now appear under the 'Public safety and public order' section in the 2010 Guidelines.
53 Paragraphs 2.1.1, 2.2.1, 2.3.1 and 2.4.1 of the Film Censorship Guidelines (2010).
54 See Chapter 4 for a discussion of the guidelines and Chapter 5 for interviewees' comments on the guidelines.
55 See Chapter 5 for more comments by the interviewees.
56 See *Paris Adult Theatre v Slaton* 413 US 49 (1973) 83.
57 See the relative sections in Chapter 4 for discussion of the censorship guidelines applied in Hong Kong and Australia. See also Chapter 5 for the interviewees' opinions of the guidelines.
58 See Chapter 5 for the Hong Kong and Australian interviewees' comments.
59 See Chapter 5 for the Malaysian interviewees' comments.
60 E. Barendt, *Freedom of Speech* (2nd edn), New York: Oxford University Press, 2005, p. 124.
61 See Chapter 5 for the Malaysian interviewees' comments on this point.
62 See Chapter 4 for discussions of this consideration in the Hong Kong and Australian guidelines.
63 See Chapter 5 for the Hong Kong and Australian interviewees' comments.
64 See the section on the legal literature in Chapter 1 for a discussion of this free speech justification.
65 D. Rolph, M. Vitins and J. Bannister, *Media Law: Cases, Materials and Commentary*, Melbourne: Oxford University Press, 2010, p. 28 and L. McNamara, 'Free Speech' in D. Butler and S. Rodrick, *Australian Media Law* (3rd edn), Sydney: Lawbook Co., 2007, p. 6.
66 E. Barendt, *Freedom of Speech* (2nd edn), New York: Oxford University Press, 2005, p. 7.
67 See Chapter 3 for a discussion of the classification categories.
68 See section 3 of the Film Censorship Act 2002.
69 The author also spoke to two film practitioners who preferred not to be interviewed on record. They were of the opinion that the 'clumsy' and 'irresponsible' censorship decisions have 'damaged good films' and made films lose their appeal, thus reducing the turnout of audiences at cinemas.
70 Article 10 of the Federal Constitution.
71 Interviews with Ahmad Puad Onah (Kuala Lumpur, 17 December 2008); Amir Muhammad (Kuala Lumpur, 15 December 2008); Khoo Eng Yow (Kuala Lumpur, 18 December 2008); Ruhani Abdul Rahman (Kuala Lumpur, 16 December 2008); Saw Teong Hin (Kuala Lumpur, 10 December 2008); Tsai Ming-liang (Kuala Lumpur, 1 February 2009); and U-Wei Haji Saari (Kuala Lumpur, 11 December 2008).
72 See the section on the legal literature in Chapter 1 for a discussion of the free speech principle and its justifications.
73 See Chapter 4 for the lists of prohibited content and portrayal under the Hong Kong and Australian systems.
74 E. Barendt, *Freedom of Speech* (2nd edn), New York: Oxford University Press, 2005, p. 7.
75 See Chapter 5 for the Hong Kong interviewees' comments and experiences.
76 In Australia, there is no similar provision allowing its film practitioners to discuss the classification category to be given to their film with classifiers.
77 See Chapter 5 for the interviewees' opinion of this procedure.
78 Interview with Ruhani Abdul Rahman, film producer (Kuala Lumpur, 16 December 2008).

79 See Chapter 5 for the interviewees' comments on the reasons provided to them as well as examples of reasons furnished by the Board.

A number of interviewees labelled the reasons given as 'shallow', 'bizarre' and 'odd', suggesting that the censors are an incompetent lot therefore underlining again the importance of appointing competent and suitable individuals to sit in the decision-making entities.

80 See Chapter 5 for the Hong Kong and Australian interviewees' feedback.

81 In Malaysia, there is no general statutory provision akin to section 13 of the Australian Administrative Decisions (Judicial Review) Act 1977 which provides that any person who is entitled to apply for judicial review may request the decision-maker for a statement of reasons for decision.

82 Interviews with Ahmad Puad Onah, film producer and distributor (Kuala Lumpur, 17 December 2008) and U-Wei Haji Saari, film director and producer (Kuala Lumpur, 11 December 2008).

83 Section 21(2) of the Film Censorship Act 2002.

84 Examples include *Zoolander* (Ben Stiller, 2001), *Bruce Almighty* (Tom Shadyac, 2003), *Daredevil* (Mark Steven Johnson, 2003) and *The Last Communist* (Amir Muhammad, 2006).

85 See Chapter 5 for the interviewees' comments.

86 E. Barendt, *Freedom of Speech* (2nd edn), New York: Oxford University Press, 2005, p. 122.

87 See Chapter 5 for an example of appeal made by lobby groups and campaigners in Australia.

88 Section 21 of the Film Censorship Act 2002.

89 See sections 17, 18 and 19 of the Film Censorship Ordinance.

90 See Chapter 5 for a description of the Australian experience where film practitioners were not allowed to reference past classification decisions.

91 An interesting example would be that of the experiences of producer-director Shuhaimi Baba. When she appealed against the censorship decision on her second film, *Ringgit Kasyorga* (*Dollar to Heaven*, 1995), she did not get the opportunity to make oral representations before the Appeal Committee but when she appealed against the censorship decision on her sixth film *Pontianak Harum Sundal Malam* (*Pontianak: A Scent of Tuberose*, 2004), she was given ample opportunity to do so. It is perhaps the case that by the time *Pontianak* was made, Shuhaimi Baba had become an established and commercially successful filmmaker in Malaysia.

92 For example, Tsai Ming-liang did not get to make oral representations before the Committee when he appealed against the Board's decision on his film *I Don't Want to Sleep Alone* (2006).

93 See Chapter 5 for the interviewees' responses.

94 See Chapter 5 for the Hong Kong and Australian interviewees' opinions of this issue.

95 See Chapter 4 for a discussion of these provisions and Chapter 6 for a discussion of the effect of ouster clauses in Malaysia.

96 The Malaysian interviewees questioned the justification of having these ouster clauses. For example, Amir Muhammad noted: 'the decisions of the Appeal Committee cannot be challenged under judicial review which, you know, why make these people so infallible? Why can't a judge look at the decision?' (Kuala Lumpur, 15 December 2008).

97 See article 10 of the Federal Constitution.

98 Interviews with Khoo Eng Yow, film director and producer (Kuala Lumpur, 18 December 2008) and Leonard Tee, film distributor (Kuala Lumpur, 18 December 2008).

99 See Chapter 5 for the interviewees' opinions of the availability of judicial review.

100 See the final section of Chapter 6 for the Malaysian interviewees' responses.

101 See Chapter 3 for a discussion of the six censorship elements provided in the Film Censorship Guidelines for Censors. Inconsistencies of application are found only with regards to 'Language', as in the use of coarse language in films, and not with the rest of the censorship elements.

102 It is interesting to note that the Public Opinion Survey on Film Classification System 2011 reported that 'for contents on offensive language, the respondents [of the 2011 survey] tended to be more tolerant of expletives in English films but applied stricter standards in Cantonese films in particular towards language carrying strong sexual connotations'. However, no explanation was offered in the report to shed light on why such a tendency exists amongst the respondents.
103 Section 10(1) of the Film Censorship Ordinance.
104 Section 10(6) of the Film Censorship Ordinance.
105 Paragraph 8 of the Schedule to the Film Censorship Act 2002.
106 Section 58(5) of the Classification (Publications, Films and Computer Games) Act 1995.
107 Section 58(6) of the Classification (Publications, Films and Computer Games) Act 1995.
108 Section 58(7) of the Classification (Publications, Films and Computer Games) Act 1995.
109 Interviews with Bill Kong, film producer and distributor (Hong Kong, 26 March 2009) and Winnie Tsang, film distributor (Hong Kong, 1 June 2009).
110 See the section concerning the Australian system in Chapter 3 for a discussion of the classification categories.
111 Section 38 of the Classification (Publications, Films and Computer Games) Act 1995.
112 Section 39 of the Classification (Publications, Films and Computer Games) Act 1995.
113 Section 40 of the Classification (Publications, Films and Computer Games) Act 1995.
114 One of the more well-known examples is Pier Paolo Pasolini's *Salo o le 120 giornate di Sodoma* (*Salo, the 120 Days of Sodom*, 1975) which has undergone no less than three reclassifications. Another example would be *Caligula* (Tinto Brass, 1979) which was initially classified for release in 1981 but later refused classification after the Classification Board called the film back for reclassification.
115 Ray Lawrence, for example, remarked that he has no issue with reclassification of films 'as long as they classify down but not up', referring to the order of the classification categories.
116 Interview with Tony Ayres, film director and producer (Melbourne, 9 October 2009).
117 Interview with Rolf de Heer, film director and producer (Telephone interview, 6 October 2009).
118 This view is shared by another interviewee who requested anonymity. The interviewee noted that 'once a film has gone through the process and classified, that should be the end of it'.

Bibliography

Ahmad, M., 'Colonial Policies, the Marketplace and the Malaysian Film Industry', in L. Feilberg (ed.) *Film Industries in Asia and Europe: A Platform for Experiences' Sharing*, Singapore: Asia-Europe Foundation, 2005, 16

Ahmad, W. A. and Badri, A. A., *Judicial Review Handbook*, Kuala Lumpur: Lexis Nexis, 2003

Anand, A. S., 'Protection of Human Rights through Judicial Review', in M. Andenas (ed.) *Judicial Review in International Perspectives*, Boston, US: Kluwer Law International, 2000, 381

Andaya, B. W. and Andaya, L., *A History of Malaysia* (2nd edn), London: Macmillan, 2001

Aronson, M., Dyer, B. and Groves, M., *Judicial Review of Administrative Action* (3rd edn), Sydney: Lawbook Co., 2004

Ashworth, A., *Principles of Criminal Law* (6th edn), Oxford: Oxford University Press, 2009

Asian Development Bank, *Key Indicators for Asia and the Pacific 2010* (41st edn), Manila: Asian Development Bank, 2010

Australian Film Commission, *The Economics of Films and Television in Australia*, Sydney: Australian Film Commission, 1993

Australian Law Reform Commission, *Censorship Procedure*, Report No.55, Sydney: Australian Law Reform Commission, 1991

Australian Law Reform Commission, *Classification – Content Regulation and Convergent Media*, Sydney: Australian Law Reform Commission, 2012

Baker, C. E., *Human Liberty and Freedom of Speech*, New York: Oxford University Press, 1989

Balaraman, N., 'The Legislative System to Support Cinema: Instruments and Policies', in L. Feilberg (ed.) *Film Industries in Asia and Europe: A Platform for Experiences Sharing*, Singapore: Asia-Europe Foundation, 2005, 12

Barendt, E., *Freedom of Speech* (2nd edn), New York: Oxford University Press, 2005

Beloff, M. J., 'Who Whom? Issues in *Locus Standi* in Public Law', in M. Andenas (ed.) *Judicial Review in International Perspective*, Boston, US: Kluwer Law International, 2000, 275

Bertrand, I., *Film Censorship in Australia*, St. Lucia, Queensland, Australia: University of Queensland Press, 1978

Bertrand, I., 'Finance', in B. McFarlane, G. Mayer and I. Bertrand (eds) *The Oxford Companion to Australian Film*, Melbourne: Oxford University Press, 1999, 156

Bollinger, L. C. and Stone, G. R., *Eternally Vigilant: Free Speech in the Modern Era*, Chicago, US: University of Chicago Press, 2002

Bordwell, D., *Planet Hong Kong: Popular Cinema and the Art of Entertainment*, Massachusetts: Harvard University Press, 2000

Bronitt, S. and McSherry, B., *Principles of Criminal Law* (2nd edn), Sydney: Lawbook Co., 2005

Butler, D. and Rodrick, S, *Australian Media Law* (3rd edn), Sydney: Lawbook Co., 2007

Campbell, T., 'Rationales for Freedom of Communications', in T. Campbell and W. Sadurski (eds) *Freedom of Communication*, Aldershot, UK: Dartmouth, 1994, 17

Cane, P., 'Understanding Judicial Review and Its Impact', in M. Hertogh and S. Halliday (eds) *Judicial Review and Bureaucratic Impact: International and Interdisciplinary Perspectives*, New York: Cambridge University Press, 2004, 15

Chan, J., 'Film Censorship Ordinance 1988', *Hong Kong Law Journal*, 18, 1988, 457

Chan, J., 'Freedom of Expression: Censorship and Obscenity', in R. Wacks (ed.) *Civil Liberties in Hong Kong*, Hong Kong: Oxford University Press, 1988, 208

Chaudhuri, S., *Contemporary World Cinema: Europe, the Middle East, East Asia and South Asia*, Edinburgh: Edinburgh University Press, 2005

Chen, A. H. Y., 'Some Reflections on the "Film Censorship Affair"', *Hong Kong Law Journal*, 17, 1987, 352

Chen, A. H. Y., 'The Concept of "One Country, Two Systems" and Its Application to Hong Kong', in S. Hsu (ed.) *Understanding China's Legal System*, New York: New York University Press, 2003, 353

Ching, F., 'Hong Kong Plays Political Censor for China', *Asian Wall Street Journal* (Hong Kong), 17 March 1987, 1.

Coldham, S., 'Reports of the Committee on Obscenity and Film Censorship', *Modern Law Review*, 43, 1980, 306

Collins, D., *Hollywood Down Under: Australians at the Movies – 1896 to the Present Day*, North Ryde, Australia: Angus & Robertson, 1987

Collins, F. and Davis, T., *Australian Cinema after Mabo*, Melbourne: Cambridge University Press, 2004

Committee on Obscenity and Film Censorship, *Report of the Committee on Obscenity and Film Censorship* (Cmnd 7772), London: HMSO, 1979

Commonwealth, *Parliamentary Debates*, House of Representatives, 22 September 1994, p. 1381 (Michael Lavarch, Attorney-General)

Courtauld, C. and Holdsworth, M., *The Hong Kong Story*, Hong Kong: Oxford University Press, 1997

Creyke, R. and McMillan, J., 'Executive Perceptions of Administrative Law – An Empirical Study', *Australian Journal of Administrative Law*, 9, 2009, 163

Curtin, M., *Playing to the World's Biggest Audience: The Globalization of Chinese Films and TV*, Berkeley, US: University of California Press, 2007

Dannen, F. and Long, B., *Hong Kong Babylon: An Insider's Guide to the Hollywood of the East*, London: Faber and Faber, 1997

Denoon, D., Mein-Smith, P. and Wyndham, M., *A History of Australia, New Zealand and the Pacific*, Massachusetts: Blackwell Publishers, 2000

Dermody, S. and Jacka, E., *The Screening of Australia: Anatomy of a Film Industry*, Sydney: Currency Press, 1987

Douglas, R., *Administrative Law* (6th edn), Sydney: The Federation Press, 2009

Dworkin, A., 'Against the Male Flood: Censorship, Pornography and Equality', *Harvard Women's Law Journal*, 8, 1985, 1

Dworkin, R. M., 'Is There a Right to Pornography?', *Oxford Journal of Legal Studies*, 1, 1981, 177

Easton, S. M., *The Problem of Pornography: Regulation and the Right to Free Speech*, London: Routledge, 1994

Endicott, T. A. O., 'The Impossibility of the Rule of Law', *Oxford Journal of Legal Studies*, 19, 1999, 1

Faruqi, S. S. and Ramanathan, S., *Mass Media Laws and Regulations in Malaysia*, Singapore: Asian Media Information and Communication Centre, 1998

Fish, S., 'There's No Such Thing as Free Speech, and It's a Good Thing Too', in H. A. Veeser (ed.) *The Stanley Fish Reader*, Oxford, UK: Blackwell Publishers, 1999, 145

Gan, C. C., 'Administrative Law and Judicialized Governance in Malaysia', in T. Ginsburg and A. H.Y. Chen (eds) *Administrative Law and Governance in Asia: Comparative Perspectives*, London: Routledge, 2009, 257

Gan, C. C., *Disciplinary Proceedings against Public Officers in Malaysia*, Selangor, Malaysia: Lexis Nexis, 2007

Gan, C. C., 'Privative Clauses: Post-*Fire Bricks* Development and Trend', *Journal of Malaysian and Comparative Law*, 18, 1991, 109

Gifford, D. J., *Understanding the Australian Legal System*, Sydney: Cavendish, 1997

Gonski, D., *Review of Commonwealth Assistance to the Film Industry*, Canberra: Department of Communications and the Arts Australia, 1997

Groves, M., 'Substantive Legitimate Expectations in Australian Administrative Law', *Melbourne University Law Review*, 32, 2008, 470

Gutman, T., 'Lolita's Lesson Learned', *Communications Update*, 155, 1999, 18

Halliday, S., 'The Influence of Judicial Review on Bureaucratic Decision-making', *Public Law*, 2000, 110

Hamzah, W. A., *Malaysian Legal System*, Selangor, Malaysia: Oxford Fajar, 2003

Harding, A., *Law, Government and the Constitution in Malaysia*, Selangor, Malaysia: Lexis Nexis, 1996

Harris, B., 'Censorship: A Comparative Approach Offering a New Theoretical Basis for Classification in Australia', *Canberra Law Review*, 8, 2005, 25

Hawkins, G. J., 'The Problem of Pornography', *Sydney Law Review*, 5(2), 1966, 221

Hinchy, R., *The Australian Legal System: History, Institutions and Method*, Sydney: Pearson, 2008

Hodsdon, B., *Straight Roads and Crossed Lines: The Quest for Film Culture in Australia?*, Shenton Park, Australia: Bernt Porridge Group, 2001

House of Representatives Standing Committee on Communications, Information Technology and the Arts, Parliament of the Commonwealth of Australia, *From Reel to Unreal: Future Opportunities for Australia's Film, Animation, Special Effects and Electronic Games Industries*, Canberra: Australian Government Publishing Service, 2004

House of Representatives Standing Committee on Environment, Recreation and the Arts, Parliament of the Commonwealth of Australia, *Report of the Moving Pictures Inquiry*, Canberra: Australian Government Publishing Service, 1992

Hunnings, N. M., *Film Censors and the Law*, London: Allen & Unwin, 1967

Information Services Department of the Hong Kong Special Administrative Region, *Hong Kong Yearbook 2009*, Hong Kong: Information Service Department of the Hong Kong Special Administrative Region, 2010

Jain, M. P., *Administrative Law of Malaysia and Singapore* (3rd edn), Kuala Lumpur: Butterworths, 1997

Jain, M. P., *Indian Constitutional Law* (5th edn), New Delhi: Wadhwa and Co., 2003

Jain, M. P. and Jain, S. N., *Principles of Administrative Law* (4th edn), Bombay, India: N. M. Tripathi Private Ltd., 1986

Jones, R., 'The Australian Film Distribution and Exhibition Industry and Competition Law and Policy', in M. Alderson (ed.) *Current Issues in Film Law*, Sydney: Prospect Media Ltd., 2007

Kenyon, A. T., 'What Conversation? Free Speech and Defamation Law', *Modern Law Review*, 73(5), 2010, 697

Khan, H. A., *The Malay Cinema*, Selangor, Malaysia: National University of Malaysia Press, 1997

Khoo, G. C., *Reclaiming Adat: Contemporary Malaysian Film and Literature*, Vancouver, Canada: UBC Press, 2006

Law, K. and Bren, F., *Hong Kong Cinema: A Cross Cultural View*, Lanham, US: Scarecrow Press, 2004

Leyland, P. and Anthony, G., *Administrative Law* (6th edn), Oxford: Oxford University Press, 2009

Luhr, W., *World Cinema Since 1945*, New York: Ungar, 1987

McDonald, N. 'Australia' in W. Luhr (ed.) *World Cinema Since 1945*, New York: Ungar, 1987

Macintyre, S., *A Concise History of Australia*, Melbourne: Cambridge University Press, 2000

MacKinnon, C., 'Pornography, Civil Rights and Speech', *Harvard Civil Rights – Civil Liberties Law Review*, 20, 1985, 1

MacMillan, P. R., *Censorship and Public Morality*, Aldershot, UK: Gower Publications, 1983

McNamara, L., 'Free Speech', in D. Butler and S. Rodrick, *Australian Media Law* (3rd edn), Sydney: Lawbook Co., 2007

Malaysia, *Parliamentary Debates*, House of Representatives, 6 December 2001, p. 106 (Chor Chee Heung, Deputy Minister of Home Affairs)

Marr, D., 'Censored: Attorney-General vs. "aggrieved person"', *Art + Law*, 9, 2001, 1

Matthews, T. D., *Censored: The Story of Film Censorship in Britain*, London: Chatto & Windus, 1994

Meiklejohn, A., *Political Freedom: The Constitutional Powers of the People*, New York: Harper, 1960

Meyerson, M. I., 'The Neglected History of the Prior Restraint Doctrine: Rediscovering the Link between the First Amendment and Separation of Powers', *Indiana Law Review*, 34, 2001, 295

Morgan, J., 'Policy Reasoning in Tort Law: The Courts, the Law Commission and the Critics', *Law Quarterly Review*, 125, 2009, 215

Murray, S., *Australian Cinema*, Sydney: Allen & Unwin, 1994

Muthalib, H. and Wong, T. C., 'Malaysia: Gentle Winds of Change', in A. Vasudev, L. Padgaonkar and R. Doraisamy (eds) *Being and Becoming: The Cinemas of Asia*, New Delhi: Macmillan, 2002, 301

O'Regan, T., *Australian National Cinema*, London: Routledge, 1996

Poole, T., 'Of Headscarves and Heresies: The Denbigh High School Case and Public Authority Decision-making under the *Human Rights Act*', *Public Law*, 2005, 685

Post, R., 'Reconciling Theory and Doctrine in First Amendment Jurisprudence', *California Law Review*, 88, 2000, 2353

Rattigan, N., *Images of Australia: 100 Films of the New Australian Cinema*, Dallas, US: Southern Methodist University Press, 1991

Rayner, J., *Contemporary Australian Cinema*, Manchester: Manchester University Press, 2000

Reid, M. A., *More Long Shots: Australian Cinema Successes in the 90s*, Sydney: Australian Film Commission, 1999

Richardson, G. and Sunkin, M., 'Judicial Review: Questions of Impact', *Public Law*, 1996, 79

Robertson, G. and Nicol, A., *Media Law* (5th edn), London: Sweet & Maxwell, 2007

Rolph, D., Vitins, M. and Bannister, J., *Media Law: Materials and Commentary*, Melbourne: Oxford University Press, 2010

Schauer, F., *Free Speech: A Philosophical Inquiry*, New York: Cambridge University Press, 1982

Schauer, F., 'Free Speech in a World of Private Power', in T. Campbell and W. Sadurski (eds) *Freedom of Communication*, Aldershot, UK: Dartmouth, 1994, 6

Schauer, F., *The Law of Obscenity*, Washington: Bureau of National Affairs, 1976

Schauer, F., 'The Ontology of Censorship', in R. C. Post (ed.) *Censorship and Silencing*, Los Angeles, US: Getty Research Institute for History of Art and the Humanities, 1998, 147

Scott, M. '100 Years of Hong Kong Cinema' Hong Kong International Film Festival Edition, Hong Kong: *Screen International*, 20 March 2009

Screen Australia, *Information for Filmmakers*, Sydney: Screen Australia, 2008

Screen Australia, *Production Guidelines*, Sydney: Screen Australia, 2008

Sheckels, T. F., *Celluloid Heroes Down Under: Australian Film, 1970–2000*, Westport, US: Praeger, 2002

Shuaib, F. S., *Powers and Jurisdiction of Syariah Courts in Malaysia*, Kuala Lumpur: Lexis Nexis, 2003

Shum, C., *General Principles of Hong Kong Law*, Hong Kong: Longman, 1992

Sunkin, M. and Pick, K., 'The Changing Impact of Judicial Review: The Independent Review Service of the Social Fund', *Public Law*, 2001, 736

Supperstone, M., 'Judicial Review after the Human Rights Act', *European Human Rights Law Review*, 3, 1999, 301

Supperstone, M., 'The Ambit of Judicial Review', in M. Supperstone and J. Goudie (eds) *Judicial Review*, London: Butterworths, 1992, 24

Strossen, N., 'A Feminist Critique of "The" Feminist Critique of Pornography', *Virginia Law Review*, 79, 1993, 1103

Tackaberry, P. and Hewitt, J., 'Towards a New Definition of Obscenity in Canada: Did *Butler* really do it?', *Entertainment Law Review*, 4(5), 1993, 152

Teo, S., *Hong Kong Cinema: The Extra Dimension*, London: BFI Publishing, 1997

Tsang, S., *A Modern History of Hong Kong*, New York: I. B. Tauris, 2004

Turnbull, C. M., *A History of Malaysia, Singapore and Brunei*, Sydney: Allen & Unwin, 1989

van der Haide, B., 'Malaysian Movies: The Shaw Brothers Meet the Pandava Brothers in the Land Below the Wind', in B. Bennett, J. Doyle and S. Nandan (eds) *Crossing Cultures: Essays on Literature and Culture of the Asia-Pacific*, London: Skoob Books, 1996, 101

van der Haide, W., *Malaysian Cinema, Asian Film: Border Crossings and National Cultures*, Amsterdam: Amsterdam University Press, 2002

Vines, P., *Law and Justice in Australia* (2nd edn), Melbourne: Oxford University Press, 2009

Wade, W. and Forsyth, C., *Administrative Law* (9th edn), Oxford: Oxford University Press, 2004

Wade, W. and Forsyth, C., *Administrative Law* (10th edn), Oxford: Oxford University Press, 2009

Walker, P., 'Irrationality and Proportionality', in M. Supperstone and J. Goudie (eds) *Judicial Review*, London: Butterworths, 1992

Watkins, D., 'Freedom of Artistic Expression and the Human Rights Act 1998', *Art, Antiquity and Law*, 2005, 147

Wesley-Smith, P., *An Introduction to the Hong Kong Legal System* (3rd edn), Hong Kong: Oxford University Press, 1998

White, H., *Anatomy of Censorship: Why the Censors Have it Wrong*, Lanham, US: University Press of America, 1997

Whiting, A., 'Desecularising Malaysian Law?', in P. Nicholson and S. Biddulph (eds) *Examining Practice, Interrogating Theory: Comparative Legal Studies in Asia*, Leiden, The Netherlands: Martinus Nijhoff Publishers, 2008, 224

Whitmore, H., 'Obscenity in Literature: Crime or Free Speech', *Sydney Law Review*, 4(2), 1963, 179

Woolf, H., Jowell, J. and Le Sueur, A. P., *Principles of Judicial Review*, London: Sweet & Maxwell, 1999

Wu, M. A., *The Malaysian Legal System* (3rd edn), Selangor, Malaysia: Longman, 2005

Yau, E., 'China', in W. Luhr (ed.) *World Cinema Since 1945*, New York: Ungar, 1987, 116

List of interviewees

Ahmad Puah Onah, film producer and distributor (Kuala Lumpur, 17 December 2008)

Amir Muhammad, film director and producer (Kuala Lumpur, 15 December 2008)

Tony Ayres, film director and producer (Melbourne, 9 October 2009)

Aziz M. Osman, film director and producer (Kuala Lumpur, 4 September 2009)

Kenneth Bi, film director and producer (Hong Kong, 26 May 2009)

Peter Campbell, film distributor (Melbourne, 14 August 2009)

Benny Chan, film director and producer (Hong Kong, 23 March 2009)

Gordon Chan, film director, producer and President of the Hong Kong Film Directors' Guild (Hong Kong, 25 March 2009)

Terence Chang, film producer (Hong Kong, 12 October 2010)

Jan Chapman, film producer (Telephone interview, 30 April 2010)

Mabel Cheung, film director and producer (Hong Kong, 28 May 2009)

Cheung Chi Kwong, film producer (Hong Kong, 2 June 2009)

Rolf de Heer, film director and producer (Telephone interview, 6 October 2009)

Greg Denning, film distributor (Telephone interview, 13 August 2009)

Richard J. Frankland, film director and producer (Melbourne, 7 October 2009)

Wellington Fung, Secretary General of the Hong Kong Film Development Council and film producer (Hong Kong, 26 May 2009)

James Hewison, film distributor (Melbourne, 19 August 2009)

Hussain Shafie, Chairman of the Board of Censors (Putrajaya, 6 January 2009)

Khoo Eng Yow, film director and producer (Kuala Lumpur, 18 December 2008)

Bill Kong, film producer and distributor (Hong Kong, 26 March 2009)

Ray Lawrence, film director (Telephone interview, 20 August 2009)

James Lee, film director and producer (Kuala Lumpur, 19 December 2008)

Rose May Li, Principal Entertainment Standards Control Officer (Film), Television and Entertainment Licensing Authority (Hong Kong, 24 March 2009)

Lo Chi Leung, film director (Hong Kong, 2 June 2009)

Joel Pearlman, film distributor and exhibitor (Melbourne, 4 June 2010)

Ruhani Abdul Rahman, film producer (Kuala Lumpur, 16 December 2008)

Saw Teong Hin, film director (Kuala Lumpur, 10 December 2008)

Greg Scott, Deputy Director of the Classification Board (Telephone interview, 20 July 2010)

Nansun Shi, film producer (Hong Kong, 29 May 2009)

Shuhaimi Baba, film director and producer (Kuala Lumpur, 5 January 2009)

Patrick Tam, film director (Hong Kong, 25 March 2009)

Leonard Tee, film distributor (Kuala Lumpur, 18 December 2008)
Lorna Tee, film producer and distributor (Hong Kong, 26 March 2009)
Tsai Ming-liang, film director and producer (Kuala Lumpur, 1 February 2009)
Winnie Tsang, film distributor (Hong Kong, 1 June 2009)
U-Wei Haji Saari, film director and producer (Kuala Lumpur, 11 December 2008)
Yasmin Ahmad, film director (Kuala Lumpur, 6 January 2009)

Index

www.ingramcontent.com/pod-product-compliance
Lightning Source LLC
LaVergne TN
LVHW011127300926
849160LV00008B/549